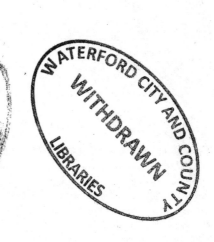
SECOND READINGS

First published in 2009 by
Liberties Press
Guinness Enterprise Centre | Taylor's Lane | Dublin 8 | Ireland
www.LibertiesPress.com
info@LibertiesPress.com
+353 (1) 415 1286

Trade enquiries to CMD BookSource
55a Spruce Avenue | Stillorgan Industrial Park
Blackrock | County Dublin
Tel: +353 (1) 294 2560 | Fax: +353 (1) 294 2564

Distributed in the United States by
Dufour Editions
Po Box 7 | Chester Springs | Pennsylvania | 19425

and in Australia by
InBooks
3 Narabang Way | Belrose NSW 2085

Copyright © Eileen Battersby, 2009
The author has asserted her moral rights.
ISBN: 978 1 905483 81 5
A CIP record for this title is available from the British Library.

Cover design by Liberties Press and Ros Murphy
Internal design by Liberties Press
Printed by Colour Books

SECOND READINGS
FROM BECKETT TO BLACK BEAUTY

Eileen Battersby

'Nothing is as Important as a Book can be' – Maxwell Perkins

For my daughter, Nadia Rogers;
best person, best friend

Contents

Acknowledgements   15

Foreword by Richard Ford   17

'The Reader in the Hammock'   25

1   One Day in the Life of Ivan Denisovich (1962)
by Alexander Solzhenitsyn   39

2   Le Grand Meaulnes (1913)
by Alain-Fournier   44

3   The Lonely Passion of Judith Hearne (1955)
by Brian Moore   48

4   The Trial (1925)
by Franz Kafka   52

5   The Violent Bear it Away (1960)
by Flannery O'Connor   58

6   Dom Casmurro (1899)

by Joaquim Maria Machado de Assis   62

7   Persuasion (1818)

by Jane Austen   67

8   Fathers and Sons (1861)

by Ivan Turgenev   72

9   All Quiet on the Western Front (1929)

by Erich Maria Remarque   77

10   Heart of Darkness (1902)

by Joseph Conrad   81

11   Cry, The Beloved Country (1948)

by Alan Paton   86

12   Wuthering Heights (1847)

by Emily Brontë   90

13   A Confederacy of Dunces (1980)

by John Kennedy Toole   94

14   To the Lighthouse (1927)

by Virginia Woolf   99

15   Ulysses (1922)

by James Joyce   104

16 Berlin Alexanderplatz (1929)
    by Alfred Döblin   109

17 The Lord of the Rings (1954-1955)
    by J. R. R. Tolkien   114

18 A Handful of Dust (1934)
    by Evelyn Waugh   119

19 So Long, See You Tomorrow (1980)
    by William Maxwell   124

20 Thérèse Raquin (1867)
    by Émile Zola   129

21 We (1920)
    by Yevgeny Zamyatin   134

22 The Great Gatsby (1925)
    by F. Scott Fitzgerald   139

23 Coming Up for Air (1939)
    by George Orwell   144

24 L'Étranger (1942)
    by Albert Camus   148

25 The Picture of Dorian Gray (1890)
    by Oscar Wilde   153

26 The Radetzky March (1932)
    by Joseph Roth   158

27 As I Lay Dying (1930)
    by William Faulkner   164

28 The Heart of the Matter (1948)
    by Graham Greene   169

29 The Expedition of Humphry Clinker (1771)
    by Tobias Smollett   174

30 Black Beauty (1877)
    by Anna Sewell   179

31 Malone Dies (1951)
    by Samuel Beckett   184

32 Great Expectations (1860-1861)
    by Charles Dickens   189

33 The Magic Mountain (1924)
    by Thomas Mann   194

34 The Optimist's Daughter (1972)
    by Eudora Welty   200

35 December Bride (1951)
    by Sam Hanna Bell   205

36 Mary (1926)
    by Vladimir Nabokov   209

37 The Tin Drum (1959)
    by Günter Grass   214

38 Nausea (1938)
    by Jean-Paul Sartre   221

39 Wide Sargasso Sea (1966)
    by Jean Rhys   226

40 Ethan Frome (1911)
    by Edith Wharton   230

41 Eugene Onegin (1833)
    by Alexander Pushkin   235

42 More Die of Heartbreak (1987)
    by Saul Bellow   240

43 The Charwoman's Daughter (1912)
    by James Stephens   245

44 Empire of the Sun (1984)
    by J. G. Ballard   250

45 Hunger (1890)
    by Knut Hamsun   256

46 Petersburg (1916)
    by Andrei Bely   261

47 Death in Rome (1954)
    by Wolfgang Koeppen   266

48 The Go-Between (1953)
    by L. P. Hartley   272

49 Oblomov (1859)
    by Ivan Goncharov   277

50 Adventures of Huckleberry Finn (1885)
    by Mark Twain   282

51 Crime and Punishment (1865/66)
    by Fyodor Dostoyevsky   287

52 The Recognitions (1955)
    by William Gaddis   293

Brief Suggested and
Selective Reading List   299

Acknowledgements

All gratitude to Brian Kilmartin, without whose astute editing, patience, exacting intelligence and generosity, this book would never have been written; to Cormac Kinsella, great reader, great friend for his support; to writer Richard Ford for his gracious introduction; to Dan Bolger of Liberties for his Philadelphian good humour and meticulous attention to detail; to Peter O'Connell of Liberties for his enthusiastic approach and to Caroline Walsh of *The Irish Times* and Seán O'Keefe of Liberties who decided between them that the series should grow into a much bigger project, a book. Huge thanks to all the writers for writing such wonderful novels; to the readers who want to read them; to former *Irish Times* literary editors Brian Fallon and novelist John Banville for encouraging me to review fiction from all over the world; to poet Gerard Smyth for being so supportive as an arts editor; to Gary Quinn of *The Irish Times*; to Professor Seamus Deane, my thesis supervisor, for telling me "you're a good reader"; to Dr Jerusha McCormack who made my move from law to arts so easy; to Prof Anngret Simms for being her kind and perceptive self; to Dr Frank Callanan for our many conversations about Joyce and Wilde; to my pal Jeni Glasgow and thank you to my daughter Nadia for already loving reading as much as I do and who urged me to include *The Lord of the Rings*, a battle easily won, not only because of Tolkien's magical book but because of my great dogs, Bilbo and Frodo, who knew all about stories and featured in so many.

Rereadings

Richard Ford

Years ago, when I was an under-aspiring and entirely unlikely college professor in America, there used to be an insider joke I shared with myself around the English Department Xerox machine, and that always sent me away entertained. Whenever any one of us "esteemed faculty members" would ask another if he'd read such-and-such a book – let's say it was *Daniel Deronda* (unopened by me to this day) – one's rumpled, tweedy, pipe-clenching colleague would go all evil-eyed and twitchy and found-out-looking, and with a half-dismissive, half-stricken smile, answer: "Oh, yes. Of course. You know I really must reread that." And off to class Professor Dottle would go, coat-tails a-wiggle, crepe soles squeaking, old exam papers and CVs fluttering from his book satchel.

By this measure, everyone had already read everything at least once, and life's jolly onward course was understood to be nothing more than revisiting these worn old faves, savouring prior underlinings, and – because we only read great books – having our most important judgements burnished and re-certified by the deeper delve.

Oh, I know there're people who've read everything. Really everything. Some time later, when I fleetingly taught at Harvard, I regularly lunched with a man named Walter Jackson Bate, who by then was elderly, retired and made extremely weary by his young literary-theorist colleagues – weary enough that having soup 'n' sandwich with a visiting novelist from New Orleans seemed not that bad an idea. Jack Bate had been the teacher of a teacher of mine, which was why I'd embraced the temerity to introduce myself. And he was also the great biographer of Keats and Samuel Johnson and Coleridge, and the brains behind plenty of other revered and recondite books. If knowing a lot makes you smart, he was probably the smartest man I'd ever met.

Bate had read everything. And occasionally, when we were joined for lunch by another of his emeritus colleagues, they would talk about it. About everything – at least everything where books were concerned. Norse mythology. Sanskrit poetics. The life of every small and large post-Raphaelite poet who ever drew breath. About hermeneutics. About Icelandic sagas. About Steinbeck. About Gainsborough. About theories of the sublime. About Kant, Li Po, Chaucer. They'd quote – always apposite, always spot-on (at least I thought so) – Dante, Shakespeare, the Venerable Bede, Congreve, Raymond Chandler, Joel Chandler Harris, Langston Hughes, Richard Hughes, Spenser, Milton, Mrs Gaskell, Mrs Woolf, La Rouchefoucauld, Merleau-Ponty, Ortega y Gasset, Burke, Locke, Ibsen, Cotton Mather, Jerry Mathers, Goethe, Roethke, Racine, Rimbaud and whoever wrote *Beowulf* – anybody you could name, really. Anybody who even had a name. Everything was their specialty. And I promise you it was never boring for one second to hear what they said. It was great just to be there – like having my birthday every day. It pleased me no end that here were these old boys who'd done the job right (unlike how I and my previous poky colleagues had done it) and were now happy to toodle along the way I just said – delving around and, as they spooned up their chicken-noodle soup, feeling the fond caress of literature, which had held them fast all those years. If Jack Bate said he'd reread something – *Daniel Deronda* – he'd goddamn well reread it. Probably twice.

If we've ever read any books at all, we'd probably like to read at least a few of them again. We were almost certainly too young to get most of the jokes in *Ulysses* the first time – if we made it through. And once you've read *The Waste Land* twenty or thirty times (it's better read out loud), it becomes just like a man talking to you – and making sense. Because we've been around more now, we're less gullible, more seasoned, less likely to be overpowered by showy virtuosity. Therefore, many of the brilliant but murky parts wouldn't seem as murky, and there'd be fewer of them. More of the best parts would finally make it into our brains.

The standard claim-to-seriousness by a certain kind of chin-pulling, Middle-western American university graduate – this person can be a woman or a man – is that they read *The Great Gatsby* every year. The point apparently is that as these young readers move wide-eyed-but-steadily-on from one mysterious life-phase to another, Fitzgerald's sleek, seemingly straightforward little tragedy of Nick and Daisy and the enigmatic Gatz, all lethally frolicking around in big Long Island houses and swimming pools and speeding cars, just keeps on turning up wonders which prior readings gave few hints of. Or else prior readings gave up only hints, which demand ever-greater seasoning in life's rigours and furious nuances before they'll surrender their fullest import.

The entire idea of rereading implies an attractive, progressive trope about life, one that's meant to keep us interested in it: namely, that as you get further along, you find out more valuable things; that familiarity doesn't always give way to dreary staleness, but to mystery and celestial understandings; that life and literature both are layered affairs you can work down through; and that, as Henry Moore once optimistically observed, we should never think of a surface but as the extension of a volume.

We mostly don't have time to reread books, of course. I don't. Mostly only teachers do, and then only because they have to teach them to make a living. But most of us aren't professors. Most of us, in fact, are slow readers, and spend our days scratching our heads and furrowing our brows at the mirage of some horizon line we wonder how we'll ever reach. Rereading's actually an expensive and oddly baulky luxury. For starters, our road's already lined with all those volumes we haven't even read once yet, but have meant to ever since we made a mental note years ago. *A Man Without Qualities*. *The Good Soldier Svejk*. *Under the Volcano*. And then there's Henry

James (except for *The Turn of the Screw*). These are books you need to be older, more patient, perhaps smarter to read.

Plus, rereading requires a kind of confiding, suspension-of-native-reluctance – assuming you don't unexpectedly hate the book you're rereading and never want to open it again (which can happen). To read a good book twice – even if our hearts swell at the patented opening words – we still have to re-subject ourselves to the novelist's now-transparent inaugural shenanigans, designed to get the unwieldy enterprise up and going for all those first-time readers who're forever threatening to put the book down. "We get it, we get it. Okay. It's India," we shout out (silently). "Just get us to the Marabar Caves part."And of course there are all the things we never really liked in *Moby Dick* to begin with – even though we loved the the book "as a whole". There's all that whaling stuff. The extracts. The cetology? It can all seem ritualised and tedious on subsequent exposure, like the *begat*s in the Lord's book. You might just as well skip these and get along to Revelations.

But. If we're rereading it because we love it, we shouldn't be skipping big chunks, should we? And yet . . . do we really have to reread *all* of the Benjy chapter in *The Sound and the Fury* just to get to the Caddy section?

I guess the answer's yes, if we're really rereading and not just dipping in, having a sniff. Our recalled affection for a book is always woven into how we entertain and balance the really good parts with the thinly outrageous, less artful passages, or the inevitably wooden infrastructure bits the novelist couldn't bear to part with. Novels are famously forgiving forms. Good writing over here often forgives less good writing over there. Rereading all of a novel invites us to be forgiving ourselves.

The point here, unsurprisingly, is that rereading a treasured book is a different enterprise from reading one the first time. It's not that you don't enter the same river twice. You do. It's just not the same you. By the time you get to the second go-round, you probably know – and know more about – what you don't know, and are possibly more comfortable with that, at least in theory. And you come to a book the second or third time with a different hunger, a more settled sense about how far off the great horizon really is for you, and what you do and don't have time for, and what you might reasonably hope to gain. Every time I open a book for the first time, I feel I'm taking a risk. It's part of the great excitement of reading. It's like standing in the street and watching a glistening, sequined tightrope walker traverse the empty space between tall buildings. If he falls, I'm implicated because I'm watching. Though maybe he won't, and I'll be implicated in a triumph.

But with *re*reading, less is thrillingly at risk – though it can still be thrilling. Everything just seems to happen on solider ground – not high up. In that sense, rereading is more like what we originally meant by reading – an achieved intimacy, a dappled discernment, the pleasures of volition, of surrendering, of time spent lavishly, the chance of glimpsing (but not quite possessing) the heart of something grand and beautiful we might've believed we already knew well enough.

∽◌

Eileen Battersby's undertaking in this tidy, understated little book is to do us the favour of leading us gently over the shoals of rereading a year's worth of those great novels we may not have gotten back around to yet. Ms Battersby, a fellow country-woman of mine, and for some time a sage and acute book critic for *The Irish Times*, offers us here not only her own valuable, happily idiosyncratic list of books indisputably worth a second go, but also succinct, perceptive synopses and appraisals of what we can expect to find when we launch into . . . well . . . *Ulysses, Persuasion, A Confederacy of Dunces, Le Grand Meaulnes, Ethan Frome, Wide Sargasso Sea, The Magic Mountain* and (how not?) *The Great Gatsby.* Plus forty or so others.

Myself, I'm unabashedly quite a ways away from having read all these books the first time – just to keep me separate from those young fogies I used to teach with, who'd "read" everything, or at least taught it. Many readers will be in my very situation, and will employ Ms Battersby's amiable little volume (or at least its table of contents) when they find themselves unable to sleep at 3AM, and go wandering around their cold houses, peering bleakly at their bookshelves, wanting a good novel to get them on toward daybreak. ("Hmm. Wonder if *December Bride*'s really all that good?" Eileen Battersby says: "Yes. Indubitably.")

Not only is Ms Battersby's list a wonderful trove of books she loves – and we might, too – but her synoptical second readings and takes are fresh and lucid, and don't dumb down these great novels on behalf of keeping things brief. Brevity's, however, a grace note you'll appreciate, and brings each book and her view of it into sharper focus, since Ms Batteresby isn't competing with her subjects or showily trying to surround them with her own bookishness. She understands she may only have one chance to match us with a book, and aims to make the most efficient use of that chance.

As I read through these little essays, I couldn't help remembering a snowy evening many years ago, in faraway Ann Arbor, Michigan, when my wife and I had our ears turned to stone for hours by a "great American poet" dilating upon the exquisite but apparently hard-to-pinpoint virtues of, in fact, *The Good Soldier Svejk*, which had apparently changed the poet's entire outlook on life, but which neither my wife nor I had read (and of course wouldn't think of reading now). Our poet acquaintance only (sweetly) wanted to share this precious novel he loved. But he drove us into the timber with his tumid oratory. If only my wife or I could've flourished Ms Battersby's book back then (and if only she'd included it here), we could've said: "Yes, yes, I have a lovely little essay about that very book. No need to go on longer. I'll read it as soon as I get home tonight. I promise." *The Good Soldier Svejk* could've been saved for posterity with that fell good fortune, instead of living on as a dreary cocktail-party memory. I'm sure it deserves better.

In America, people say you can't spend two minutes with a liberal without having a book recommended to you. I don't know Ms Battersby's politics, but I do know that no matter how strongly and morally certain we feel, it's damn near impossible to get anybody to read anything they don't already want to read – much less to read something again. We're all, I guess, too self-directed, too driven, too suspicious of the subjective out there in life. Data are what we crave. For that reason, then, this book of second readings may be a bit old-fashioned, may hearken to a time (not that long ago) when someone we trusted could amiably say to us: "Here's a really good book I read. You'll like it." And off we'd go to the library.

I'm naturally skeptical of sentiments that long for how things were "back then". Things probably weren't that great, or even much worse. And I don't estimate Ms Battersby to be wishing for a time when books meant more (although it'd be nice). Best just to think that her book of second readings tries to cut through our clutter with a good idea, tugs at our sleeve with a gift she thinks will make our life better in the congested here and now. Surely none of us is too busy for that.

'The Reader in the Hammock'

I

Why do we read? More importantly, why do we re-read? It is difficult to say. Perhaps it's comfort, the pleasure of re-engaging with old friends who aren't going to pull any nasty surprises because we already know what those surprises will be. We read a book and then return to it because we loved it the first time round; or maybe we didn't quite get it? Could it be we just weren't ready to read it? Was the timing wrong? But it's more likely that we go back to a book because we want to know if it is still as good as we remembered; has it changed? More to the point – have we?

Perhaps we first turn to a book because it meant a great deal to someone else and now it's our turn to discover a specific time and a place, or meet a character that we think we might like, or identify with and help explain us to ourselves. And once that connection is established with a novel, we return to it. All of this is far removed from the traditional question that makes stories so compelling, that urgent "and what happened next?", or "what did she do?" "Did the hero get the girl?" or "did the bad guys get him?"

It's intriguing how the novelist relies on story and yet is equally able to bypass it, by concentrating on feeling, romantic passion, love of country or an abiding belief in justice. Novelists tell stories, but they do a great many other things as well. They create characters we believe in, even maybe want to know, or think we know, having experiences we'd like to share, or are mighty glad we're not sharing. Novels tell us what happened to people who rebelled against dictators or how a king bullied his subjects or how an eccentric old Spaniard took to the road with his ancient horse and servant on a quest to discover God knows what. There's the nervy mother in a rush to marry off five daughters to men with good fortunes; there's a poor boy made good by dubious means who wants to win back his lost love. Or how about observing a Russian aristocrat so apathetic he wants to stay in bed all day as it's so much easier than thinking? What would it be like to be living in the barren beauty of Newfoundland's harsh landscape with interwoven stories about your Scots ancestors alive in your head?

Imagine St Petersburg in the nineteenth century? Or visit Berlin in confused stagnation during the Weimar years? Think yourself to Shanghai in 1941 where the menacing Japanese forces of occupation interpret the slightest movement as a gesture of defiance? Or observe Edwardian Dublin on a hot June day? Do we empathise with the man trapped in a Berlin boarding house waiting for the arrival of his lost love who is now another man's wife? Why not share the thoughts of that young German soldier who carries his wounded friend on his back for miles through the mud to a medical station, only to be told on reaching it that his friend is already dead.

Story is important, no doubt about that. But often the complications go far beyond "what happened next?" When I was a child we used to go to a cabin in a pine forest in the mountains in California. It was the sort of place that always seemed to have a skunk lurking by the meal stores, snakes hiding beneath the logs. You had to lock, not just close, the kitchen door because a dextrous racoon knew how to push up the handle and execute speedily efficient raids. The neighbours up the valley had a bow-legged old yellow dog given to wandering about, sniffing the air or just lying sprawled in the sun. The deer weren't afraid of anybody and cranky

Mr Olmstead was so short sighted he couldn't aim to hit the barn, never mind those frantic squirrels who lived on the roof of his house.

It was there, outside our cabin, staying very still in the musty old canvas hammock for fear I would tip out of it, that my eleven-year-old self began to read *Moby Dick* (1851) and figured out pretty quickly that this was a story about a lot more than a crazy old sea captain trying to kill the white whale that had torn off his leg. *Pride and Prejudice* (1813) had been easier to understand; even at ten I had reckoned that Elizabeth Bennet liked Mr Darcy, and had noticed that grown ups tended to run around in circles for a while before they got friendly with each other. At night in the cabin as the moths crashed into the mesh screens over the open windows and the wooden floorboards creaked after the heat of the day, it was time to catch up with calculating Becky Sharp in *Vanity Fair* (1847), to find out if she was ever going to get what she wanted. And way in the distance, that eerie cry? That was a lone wolf howling and that was definite; once you had read *The Call of the Wild* (1900), you knew.

To a child in the mountains, reading brought you over those mountains, to the high seas in *Treasure Island* (1883), to Paris during the French Revolution, to the squalor of Fagin's dirty old lair. Far closer to home was to live the story of Steinbeck's red pony. Years later when reading Cormac McCarthy's *All the Pretty Horses* (1992), I remembered that red pony.

Lying rigid, straight-legged in that hammock like a Norman knight in his tomb, I imagined being David Balfour in *Kidnapped* (1886); even better, you could be Huck Finn and I was; we didn't have a river but we had a lake so big you could only imagine what was on the other side. All you needed was a raft. Huck Finn was miles better than pain-in-the-neck Holden Caulfield in *The Catcher in the Rye* (1951), although sometimes I wished I was Scout in *To Kill A Mockingbird* (1960), as she was possessed of a logical turn of phrase and her dad Atticus was the sort of calmly wise father I wanted to have instead of a golf pro with a hands-off jazz collection. The haunted shack up near our ridge was just as spooky as the Radley place, although we didn't suspect any real person was actually living in it. Instead, we guessed a heart had been buried under the floorboards, just like the one in Poe's story, and of course it pounded loudest at night.

Just because you already know the story it doesn't spoil the re-reading; you still cry when Ginger dies in *Black Beauty* (1877), the shadows still dance in the flames at the end of *Jane Eyre* (1847). On the second or third reading the mechanics of the writing begin to assert themselves; this is when the language is tested, the imagery is deconstructed, additional symbolism appears. Novelists know the tricks, and describe the characters, summon the images, evoking mood and atmosphere. They tell the story but they also make their point and Tolstoy made many. It is odd how we accept being lectured to by a good writer telling a story; Dickens and Orwell attacked society and power, but they didn't allow the message to obscure the story. If we don't feel sorry for Meursault it is because the outsider isn't capable of feeling and is about to die because of his failure of emotion. Camus is concerned with exploring our perception of right and wrong. Although Emily Brontë may not be trying to instruct us in *Wuthering Heights* (1847), she does teach us all about the power of story when it is driven by an ungodly, destructive passion.

The more we read the more we want to read, *need* to read and re-read. Reading is the well that never runs dry, the list that keeps growing. One novel begets a further ten. The world is full of books, many of them great, and time is short. There is also the fact that for every writer who wrote only one book, many more produced large bodies of work. How grateful we should be to the mighty Dickens who despatched more words in English than any other published writer. Not only does he tell complex bustling tales, he also conjures up a world, nineteenth century England, and in particular nineteenth century London. English social history is contained within his stories, as is Paris in the works of Hugo and Zola. I always cringe on hearing a book being dismissed as "only a novel". Great fiction helps the historian to teach us about the past because at its best, it recreates it. Beyond the historical facts, it calls up a specific place; the sounds, the preoccupations and the people.

II

Readers are greedy, and this is a reader's book written by a reader, not a writer, and readers make no apology; walking into a library or a book store is the equal of walking into a chocolate factory. Part of the excitement is fuelled by sheer panic, the avid reader's compulsion to read everything. I once pretended to have a sore throat to stay at home from school to read *War and Peace* (1863-1869), it was the best lie I ever told. People read at night, on the train, on the bus, at work, at school, maybe not in church, but at meals, in restaurants, on the beach, when waiting for the washing machine to empty, for the bread to bake, for the mechanic to service the car, for the windows to somehow manage to wash themselves – and all because there isn't enough time to read all we want to.

The fifty-two novels gathered here are a mixed bunch of random wonders. There is no agenda, no definitive claims being made that they are the divine elect, although I think they're pretty good. It is not an absolute selection. How could there be one? All these fifty-two novels have in common is that they are, in my opinion, great. Some are famous, others are not. Some of the authors included are more famous for other novels. Everyone appears to have read *Animal Farm* (1945) and *Nineteen Eighty-Four* (1949), but far fewer are familiar with Orwell's engaging *Coming Up For Air* (1939), one of the first great novels I read. I remember finding a Penguin paperback edition in a coffee shop. It had a smooth white cover splashed with a water colour illustration and was looking abandoned, the sole book on a stand packed tightly with postcards and stationery – just waiting for me and that's how I first made the acquaintance of George Orwell. Much the same happened with Aldous Huxley. I read *Point Counter Point* (1928) and his best book, *Antic Hay* (1923), before reading *Brave New World* (1932) which I was disappointed with, because, by then, I had already read Yevgeny Zamyatin's riveting *We* (1921), a tale about living as a dehumanised number.

When I suggested doing a series in *The Irish Times* about great books, titles danced into my mind, a world to revisit. I had not read

Smollett's *The Expedition of Humphry Clinker* (1771) since my second year at university. Would it still make me laugh? It did and louder. Returning to Hermann Hesse's cult quest *Steppenwolf* (1927) proved mortifying; I couldn't believe I had ever read it in the first place. It made me wary of re-reading *The Glass Bead Game* (1943), but I will, just not yet. I picked up *Nausea* (1938), a novel I had loved at thirteen; how bad would this be? Re-reading it was wonderful; it is brilliant, even better than I remembered. And yes, it's in this selection, as is Nabokov's *Mary* (1926), his beautiful first novel which looks so intently to the Russian tradition. Solzhenitsyn's *One Day in the Life of Ivan Denisovich* (1962) is as convincing as ever. V. S. Naipaul's finest achievement, *The Enigma of Arrival* (1988), a haunting, evocative work, presented a claim for inclusion that was strong, but not strong enough.

Smollett's comic picaresque was not the only book to make me laugh. *A Confederacy of Dunces* (1980) continues to shine and roar. It's just as well, as it is difficult not to notice the amount of unhappy narrators and tragic central characters populating literary fiction. Far less dangerous a man than Heathcliff and a great deal less complex is Ethan Frome who paid dearly for love; narrators such as Nick Carraway and Marlow have acquired sombre wisdom while in two fine novels, *So Long, See You Tomorrow* (1980) and *The Go-Between* (1953), the narrators as older men painfully revisit their respective boyhoods. Great fiction makes effective use of human torment and that's a fact. Do we as readers engage more closely with grief, nostalgia, pain, violence, alienation, loneliness, regret than with happiness? Possibly? After all, what comic novel could expect to overwhelm a reader the way *Wide Sargasso Sea* (1966) does?

Mention of Jean Rhys reminds me that *The Good Soldier* (1915), a classic work for sure, by her one-time lover, Ford Madox Ford, seemed as polished as ever, if less compelling on return than I had expected. It is a cold, somewhat mannered narrative. Not that novels have to be nice to be great. Among the finest novels I have read is Patrick White's *The Vivisector* (1970), based on the life of artist Sidney Nolan. Some would argue it is savage, yet it is also wonderful, as is his epic *Tree of Man* (1956). No, novels don't have to be *nice*; people don't tend to be all that nice.

Sad and tragic, these are the qualities that remind us we are humans; it is true although for much of Mann's dialectic opus, *The Magic Mountain* (1924), the narrative is not particularly sad. Hans Castorp is engaged on a journey of self-discovery. That's what reading is, a journey. Every great novel brings us on a meaningful odyssey, teaching us about the business of living, the often horrible comedy of it all, as Beckett's Malone reflects, lying there in his death bed. How come Thomas Hardy's Tess and Jude are not as sympathetic on the third or was it fourth reading as I remembered? Although Michael Henchard's desperate life as described in Hardy's finest novel, *The Mayor of Casterbridge* (1886), remains a convincing Greek tragedy. If much of Hardy's fatalistic fiction appears more laboured than I had imagined, Jane Austen's, written more than eighty years earlier, continues to seem as fresh as if it were published yesterday. That is one of the many wonders of fiction, how writers as different as say Austen and Evelyn Waugh can examine their societies so closely, through such contrasting styles, yet still reflect human behaviour so accurately.

When writing the original series in the newspaper, time as well as space, and of course, who to include, became the enemy; fifty-two is very few, too few. A book seemed to offer far more freedom. Even as I write this I still can't figure out what happened to *The Portrait of a Lady* (1881). Günter Grass's masterpiece *The Tin Drum* (1959) argued its case, and won. There it was, as relentless as a drum beat, and in the magnificent new translation that Grass has sought for more than thirty years. But I still got to re-read *The Portrait of a Lady*, stately, deliberate, chilling and relentlessly accurate. Yes, this is how people conduct themselves.

So, no Henry James? If defeated by numbers he is present throughout this selection. Where are so many favourites? William Trevor? John Updike? John McGahern? John Cheever? Absent, along with Chekhov, Alice Munro, Mavis Gallant and Tobias Wolff, are they all, but for a good reason; they are all masters of the short story. Updike could well have got in with *Roger's Version* (1986), or *Rabbit at Rest* (1990), or *Towards the End of Time* (1998) but the fact remains his greatest achievement is the remarkable, quasi-autobiographical short story, 'A Sandstone Farmhouse' (from *The Afterlife*, 1994). Updike, as with Trevor, is a supreme short story writer.

Similarly with John McGahern. I once said to him that I thought his greatest work was the long short story, 'The Country Funeral'. McGahern thought for a moment and replied, "Yes, I like that." And writer to reader it was John McGahern who alerted me to a gifted, though neglected American writer, John Williams, who wrote four novels including the 1973 National Book Award-winning *Augustus*, and a subtle masterpiece, *Stoner* (1965). It is the story of a farmer's son who becomes a college professor. It is about love and about work, responsibility. McGahern was a great writer; he was also a great reader.

Then there is John Cheever. *Falconer* (1977) is his finest novel, a work that is there in the shadows when you read Annie Proulx's *Brokeback Mountain* (1997), yet Cheever's short stories are among the best you'll find. *Falconer* was jostling for space with William Gaddis and *The Recognitions* (1955) won – on the day. The thirty-fifth entry of the year-long series coincided with the Halloween weekend and *Dracula* (1897) was an obvious choice. Such an iconic work would not suffer by conceding its place to another Irish classic, *The Charwoman's Daughter* (1912), by James Stephens, a fascinating individual who brought astute insights to the story of a young girl and her hard-working mother. Its inclusion, along with that of Sam Hanna Bell's *December Bride* (1951), was well deserved.

Alfred Döblin's urgent, cinematic *Berlin Alexanderplatz* (1929) pushed its way into the reckoning. Ironically, Ernest Hemingway looked a likely choice with his finest work, *The Sun Also Rises* (1926), known to some readers as *Fiesta*. But he was never going to challenge Faulkner or William Maxwell's *So Long, See You Tomorrow*, with its assured use of the first-person voice that sets a formidable standard for the American short novel.

Looking at the US fiction featured certainly alerts one to the strength in depth of the Southern writers and their tradition so well upheld by Richard Ford. Flannery O'Connor – admittedly a short story writer who did sneak in with *The Violent Bear it Away* (1960), the second of her two novels – Eudora Welty, Thomas Wolfe and the great Faulkner are all virtuosos. It wasn't easy leaving out Peter Taylor. Hopefully though, readers will seek out *A Summons to Memphis* (1986) and *In the Tennessee Country* (1992); yet he too is primarily a superlative short story writer as evident from the stories of *In the Miro District* (1977).

III

No doubt about it, this selection could have been dominated by great Americans. The more I wandered among my book cases, it could easily have been a selection of nineteenth century Russians and twentieth century German-language writers, or only Russian writers, from Pushkin to Bulgakov; from the tsarist Gogol of the doomed *Dead Souls* (1842), to the post-revolutionary Andrey Platonov (1899-1951) and *The Foundation Pit* (1929-1930), which was not published in Russia until the late 1980s, and Andrei Bitov's subversive summation of a nation's literature, *The Pushkin House* (1978). The Russian achievement is overwhelming whether you are reading Turgenev or Solzhenitsyn. Tolstoy tells great stories and deals in epic truths, his personal contradictions retreating to the background because he knows all about people in crisis. However widely one reads world fiction, it is impossible to shake off the psychological influence of Dostoyevsky. Is he the giant at everyone's shoulder? From Hamsun to Kafka and Conrad and beyond.

Mention of the Russians introduces one of the most contentious issues facing literature, translation. While some of us can summon sufficient French, or German or Italian or Spanish, far fewer can claim good reading Russian. You hear purists announce that they only read in the original, but unless they read Russian, they are missing out on wonders the rest of us have enjoyed thanks to translations. The greatest friends readers have, aside from the writers, are the translators who open the doors of great books.

Thanks to translation we are now beginning to benefit from the wealth of recent Chinese and Japanese fiction; novels such as Ma Jian's *Beijing Coma* (2008) or Gao Xingjian's profound odyssey, *Soul Mountain* (1990) and Jiang Rong's *Wolf Totem* (2004) as well as Saiichi Maruya's *Singular Rebellion* (1972) – which was not translated into English until 1988 – and the lively and ever-expanding ouvre of the prolific Haruki Murakami.

There was another extraordinary body of national literature threatening to take over the selection: novels written in German. Kafka the enigmatic Czech raced into the selection in the company of Thomas Mann with *The Magic Mountain* (1924). Mann's unhappy son Klaus had also been included in the original series with his satirical indictment of Nazi evil, *Mephisto* (1936). But on a more practical level, with the introduction of individual author essays, Klaus's sad personal story is closely bound to that of his father.

Joseph Roth is in the selection; *The Radetzky March* (1932) was one of the first novels I reached for; his rival, fellow Austro-Hungarian Robert Musil, is not, although I can boast of reading *The Man Without Qualities* (1930-1932) twice (the second time to review a new edition), and enjoyed it both times. Roth surpasses Musil's admittedly magisterial if cold opus. Ultimately, the self-absorption of Ulrich, Musil's anti-hero, is a barrier to the book despite Musil's irony and genuine perplexity at the chaos of human emotions. Viennese Hermann Broch, who shared his first English language translators, the Muirs, with Kafka, is one of my most glaring omissions; how I fretted over *The Spell* (1935), *The Death of Virgil* (1946) and the 'Sleepwalkers' trilogy. The only consolation for leaving out the Dutch-born but Austrian-bred Thomas Bernhard is that his finest book is his autobiography, *Gathering Evidence* (1985).

German language fiction has extraordinary range from Goethe and Theodor Storm to Walser and Koeppen and the Austrian Stefan Zweig, to another of my absolute heroes, W. G. Sebald, who through magnificently singular works such as *The Emigrants* (1993), *Austerlitz* (2001) and his exceptional meditation, *The Rings of Saturn* (1995), introduced his admirers to the glories of the eighteenth century novel of ideas.

Sebald understood the relentlessness of memory; his work is difficult to classify but its relevance is monumental and its artistry inspirational. He is a vital element in the extraordinary mosaic created by German writers such as Thomas Mann, Hans Fallada, Wolfgang Koeppen, Gert Ledig, Gert Hofmann and Grass, who at time of writing, is still at work.

Post-communist Central and Eastern Europe continues to unearth revived classics and new writing. The translation in 2002 of rediscovered Hungarian Sandor Márai's *Embers* (1942) was a cause for celebration, as was the subsequent 2007 translation of *The Rebels* (1930). The past continues to live and always war, in particular, the second World War, remains as important to writers as the enduring themes of love and death and truth.

One of the most fascinating stories in modern fiction is the impressive emergence of Indian and Pakistani writers who have mastered the balance between story and polemic, whether writing from the sub-continent, or from North America and multi-cultural Britain.

Latin American writing asserted itself by the mid-twentieth century. Alejo Carpentier (1904-1980), the Cuban-born son of a French father and a Russian mother, was a great storyteller. It was Carpentier, through works such as *The Lost Steps* (1953), *The Chase* (1956) and his fantastical novella, *Baroque Concerto* (1974), who pioneered magic realism, a genre which influenced many writers including Angela Carter and Grass, but found its most cohesive expression among the writers of Latin America such as Colombia's 1982 Nobel Literature Laureate, Gabriel García Márquez, who elevated the style to baroque richness in *One Hundred Years of Solitude* (1970), *Chronicle of a Death Foretold* (1982) and *Love in the Time of Cholera* (1988).

Isabel Allende followed Márquez with her debut *The House of the Spirits* (1985). Many Latin American writers work within the heady mix of politics and narrative innovation adopted by Peruvian Maria Vargas Llosa and shared for so long by the eastern European writers of protest. The kaleidoscopic posthumous publications from Chilean writer Roberto Bolaño in recent years continues to excite readers, but is he an original? Was not Gaddis there before him, as Gaddis pre-empted Pynchon? Considering the internationally established wealth of Latin American writers, I guess the inclusion of an earlier master, the Brazilian Joaquim Maria Machado de Assis (1839-1909), to represent this tradition may be unexpected, and it is. He will be a fascinating discovery for some readers.

The swell of books, new or old, is there waiting to be discovered. Influences defy frontiers. It is exciting to see Goncharov's *Oblomov* (1859) echoed in Israeli Amos Oz's *Fima* (1991); Dostoyevsky shaping J. M. Coetzee's *The Master of Petersburg* (1994), or Camus's *The Fall* (1956) re-emerge through the voice of Moshin Hamid's narrator in *The Reluctant Fundamentalist* (2007).

Stories are told and continue to be told. Language moves around the world, narrative seduces and informs. The reader has no choice. Nor is there a better one, than to select a volume and clamber back into the hammock for the next adventure – to experience, relive, share and remember by reading and re-reading.

1 | One Day in the Life of Ivan Denisovich (1962)

by Alexander Solzhenitsyn

You wake up hungry and you wake up cold. You shit in a communal bucket. Breakfast is a test of wiles, the prize a miserable bowl of watery porridge – a stinking lump of fish becomes a treasure to savour, as is the hoarded crust sewn into your secret pocket. The guards watch your every gesture; you learn to mind your tongue, your fellow prisoners will kill for your ration of stale bread or even for the rags in which you wrap your feet. Suspicion, despair and the cunning inspired by suffering is the code by which you exist. Each day is like the next, or the previous one; there is no hope, aside from the thrill of petty theft or concealing a sliver of broken blade. Life is a void. Memory is reduced to fragmented incidents or a line of poetry uttered by another voice.

Above all there is 'the naked steppe' with its frozen air and temperatures plunging towards minus forty degrees; the snow, the frost, the viciously unrelenting wind and the spectacle of watching each other rot. "As usual, at five o'clock that morning reveille was sounded by the blows of a hammer on a length of rail hanging up near the staff quarters . . . the clanging ceased, but everything outside still looked like the middle of the night when Ivan Denisovich Shukhov got up . . ."

The publication of Solzhenitsyn's starkly lyric masterpiece, *One Day in the Life of Ivan Denisovich*, in the November 1962 issue of the Russian literary journal, *Novy Mir*, shocked the world by confirming that there was yet another hell which had endured long after the liberation of the Nazi death camps. This detailed account of one man's day summed up the fate of millions of Russians under Stalin.

Here was the reality of existence in a Siberian labour camp as experienced by Solzhenitsyn and recast as art with equal measures of poetry and metaphysics which had been directly bequeathed by a prisoner of an earlier generation, Dostoyevsky.

Although told in the third person this is the story of Shukhov, an ordinary villager, no hero perhaps, but an individual who has retained his sense of humour, even honour. Everything is filtered through his thoughts, responses and observations. The genius of the narrative lies in the language which is simple, direct, folksy and often idiomatic. The tone is laconic, never satirical. Many of the exchanges are shaped by the understandable exasperation shared by victims of an inhuman, at times farcical, system.

Assigned to a work party building a power station, Shukhov more than pulls his weight as a mason, a skill he mastered because it was needed. Bantering among themselves the team become carried away; the project, though pointless, is a communal effort. Shukhov enjoys building the wall; he and his mate Senka work beyond the set time. Fearing punishment for returning late, both run back. The effort is not lost on Shukhov who thinks: "There are loafers who race one another of their own free will round a stadium. Those devils should be running after a full day's work, with aching back and wet mittens and worn-out *valenki* – and in the cold too."

Late in the narrative, Shukhov is feeling good; having done a favour for his team leader, Tsezar, he has been rewarded with a second ration of soup. Lying on his bunk, he debates God with earnest young Alyosha, who is serving a twenty-five year sentence for being a Baptist. The young man believes in prayer: "If you have real faith you tell a mountain to move and it will move." Shukhov smiles, unconvinced: "I've never seen a mountain move. Well to tell the truth, I've never seen a mountain at all."

Some hours earlier, he had playfully quizzed Captain Buinovsky, who had been imprisoned for being liberated by the Americans, on the behavioural patterns of the moon. "Listen, captain, where according to this science of yours does the old moon go afterwards?" and had delighted in announcing to the exasperated captain who had already explained that it simply becomes invisible: "In our village, folk say God crumbles up the old moon into stars." These new stars, Shukhov maintained, fill the gaps made by stars that have fallen from the heavens.

Despite subsequent major works such as *Cancer Ward* (1967), *The First Circle* (1968) and his crusading, multi-volume history, *The Gulag Archipelago* (1967), Solzhenitsyn was never again to approach the simplicity and beauty of a stoic Everyman doggedly mastering the art of survival in a Soviet labour camp.

Alexander Solzhenitsyn *(1918-2008)*

Had he died during the 1960s, instead of living until August 2008 to die of heart failure at eighty-nine, Alexander Solzhenitsyn, the 1970 Nobel Laureate for Literature, would have been remembered as a hero, a prophet and, above all, a great writer in a country of great writers. But he made one mistake; he survived. Not only did he survive the Second World War, Stalin's death camps and stomach cancer, he outlived communism.

By the time Solzhenitsyn had settled in Vermont, where his household lived in a high-security compound, the West had already discovered a far more attractive Russian, albeit Americanised, dissident – the poet Joseph Brodsky, who openly performed the role of artist, was possessed of theatrical rage, played to the gallery and would eventually, in 1987, be awarded the Nobel Prize for literature.

Solzhenitsyn, reclusive and taciturn, was very different. His soldier father, having returned from the Great War, died in a hunting accident six months before the future writer's birth – some suggested it was suicide. Whatever the truth, Solzhenitsyn was born in the shadow of a family tragedy and was left with relatives while his mother went to work in a nearby town. He was also born into revolution; his birth in Kislovodsk, a spa town in the Caucasus Mountains, in southern Russia, on 11 December 1918 coincided with a time of global upheaval. For Russia it was cataclysmic; tsarist Russia died in a blood bath and Communist Russia was born into another.

The young 'Sanya' Solzhenitsyn was clever, securing a first-class degree in maths and physics while pursuing his interest in the arts, particularly literature. Then he was called up. Already something of an intellectual he proved an arrogant soldier, serving as a gunner and later an artillery officer. Twice decorated he was soon promoted to captain. But he made a mistake; when writing a letter to a friend, he made "derogatory" comments about Stalin. The irony was cruel – having served his country well, Solzhenitsyn was then arrested as an enemy of the people in early 1945. His eight-year sentence seemed mild enough, but those eight years were spent in the hell of the labour camps – initially in the Arctic Circle where the political prisoners lived alongside criminals, and later in the harsher conditions of the "special" camps for long-term prisoners organised by Lavrenty Beria, chief of the security police under Stalin.

These experiences inspired a masterful debut, *One Day in the Life of Ivan Denisovich*. Initially published in *Novy Mir*, the literary journal, in 1962, it was the performance that would make his name, and for many, it remains his finest artistic achievement. It is written in a bleak lyricism that is both heartrending and also, at times, deeply witty. It is his most human book. For those who doubt Solzhenitsyn as an artist they need only read this short novel and experience life in the camp through the thoughts of Shukhov who survives the biting cold and the hunger.

On his release in 1951 Solzhenitsyn faced another ordeal, cancer. This experience would later inspire a compelling narrative, *Cancer Ward* (1967). With *The First Circle*, published in 1968, he proved that he too was privy to the literary power that had elevated the nineteenth century Russian novel. Meanwhile Solzhenitsyn the artist was being pushed aside by Solzhenitsyn the campaigner. Setting out to expose the horrors of the Soviet system he began his monumental work, *The Gulag Archipelago*, the defining history of the political oppression and personal suffering that destroyed millions of Russians. It is a three-volume labour of courage. In 1967 he revised and re-typed the entire text, which runs to more than 1,500 pages. At that time he had some support within Russia; he could also draw on Pasternak's legacy and the international success of *One Day in the Life of Ivan Denisovich*. It was a useful shield; he did not "disappear" but was merely expelled from the Soviet Union, initially arriving in Bonn, then West Germany, before moving on to Zurich and later the United States, where he remained for more than twenty years.

There is no disputing his contribution towards the collapse of communism – he exposed the system. He had also demolished the myth of Lenin with his boldly ironic, *Lenin in Zurich* which was first published in Paris in 1975. By then he had already been honoured with the Nobel Prize, although he had not been able to accept it in person in 1970. His fiction was being read all over the world but he was grimly devoting himself to the story of Russia. The witness, the writer, had become an historian. Unfortunately, unfairly for Solzhenitsyn, he had outlived his usefulness. No longer regarded as a prophet, he was increasingly dismissed as a polemicist and a crank.

In addition to survival, his love of Russia proved another mistake. After the fall of communism, he decided in 1994 to return home to a changed country which greeted him with indifference not affection. His books were dismissed as boring and his use of Russian was considered ugly and graceless. If his country lost interest in him as both a writer and a polemicist, the West continued to take him seriously, although US opinion of him was damaged by his reclusiveness.

Solzhenitsyn did outlive his time; the country he loved and tried to save rejected him. Yet his achievement remains. For all the truths contained in his non-fiction and autobiographical writings, *Cancer Ward* and *The First Circle* are compelling, important novels, although overshadowed by his masterpiece, *One Day in the Life of Ivan Denisovich*. The prophet may have been forgotten but the novelist will endure.

2 | Le Grand Meaulnes
(1913)
by Alain-Fournier

Mystery, romance and unbearable sadness haunt this graceful, elegiac study of the passage from boyhood – that lost domain of dreams – to the adult world. Few novels so beautifully evoke the mood of the past as well as of a period intense with restless longing and an indefinable need for new adventures. François Seurel, the immensely sym- pathetic narrator, recalls his younger self, the sickly son of a country school master, and his early days spent attending class, during which he would address his father as "Monsieur Seurel". Millie, his mother, who taught the younger boys, was by nature a tenacious housewife, forever bemoaning the inferior accommodation which came with each new appointment.

Yet this time, it would be different; the long red building with the Virginia creeper and the courtyard really did become home, as the narrator's father stayed on at the same country school for ten years. One cold winter day, a wealthy widow arrived, hoping that her son, whom she considered exceptional, could not only attend the school, but lodge with the school master's family. The newcomer was, to the eyes of the then fifteen-year-old narrator, "a tall youth, about seventeen. It was too dark to make out much more than his peasant's hat of felt pushed back on his head and a black smock tightly belted in like a schoolboy's. But I could see that he was smiling."

The smile belonged to Augustin Meaulnes. He captured the attention of the family and for François, the elusive Meaulnes became his hero, and his friend. It was an important time, not only had the narrator finally recovered from the weak knee which had left him "timid and forlorn" and unable to play with other children, the arrival of Meaulnes changed his life. Instead of spending the evenings sitting in with his parents, he began to join the senior boys who huddled around Meaulnes. They debated and argued, and although Meaulnes said very little, the boys sought his company, and his approval.

One day, when entrusted with an errand, Meaulnes disappeared. On his return, exhausted, four days later, he brought with him a heightened air of mystery and a silken waistcoat. Everything begins to change; Meaulnes believes himself to have become different: ". . . that strange adventure . . . was my one reason for living, my only hope in the world."

His story is dream-like, vivid, strange and immediate. Having become hopelessly lost he had by chance happened upon a marvellous gathering at a mansion, a place which will acquire symbolic resonance in the narrative. A stranger among strangers, he too put on fancy dress and joined in. The occasion had been planned to celebrate the son of the great house who was bringing his fiancée home. The description of the festivities, the rambling house, the gardens, the costumes, the players ready to entertain the guests, the fairytale heroine, the sheer ease of it all, is like nothing else in literature. But Frantz de Galais, the wilful, indulged son of the great house, returned without his beloved and fled, causing everything to collapse into disarray.

Meaulnes had vowed to find Frantz's intended, but he is also seeking something for himself. His quest transforms him into an obsessive knight of old. His restlessness, as much as the burden of a promise given, takes over his life – and the story. The narrator, François, watches, is privy to some of it, befriends Yvonne de Galais, Frantz's sister, and ultimately plays some part in the story. In the course of his search Meaulnes experiences his own romance which ends in tragedy. It is as if the narrator and Meaulnes are two sides of the one person; François, in telling the story, makes clear that he accepts the life fate has given him, while Meaulnes pursues his dreams.

Alain-Fournier's psychological journey into the subconscious explores the passage from childhood fantasy to adult realities with terrifying beauty. As if by way of an eerily appropriate postscript to the novel, Alain-Fournier went to war and was killed in action. His enigmatic only novel is subtle and atmospheric; as lovely as a flower, as unforgettable as a plaintive melody.

Alain-Fournier (1886-1914)

Many ironies, most of them sad, surround Alain-Fournier. His haunting novel, *Le Grand Meaulnes,* represents boyhood idealised and innocence lost. Its central hero becomes a wanderer in search of many things. Alain-Fournier personifies the wartime Lost Generation in a way that transcends the more immediate tragedies of Rupert Brooke or of the great Wilfrid Owen. While Owen died the week before the Armistice, Alain-Fournier was killed in the opening weeks of the war. There is nothing war-like about him, no famous images of him in uniform. There is no rhetoric, no lamentation, no sense of conflicting loyalties.

He was born Henri Alban-Fournier on 3 October 1886 in central France and had a country upbringing, in the flat, marshy landscape of Bourges, in Cher. His father, as with Monsieur Seurel, the narrator's father in the novel, was a school teacher. Alain-Fournier understood country ways, and, having initially abandoned them as he became more immersed in a literary life, later reclaimed his heritage, making much of being "un paysan", a peasant. This would play an important part in his novel. He would recreate from memory the freezing winter days in a classroom full of boys wearing damp clothing.

He was a hard-working though not outstanding student and set out to become a teacher. At nineteen he had an encounter which deeply affected him and was to prove central to his novel as well as to his life. While out walking along the Seine on 1 June 1905, he met Yvonne de Quievrecourt. They spoke, he felt he was in love, but she was far more detached. As the day marked a church holiday, he decided he would walk in the same place on the same day, the following year. She did not appear. This disappointment became his personal tragedy. By the time they next met, eight years later, she was married and had two children, and was farther away from him than ever. Still, he had his muse; she would be immortalised as Yvonne de

Galais, with whom François Seurel, the narrator of the novel, has an obviously platonic relationship.

Before this fateful meeting, Alain-Fournier had completed his military service in 1909. He had already begun a friendship with the future critic Jacques Rivière who married his sister. Alain-Fournier began publishing poems and short stories, and in about 1910 emerged as a literary journalist writing for *Paris Journal*. He became friendly with novelist Andre Gide and the poet Paul Claudel.

Then, in 1912, he made what seemed an odd career move, becoming personal assistant to a politician. It may have been a way of financing his writing while avoiding the distractions of having to undertake other literary work. It is known that during this period he was working on *Le Grand Meaulnes*. It first appeared in serialised form in the *Nouvelle Revue Française* between July and October 1913, and was then published in book form. Although nominated for the major literary award in France, the Prix Goncourt, it failed to win.

He had begun work on a second novel, *Colombe Blanchet*, but it was unfinished when he joined the army in August 1914. Within a month, he was dead, having fallen on 22 September 1914 on the Meuse. For years, Alain-Fournier was mourned, his body lost. His remains were finally recovered in 1991. *Miracles*, a volume of essays and poems, was published in 1924, and his correspondence with Rivière two years later. His letters reveal him to be romantic and self-dramatising, conscious of the literary world he had entered. His sensitive, artistic perception shaped a defining, dream-like Symbolist narrative that reads as a life experience unfolding.

3 | The Lonely Passion of Judith Hearne (1955)

by Brian Moore

Judith Hearne, alone and lonely, unpacks, yet again. The silver-framed photograph of her dead aunt is positioned in a place of honour, as ever, on the mantelpiece of "whatever bed-sitting-room Miss Hearne happened to be living in." Within sentences, Brian Moore, in this his first (officially) and finest novel, leaves no doubts; his anti-heroine appears to be as hopeless as is her new room in this 'run-down part of Belfast.'

A second picture is unwrapped, a coloured oleograph of the Sacred Heart, 'His eyes kindly yet accusing.' The clues are already mounting, Judith Hearne, clearly beaten by life, continues to be dominated by that dead, still all-seeing aunt, and by a religion that for her is more concerned with ritual than belief. Judith addresses the aunt's photograph, informing her that this once smart residential area has become flatland. Quickly, Ms Hearne moves on to more practical matters. She has brought picture hooks with her but needs a hammer before she can hang the Sacred Heart over her bed. The quest brings her downstairs to her new land lady, Mrs Henry Rice. There she meets Bernard, the repulsive son "all bristly blond jowls, tiny puffy hands and long blond curly hair, like some monstrous baby swelled to man size." Judith is shocked that this "ugly pudding" should possess a "soft and compelling" speaking voice.

So adroitly does Moore enter the often bizarrely jaunty mind of Judith Hearne, unloved, though genteel spinster, that it seems as if she is speaking directly to us. Like an animal accustomed to being kicked, she expects to be rejected by any male she encounters.

Moore's approach to the telling, the precise evocation of a decay shared by most of the characters, as well as Belfast itself, appears initially to share something of the tone of Joyce's *Dubliners* (1914) – and Joyce is obviously an influence. Yet this novel is far closer to William Trevor's vision of boarding house life in London. Judith's hopeless predicament is pathetic and partly traceable to her aunt's domineering influence, as well as, of course, to Judith's destructive weakness for invariably turning, at times of crisis, to alcohol.

Moore remains detached and is as interested in Judith's plight as he is in exposing the religious hypocrisy, cruel gossip and repressive social attitudes prevailing in Belfast, the native city he fled yet always admitted to never having fully escaped. Despite her self-pity, she is a fantasist, with a flair for subconscious self-delusion. With the arrival of Jim Madden, the landlady's widower brother, back home after some thirty years in New York, Moore develops this theme of self-delusion. Unlike Judith with her shaky grasp of correct behaviour, Madden is incontestably crude. For her, he is a possibly attainable, if lame and no longer young, future husband; for him, she is a potential business partner, no more.

Throughout the narrative Moore intuitively shifts the viewpoint between characters who always think and act true to themselves. Among the many inspired set pieces are the Sunday afternoon teas at Professor O'Neill's home, during which Judith is endured rather than enjoyed. Published in 1955 and never out of print, this precise study of an unwanted woman's slow agony of thwarted dreams and all-too-real humiliation displays the psychological astuteness Moore would bring to his subsequent diverse, always moral fictions.

Brian Moore *(1921-1999)*

Although he first left Belfast in 1943 and moved around between Europe and North Africa throughout the war years, returning briefly to London in 1948 when he was twenty-seven – settling first in Canada and later in California – the wry, detached Brian Moore never relinquished his Irishness and in time, would admit to regarding himself as an Irish writer. Themes of sin and guilt preoccupied him; he didn't believe in God, but was interested in watching characters struggle with faith and religion. Calm and opinionated, he was a self-exile who never glamorised his outsider status. He could easily have been a spy, such was Moore's ability to merge with the background and observe the world as if it were his favourite television programme.

Neither an autobiographical nor a confessional writer, his attitude towards his work was confident and practical, never pretentious. Born in Belfast in August 1921, he was the fourth child and second son, in a doctor's family of nine children, raised in a Catholic household which was also strongly nationalist, although settled in a Protestant community. His mother was a native Irish speaker. Moore attended St Malachy's College, later immortalised in *The Feast of Lupercal* (1957), where he enjoyed English, writing essays and discovering fiction.

Moore's father eventually became the head surgeon of Belfast's Mater Hospital. Two of Moore's brothers became doctors, yet he knew by the age of twenty that medicine was not for him. Opposed then, as he would remain throughout his life, to Ireland's neutrality, he set off for the war, volunteering in a civilian capacity. Initially he served with the British Ministry of War Transport, and soon developed his father's anti-British sentiments. Posted to Algiers, he then moved on to Anzio, south of Rome where he witnessed Allied landings. After spending two years as a port clerk in Naples, he joined the United Nations Relief and Rehabilitation organisation in Warsaw.

So self-contained was Moore that he never drew on his war experiences in his writing despite having witnessed the German invasion of southern France and later the German retreat from Russia. On leaving Warsaw, he went to Canada in the vain pursuit of a Canadian economist, ten years his senior. After securing Canadian citizenship, he began working as a proof reader on a Montreal newspaper, soon moving on to reporting before he realised he preferred feature-writing.

He tried his luck at writing fiction. Much has been written of his first novel, *The Lonely Passion of Judith Hearne* (1955), arguably his finest achievement. If not quite his first, he had written seven thrillers under the name of Michael Bryan – all of which he subsequently disowned – it remains unique. He always maintained it had been inspired by a chance remark he overheard made by a woman speaking with his mother who mentioned "my brother-in-law who was to have been." *The Lonely Passion of Judith Hearne* was followed by *The Feast of Lupercal* and *An Answer from Limbo* (1962), *The Emperor of Ice-Cream* (1965), *I am Mary Dunne* (1968), *The Doctors Wife* (1976) and another major work, *Black Robe* (1985), about the tensions threatening a community of Jesuit missionaries in seventeenth-century Canada.

His earlier fiction has echoes of William Trevor. But from *The Colour of Blood* (1987) onwards, Moore looked increasingly towards the political thriller genre. It suited his cinematic eye and spare prose. As the years passed, themes and issues interested him more than character. In October 1995, the publication of *The Statement*, in which Moore openly took on French history and the wartime crimes perpetrated by the Vichy government, incited much debate. Most of all, he explored the anti-Semitism of the French Catholic church.

The Magician's Wife (1997), set in mid-nineteenth century France and Algeria, is a study of religion, politics and love. In it, he balanced Islamic ways against those of the West. He loved researching and investigating, always with a moral dilemma as the central theme. There are two novelists at work within him, the storyteller and the professional investigator.

Witty and relaxed, with an expressive, fine-boned, almost bird-like face, he was quietly astute. In 1990, I stood with him in Clifton Street, Belfast, outside his old family home, by then long derelict. It faced on to an equally derelict Orange Hall, overlooked by a bronze statue of King William astride a horse up on the roof. Moore studied his former home thoughtfully, as if slowly adjusting an imaginary lens to re-focus on something he thought he had forgotten but obviously had not.

4 | The Trial
(1925)
by Franz Kafka

"Someone must have been telling lies about Joseph K., for without having done anything wrong he was arrested one fine morning." The opening sentences of Kafka's symbolist parable establish the tone for a vividly choreographed nightmare about life in an increasingly inhuman, modern society. This novel is as terrifying as it is blackly, relentlessly funny – and timeless. Poor Joseph K., a relatively successful bank employee, an assessor, is a somewhat peevish Everyman at the mercy of cruel logic, the chill reasoning that dominates a narrative which is undoubtedly bizarre but also obliquely erotic – Joseph K. believes women can help him and his habitual sexual abandon is later used against him.

Written in that flat, deadpan German that Kafka uses to such brilliant effect, *The Trial* is a metaphysically charged fable of blatant strangeness and complex syntax. It is interesting that although Joseph K. has been arrested, he is then free to go to work. Aware of his innocence, this certainty does not prevent him from feeling guilty. Alienation was one of Kafka's prevailing themes and as a German-speaking Jew living in Prague he had been born into a minority within a minority. His poor health also set him apart. In addition to his contradictory personality and multiple insecurities, he was living in a time of great change. The introspective, obsessive Kafka, though not as aware of the political and cultural changes affecting his world as was the Austro-Hungarian Joseph Roth, must have absorbed the turmoil. When Kafka began writing *The Trial* in August 1914, the society he knew, that of the Austro-Hungarian Empire, was collapsing; on a larger scale Europe was staring at world war.

Joseph K. is far less passive than Gregor Samsa, the hapless hero of Kafka's *Metamorphosis* (1912), whose most pressing concern on having been transformed overnight into a huge insect is his inability to get to work. By comparison, Joseph K.'s initial dilemma, the failure of his landlady's cook to bring his breakfast, appears rather petty and doesn't quite equate with losing one's human body. Instead of the cook materialising on schedule, a man wearing a black suit "like a tourist's outfit" enters Joseph K.'s bedroom, carrying the expected tray. The intruder has a companion. Together they delight in informing our hero of his arrest. They also gobble down his breakfast.

Kafka ensures that Joseph K. remains outraged and bewildered. On returning to his boarding house after his day's work, Joseph K. feels compelled to inform his fellow lodger, Fräulein Bürstner, that he had earlier undergone an interrogation, conducted in her room. They discuss his alleged guilt. Although reluctant to offer an opinion, she says: "Yet as you are still at large – at least I gather from the look of you that you haven't escaped from prison – you couldn't really have committed a serious crime." Their conversation becomes sexually charged, as do most of K.'s encounters with women.

One day his uncle arrives and offers some suggestions about his forthcoming trial. Joseph K. begins a crazy search for good legal advice which leads him to another female, Leni, who is only attracted to guilty men. Then one of K.'s clients sends him to Titorelli, the law court artist, who offers him confused advice and the chance to buy some dusty paintings.

Through a hall of distorted mirrors, satirising the law as well as bureaucracy everywhere, K. stumbles looking for reasons but finds only logic. His quest culminates in an encounter in the Cathedral with a priest who turns out to be the prison chaplain. It is he who reveals the mythic core of the narrative, a story about a man waiting outside the door of the Law Court which cleverly illustrates the impenetrable nature of the inflexible rules governing us all. It sounds almost Talmudic and suggests how strong a hold his religion apparently still had on Kafka. The priest, of course, also belongs to the court. By the close of an absurdist year-long odyssey which begins with his arrest and ends with his execution, Joseph K. has discovered that logic always wins.

Published in the year following Kafka's death at the age of forty-one, *The Trial* had a difficult history on the way to becoming a modernist masterpiece. Banned by the Nazis, it was then, in turn, disregarded by Communist regimes throughout Europe.

There are several translations yet the pioneering literary version completed by Edwin and Willa Muir in 1935 best conveys Kafka's elegant irony and his controlled whimsy in the face of the nonsensical. The heir to Dostoyevsky's complex consciousness, he remains a writer's writer – particularly for Beckett, who knew Kafka had noted all the ironies, terrors and comic ambiguities confronting the individual in a world invariably run by the enemy.

Franz Kafka *(1883-1924)*

"Everything I leave behind me . . . is to be burned unread and to the last page." So directed writer Franz Kafka, a man intent on never making life too easy for anyone, least of all himself. The haunted face with the staring eyes seems to explain why he could have written so precisely about traumatised states of mind. If Kafka, on the basis of three remarkable novels, and a handful of stories, is the heir to Dostoyevsky, then he in turn is the guiding influence of many writers. He is a shaper of consciousness; the modern novelist, possessed, assured and with a cautionary message to deliver.

That we have his work at all is thanks to his friend and literary executor Max Brod. The two met while students at the German University in Prague. Later they went into government service together and both became immersed in the Prague literary scene. Kafka's work came out of two sources of turmoil. The first was his own, his personal unease as the sickly, only surviving son of a dynamic father who had come from the country and made a success of life as a merchant in Prague. The other was the upheaval going on around him. As Kafka began writing *The Trial* in August 1914, just as the Great War was starting, his own world, that of the Austro-

Hungarian empire, was beginning to die. Even if Kafka was as self-absorbed as he appears to have been, he could not help noticing that collapse.

But there were other dilemmas facing him; the sexual chaos which was his personal life invariably cast him in the dual roles of pursued and pursuer, while the first signs of the tuberculosis which would kill him had appeared. To suggest he was complex is an understatement, but for all the terror and gloom of his prophetic work, as well as his apparent paranoia, he was also very funny. In person he was said to be good company and a talented mimic. Both in life and certainly in his writing, Kafka knew all about black comedy.

The Trial was published by Max Brod in 1925, a year after Kafka's death. It was followed by *The Castle* (1926) and *America* (1927); three unfinished novels, yet sufficient to make him immortal.

Here was a writer more interested in fable than in character and yet his beleaguered central figures are invariably Everyman characters whose battle is our battle. His narratives are nightmare worlds dictated to by logic. Sometimes that logic may not appear all that obvious, but it is there – even in his great story, *Metamorphosis*. Gregor Samsa is an ordinary man; his life is devoted to supporting his family, his father's business having failed. He also wants to send his sister to a music school where she will mature as a violinist. Gregor is a good man; he is also a natural underdog, eager to please and intent on approval, so intent that he is servile. Ultimately, this destroys him.

On waking to discover he has been transformed into a giant insect, his initial response is panic – how will he get to work? Far more passive than the arrogant Joseph K. of *The Trial*, Gregor accepts the disdain of everyone, sees contempt as his due and dies without protest, ending up "quite flat and dry." Consistent with Kafka's theme of the individual under threat and denied privacy, Gregor's story begins in his bedroom, as does Joseph K.'s.

"If someone else is observing me, naturally I have to observe myself too; if none observes me, I have to observe myself all the closer" – this could well have been uttered by Gregor or Joseph K. but it was Kafka who wrote it in his diary. This was a man at the mercy of his imagination. Yet although Kafka's writing appears to present him as a victim, he seems to have been in control of himself, and more importantly, of others – particularly the various women in his life – most notably a young Berlin woman, Felice Bauer, to whom he wrote incredible letters filled with alarming levels of self-accusation. There was also an element of performance about these letters; Kafka had a well-developed sense of the dramatic.

His detachment could be breathtaking. A diary entry reads: "August 2. Germany has declared war on Russia – Swimming in the afternoon." He recruited Felice's friend Grete Boch who lived in Vienna as a go-between, and then began to send her explicit correspondence. In an essay, Bulgarian Noble Prize winner Elias Canetti suggested that *The Trial* is partly a metaphor for Kafka's fear when he became engaged; the engagement equals the arrest. It is a plausible theory, not least because Kafka's irony is invariably direct. Then there was his tormented relationship with Milena Jesenká, an unhappily married Czech woman, and finally Dora Dymant, with whom he lived in Berlin.

It is difficult to think of a writer who has consistently fascinated critics in the way that Kafka continues to. The Joyce industry, after all, is far more concerned with the textual history of his work than it is with his life. But Kafka is different; very strange, troubled, doomed. His fiction is perplexing precisely because its nightmare madness is so real. He lived the worlds of *The Trial* and *The Castle* and has kept literary critics, particularly scholars of German-language literature, very busy, even bewildered. His literary influence is everywhere; Kafkaesque has become a standard adjective used when dealing with bureaucracy. Readers share the terrors experienced by his protagonists.

But there is the other Kafka, the playful one who comes to life in an engaging story. During his final months he stayed for a while in Berlin. While out walking he met a little girl distressed about the loss of her doll. According to Pietro Citati in his wonderful biography of the writer, Kafka assured the child that her doll was not lost but had gone travelling. He said that the doll had written him a letter. The child wanted to see it. Kafka said he would bring it the next day and went home to write it. The following day, the child was waiting in the park for Kafka. There then began over a three-week period, days filled by Kafka's accounts of the doll's adventures as relayed through the letters.

The little girl became more interested in the exciting life the doll was having than in its loss. Eventually Kafka decided that the doll should get married. Having described her new life, her fiancé, the wedding plans and the new house, the doll, through Kafka, announced that she and the child would no longer be able to see each other. It is not that surprising that Kafka involved himself in the doll's experience. His work is dark and terrifying, but it is also very funny and consummately human.

5

The Violent Bear It Away (1960)
by Flannery O'Connor

An orphan boy is raised by his ancient great-uncle, a self-styled preacher of powerful, one might say, extreme religious convictions. Something of a self-styled prophet, Mason, the demented old moonshine maker had groomed the boy, Tarwater, as his successor, and had entrusted him with the mission of preaching God's message through the ritual celebration of Baptism.

Mayhem reigns in the magnificently rhythmic opening sentence: "Francis Marion Tarwater's uncle had been dead for only half a day when the boy got too drunk to finish digging his grave and a Negro named Buford Munson, who had come to get a jug filled, had to finish it and drag the body from the breakfast table where it was still sitting and bury it in a decent and Christian way, with the signs of its Saviour at the head of the grave and enough dirt on top to keep the dogs from digging it up" – and that state of chaos never settles.

The deceased was his great-uncle, and, all the while in the background, Tarwater's uncle, Rayber, a schoolteacher and brother of the orphan's dead and disgraced young mother, has never stopped trying to grab the boy back from the old man.

Welcome to Powderhead, Tennessee. Better still, welcome to the black-as-night comic, but always humane, satire of Flannery O'Connor's unforgettable second novel. It soars through prose, which as poet Elizabeth Bishop noted, is "clear, hard, vivid" possessing "more real poetry than a dozen books of poems."

Long after having initially lost his nephew to the old man, Rayber the schoolteacher, now the father of Bishop, a mentally challenged little boy, seeks control over young Tarwater more than ever. The clashes between the old man and the schoolteacher are vividly recalled. It had been a fight to the death and the old man's passing dominates the narrative: "The morning the old man died, he came down and cooked the breakfast as usual and died before he got the first spoonful to his mouth." Just in case you begin feeling too sorry for the again-abandoned boy, do note that he knew the old man was dead: "and he continued to sit across the table from the corpse, finishing his breakfast in a kind of sullen embarrassment as if he were in the presence of a new personality and couldn't think of anything to say." Though the story may be bizarre, even sinister, O'Connor's flamboyant narrative skills are superbly well served by her fluid, visceral prose.

O'Connor, who was from Savannah, Georgia, spent her short life under the shadow of lupus, an inherited disease. She looked at the world through open eyes with a diviner's feel for humour. The narrative abounds with inspired set pieces, such as a visit to the old man's lawyer, while several comic sequences draw upon the battle of wills between the narrow-minded, exasperated schoolteacher and his wary nephew.

Before arriving at his uncle's home, young Tarwater, unable to dig the grave, decides instead to burn down the house he had lived in with his grand-uncle, thus disposing of the body. Convinced he has cremated the old man, he flees. Hours later he hitches a ride with a tired travelling salesman named Meeks who orders the boy to talk as a way of keeping him awake at the wheel. The far-from-stupid salesman reckons Tarwater is a runaway and, in an offbeat conversation worthy of the Coen Brothers, lectures him about life. Having quickly sized up his passenger, the salesman announces: "You belong in the bobby hatch. You ride through these states and you see they all belong in it. I won't see anybody sane again until I get back to Detroit."

On arrival at his uncle's house, Tarwater wages a war of angry silence. The schoolteacher brings his son Bishop and the newcomer to a beach resort. Once there, a dramatic power struggle develops into which Flannery O'Connor, firm in her belief that a prophet is doomed to suffer in this life, injects complex religious symbolism which culminates in a fatal baptism.

This singular Southern Gothic which took O'Connor seven years to write, allows horror and comedy to run full circle, and proves a more than worthy successor to her explosive debut, *Wise Blood* (1952). There are no heroes. Circumstances prove too much for all of the characters.

Flannery O'Connor *(1925-1964)*

Flannery O'Connor's South, inhabited by crazed preachers and fanatical misfits, is a strange world at the mercy of an often demented, frightened religiosity, born of traditional Catholicism. Her complex attitude to religion is explosively obvious in her episodic first novel, *Wise Blood* (1952). Although less inventive than *The Violent Bear It Away*, and lacking its humanity, *Wise Blood* captures the essence of Southern Gothic and provides a dramatic, convincing entry into O'Connor's surreal world. It is also worth noting that three of her earliest stories, 'The Train', 'The Peeler' and 'The Heart of the Park', appear as self-contained chapters in *Wise Blood*.

Her brief life wasn't easy, dominated as it was by a vicious disease, lupus, which made her an invalid by twenty-five and was to kill her within fourteen years. Watching her father die of it when she was fifteen left O'Connor resigned – that, for her, it would always be just a matter of time. She was born in Savannah, Georgia, and graduated from the Georgia State College for Women in 1945. Two years later, aged twenty-two, she completed a master's degree in creative writing from the University of Iowa. Her illness confined her to the family's 550-acre farm where she lived with her mother and raised peacocks.

Initially intending to be a cartoonist, she remained interested in the form and felt that *Wise Blood* had elements of sophisticated cartoon. For all her fascination with the grotesque, O'Connor builds her narratives on exact, economical details. Her staunch Catholicism did not prevent her from exploring the dangerous extremes of evangelical religious fervour as battled out in the Deep South.

"The religion of the South," she explained in a letter to novelist John Hawkes, "is a do-it-yourself religion, something which I as a Catholic find painful and touching and grimly comic. It's full of unconscious pride that lands them in all sorts of ridiculous religious predicaments. They have nothing to correct their practical heresies and so they work them out dramatically. If this were merely comic to me, it would be no good, but I accept the same fundamental doctrines of sin and redemption and judgment that they do."

All the colour and atmosphere is provided by the vicious, brutally rhythmic, mutually threatening exchanges. Her characters involve themselves in religion, the very thing they wish to flee. True to his madman's logic, Haze, in *Wise Blood*, establishes his own religion, "The Church without Christ".

These are dark, exciting and frankly bizarre novels, yet the very best of Flannery O'Connor is to be found in her short stories which invariably feature in major US anthologies. Works such as 'The Artificial Nigger', 'A Good Man is Hard to Find', 'The Lame Shall Enter First' and 'Parker's Back' are among some of the strangest and most accomplished of American short stories.

6 | Dom Casmurro
(1899)
by Joaquim Maria Machado de Assis

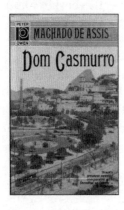

It all begins gently, sedately; the narrator, apparently an older man, recalls meeting a young acquaintance on the evening train. The younger man writes poetry and recites some of his efforts. The narrator makes the grave mistake of falling asleep which greatly offends the aspiring versifier. Within the brilliantly observed small world of the remarkable Brazilian master, Joaquim Maria Machado de Assis, who looked to his immediate experience as effectively as did Jane Austen, the smallest gesture speaks volumes.

Dom Casmurro means 'Lord Taciturn', the nickname that the outraged poet confers on Bentinho Santiago, the narrator, who appears indifferent to the insult.

He sets about introducing himself: "I live on my own, with one servant. The house where I live is my own property, and I had it built for a very special reason which I hesitate to admit, but no matter." The relaxed, conversational tone continues and without making much of a fuss he admits that in building it, he was hoping to recreate the loving home of his youth. He has his "gentle, beguiling" memories. "To be honest I don't go out much and I converse even less. I have few pastimes. Most of my time, I spend in my orchard, gardening and reading. I eat well and I don't sleep badly." Yet, aware that he is in need of an additional occupation, he decides to write.

In this unsettling novel, his finest achievement in a career which he outwardly treated as if it were a hobby, Machado de Assis prepares to continually surprise the reader through a series of subtle, initially, almost causal shifts of tone, from appearing relaxed, he then becomes reflective, melancholic.

Having considered writing a *History of the Suburbs* Santiago drifts into telling his own story. Looking back over a distance of some forty years, he evokes his boyhood self - the adored son of a beautiful, kindly widow who made a grateful pact with the Lord. Dona Glória has vowed that her only child will become a priest. The household is also home to the gregarious José Dias, an inherently conspiratorial former dependent of the narrator's dead father. Old Dias "loved superlatives" – and in a characteristically inspired flourish Machado de Assis continues - "they served to give grandiosity to his ideas and, when these were lacking, to prolong his sentences."

Old Dias likes to be involved in any decision-making, and he quickly develops into one of the several vividly drawn characters who play their part in shaping the man the narrator will become. All talk is of the day the youth will set off for the seminary and his destiny.

There are complications; the boy's closest friend is Capitu, the girl next door. As our hero becomes increasingly confused by his changing emotions, she responds with impressive resourcefulness. It is not surprising that she has remained one of the central characters of Brazilian literature. She is intriguingly ambivalent, and this quality heightens the emerging darkness of a narrative which had begun as a charming memoir fraught with furtive teenage romance. The narrator does attend the seminary for a time and becomes friendly with Escobar, who doesn't have a vocation either. Their friendship is so intense that their subsequent respective marriages are absorbed into it and are regarded as merely secondary arrangements.

On being released from a future in the church Bentinho Santiago becomes a lawyer. It is fittingly consistent with his deliberate personality that he approaches the story as if it was a legal case. The facts are presented, and then considered. By the time he marries Capitu, he sees marriage as more of a social statement than an expression of passion. He describes the day he experienced, to his amazement, a frisson of sexual interest in Sancha, Escobar's wife. He then detects that this interest is reciprocated. "Frankly I was far from happy, caught between friendship and the attraction I felt." Far worse is to follow when Escobar dies in a swimming accident and the narrator observes Capitu's grief. Santiago's suspicions are compounded when he suspects that he is not the father of Ezequiel, their long-awaited son, and only child. He takes action.

Throughout the novel, Machado de Assis has his narrator pause to address the reader, as if she – and he does presume that the reader is female – is the jury in judgment. As the extent of Santiago's cold retreat becomes terrifying clear, the plot twists are worthy of Stendhal or Somerset Maugham.

Machado de Assis writes with the ironic elegance of Turgenev, while the harsh social realities of the Brazil of his day including slavery – Dona Glória keeps slaves – and leprosy are merely referred to in passing. Although he conveys a sense of Rio de Janeiro, he avoids the linguistic opulence characteristic of South American writers.

Reading this quietly sophisticated and ultimately chilling account of one man's personal journey makes it easy to understand why Dom Casmurro continues to set the standard not only for Brazilian fiction, but for all fiction.

Joaquim Maria Machado de Assis (1839-1908)

Brazilian master Joaquim Maria Machado de Assis specialised in writing narratives that appeared to suggest to the reader "now you see it, although possibly you don't". His literary style, with its blend of grace and power, kept the frequently sinister content at bay. Far closer in tone and irony to nineteenth century Russian writers, particularly Turgenev, than to his Latin American counterparts, Machado de Assis had conversational, anecdotal flair and a quality of amused curiosity. His narratives were sharp, elegantly understated slices of controlled madness. He looked at the world through a glass that magnified the unfailing absurdity of everything. His narrative voice, and that of his narrators, lures the reader into worlds that are small, potentially touched by menace, guilt, and even shame.

In a typical story two men are gossiping outside a church, they are discussing a woman. "Do you see that lady over there, going into the Holy Cross Church?" asks one man of his companion. ". . . she wasn't a seamstress, she didn't own property, she didn't run a school for girls; you'll get there, by process of elimination . . ."

Machado de Assis had his own story. Born into poverty in a slum district of Rio de Janeiro in 1839, he was a mulatto and so was caught between the black and white communities, belonging to both and neither. After working as a newspaper reporter, he joined the civil service assigned to the Ministry of Agriculture. He married the sister of an established poet with whom he was friendly. The logic and realism that drive his fiction must have been second nature to him. Machado de Assis was a likeable character; he appears to have succeeded in life without either irritating or offending. Once married, he and his wife settled into a quiet neighbourhood just outside Rio – and never left. In 1897 he co-founded the Brazilian Academy of Letters and was elected its first president.

He suffered from epilepsy but as to whether he was born with the condition or developed it later in life is unclear. However it affected him, he never complained and also managed to deal with a speech impediment that gradually began to trouble him. Machado de Assis had a happy marriage, his life was contented. He left no children. When not working he devoted his free time to writing, and wrote more than two hundred short stories, most of which were originally published in newspapers and magazines. There were nine novels including *Yaya Garcia* (1878), *Epitaph of a Small Wonder* (1881), *Philosopher or Dog?* (1891), *Esau and Jacob* (1904), *The Wager* (1908), as well as *Dom Casmurro*, with its echoes of *Othello*.

After a guarded initial reception, probably due to its themes of adultery, betrayal and cold revenge, Dom Casmurro would become Brazil's most revered novel. Machado de Assis wrote up until the last two years of his life. He died in 1908, aged sixty-nine and inspired such regard that the nation as one mourned his passing. Large crowds attended his state funeral.

As a writer he succeeded in looking to the nineteenth century

Russians, while also arriving at that elusive offbeat surrealism that Paul Auster has spent his career pursuing. If Machado de Assis has a literary heir it is Portugal's 1998 Nobel Literature Laureate José Saramago whose finest novel, *The Year of the Death of Ricardo Reis* (1984), could almost have been written by the great Brazilian. As discreet as he was astute, Machado de Assis intrigues on many levels. This most sophisticated of South American writers is consummately European, often original and invariably unsettling.

7 | Persuasion
(1818)
by Jane Austen

Marriage was far more than the stuff of romantic fantasy in the society in which Jane Austen lived and wrote; it was a pragmatic reality, a necessity. For all the wit and shrewdly observed social comedy in her work, there is always the terror of spinsterhood. A girl who failed to attract a husband was facing a shadowy life as, at best a companion, at worst a dependent and living example of what every girl dreaded most. Anne Elliott, the heroine of Austen's posthumous, darkest and most mature novel, has to contend with a sensation even worse than failure: regret.

She is twenty-seven, and the unassuming middle daughter of the ridiculous Sir Walter Elliott, an impoverished baronet. He is famously vain and had apparently managed to beguile his late wife with his good looks. As Austen reiterates throughout the narrative, he judges people on their physical appearance. The freckled Mrs Clay, a woman with designs on him, is in his opinion, sadly disfigured. His selfishness and snobbery has been duly passed down to his eldest daughter, Elizabeth, who ranks among Austen's coldest creations.

Already disappointed in her efforts to marry her father's nephew and heir, William Walter Elliott, who had instead wed a rich woman of inferior birth, who later died, Elizabeth is a study in angry panic, particularly as her equally self-centred youngest sister, Mary, a variation of Lydia in *Pride and Prejudice* (1813), is already married. But Anne is different; gentle and quiet, she is resigned to having lost her early bloom, and with it, any chance of happiness – or possible escape from her father and elder sister.

As the novel opens Sir Walter is finally accepting that he must rent the family seat, Kellynch Hall. The new tenants represent an emerging breed. Admiral Croft is not a landed gentleman; he is a naval careerist who has risen through the ranks to status and material comfort. His face, much to Sir Walter's horror, is weather-beaten from years at sea – but the admiral, unlike its owner, can afford to lease Sir Walter's house.

Admiral Croft's wife has two brothers, one of whom is Captain Wentworth, a now successful, highly eligible man, who had been rejected years earlier by Anne then under pressure from her family's adviser, the well-intentioned Lady Russell: "She was a benevolent, charitable, good woman, and capable of strong attachments . . . She had a cultivated mind . . . but she had prejudices on the side of ancestry; she had a value for rank and consequence which blinded her a little to the faults of those who possessed them."

Just as she had "protected" Anne from an early inferior marriage to an impoverished young Wentworth, Lady Russell is now preoccupied with preventing Sir Walter falling prey to Mrs Clay. Quite by chance, Anne, who is well accustomed to living within the noisy family society of the Musgroves, into which Mary has married – Anne having declined that offer – discovers that the Wentworth mentioned in a conversation she overhears, is none other than her former suitor.

The arrival of Frederick Wentworth proves initially crushing for Anne. Mary is quick to report that he had mentioned to one of the Musgroves that Anne had changed, encouraging Mary to announce with obvious glee: "You were so altered he should not have known you again." Wentworth, still resentful at the rejection, is polite but detached.

Austen lays aside her characteristic repartee and concentrates, incisively, on charting Anne's regret as it develops into acute emotional pain which intensifies as Wentworth becomes friendly with the two unmarried Musgrove girls and a match seems likely. Lady Russell may be a snob but she is not a fool: ". . . internally her heart revelled in angry pleasure, in pleased contempt, that the man who at twenty-three had seemed to understand somewhat of the value of an Anne Elliott, should, eight years afterwards, be charmed by a Louisa Musgrove."

When Louisa slips while showing-off during an outing and suffers a head injury, Wentworth looks to Anne for help. A slow, tentative reconciliation begins, assisted somewhat by the rival interest in Anne shown by the duplicitous young Mr William Walter Elliott, her father's heir, and by the revival of Wentworth's former affection for her.

Although written within the convention of social comedy, there is nothing coy about this candid novel. Anne's regret yields to despair and gradually, moves towards tentative hope. There are occasional echoes of the sharp, social observation of *Pride and Prejudice*, yet despite the ironic jabs at the less pleasant characters and her inevitable flair for comic timing, *Persuasion*, published a year after Austen's death, is subdued, subtle, intriguingly melancholic and deliberate.

Jane Austen (1775-1817)

Fame not entertainment was uppermost in the mind of Jane Austen whose literary ambitions guided her pen, leaving her formidable intelligence and irony to do the rest. The sixth of seven children born to a middle-class English country rector, she was well accustomed to watching wealthy relatives living a life that she experienced only when visiting them. History tells us that she was neither small nor all that retiring; memories of those who knew her suggest that her demeanour was more closely shaped by eighteenth century candour than the Victorian coyness posthumously attributed to her.

If she wrote in the corner while sitting in the family drawingroom, it was because it was considered sociable to be present, and there was little free space available elsewhere. Her novels did not flow effortlessly; she wrote many drafts. Write what you know is advice given to every aspiring writer, and Austen wrote what she knew best, the life and times of the country gentry; the gossip, the secrets, the matches made in the interest of social and financial security.

Austen read the fiction of Fanny Burney (1752-1840) and enjoyed the epistolary novel *Evelina*, which Burney had published anonymously in 1778. The literary fashion of Austen's day was dominated by tales of gothic horror and by popular melodrama. Austen was familiar with the trends – and would satirise gothic conventions in *Northanger Abbey*, an early work, which was eventually published in 1818, with *Persuasion*, one year after her death.

Fantasy never attracted her as a writer; she was far more intent on poised and truthful studies of social behaviour. Her father, and later her brother, dealt with publishers on her behalf. The first two novels including *Sense and Sensibility* (1811) were published anonymously with a cryptic "By A Lady" on the author line. Her third appeared under her name. "I should rather try to make all the money," announced Austen, "than all the mystery I can of it."

First Impressions was submitted to a London publisher in 1797 when Austen was twenty-two. It was rejected. She re-worked the manuscript. The new version was accepted and eventually appeared as *Pride and Prejudice* in 1813. It has become one of the most famous and popular novels of all time, opening with the oft-quoted sentence: "It is a truth universally acknowledged, that a single man in possession of a good fortune, must be in want of a wife," lines which continue to ring true in the hearts of concerned mothers the world over.

Her forensic detail and gift for writing dialogue ensure that her characters live off the page; Austen was brilliant on snobbery whether the variety practised by Mrs Bennet, desperate to marry off her daughters; or of Darcy at his most pompous; or of the repellent Lady Catherine De Bourgh, but she could also convincingly convey the mindless showing-off of young Louisa Musgrove in *Persuasion* which results in a serious accident.

Pride and Prejudice was followed within a year by *Mansfield Park*, a daring study of repression and her most underrated, if also less beguiling novel. That Austen was shrewd is obvious; did she not dedicate *Emma* (1816) to the Prince Regent, an admirer whom she openly detested?

Austen's story is fascinating for many reasons. Long before she acquired her present superstardom on the strength of attractively in-period television serialisations and movie versions, Austen enjoyed serious literary status. Her work never really disappeared; readers, writers and academics ensured she was read and respected. Her subject matter remains popular, appealing and commercial, while her sharp, elegant and precise prose ensures her literary legacy. Austen also learned to master narrative structure. Re-reading Austen is to be again struck by the irony, realism and timelessness. Admittedly a major poet, Thomas Hardy the novelist, with the exception of *The Mayor of Casterbridge* (1886), seems overly fatalistic, even heavy handed, whereas Austen's fiction remains lively and curiously modern.

One of her nephews, James Edward Austen-Leigh, wrote a well-meaning but dull memoir recalling over a period of more than fifty years the aunt he barely knew. It presented a re-invented Jane Austen as a genteel Victorian. How she would have smiled, or more probably, laughed aloud at his portrayal of her. She had no children, she never married and her final months before her death at forty-one were passed in agony. Her observation and satire confirm she watched and listened closely, but *Persuasion* suggests she also learned a great deal about regret.

8 | Fathers and Sons
(1861)
by Ivan Turgenev

A middle-aged man scans the highway, anxiously waiting for the carriage bringing his son home from university. Nikolai Petrovich Kirsanov is a landowner whose estate consists of a couple of hundred serfs – "or five thousand acres, as he expresses it now that he has divided up his land and let it to the peasants and started a 'farm'." A broken leg suffered on the very day he had received his commission prevented Kirsanov, the son of a general, from pursuing a military career – unlike his older brother. Instead, he had gone to the university in St Petersburg where he had fallen in love with his landlord's intellectual daughter – much to the fury of his parents. His father, the general, died and was quickly followed to the grave by his wife. Nikolai then married his beloved and they had a son, Arkady.

Life was kind until Nikolai's wife died. As the years passed, he in turn brought his son to St Petersburg, to enrol at the same university he had attended. Turgenev sets the scene with characteristic ease and deliberation. The arrival of Arkady also marks the entrance of Bazarov, one of the most fascinating characters in all literature. Blunt, self-assured and questioning, he encapsulates the new Russia. For Arkady, he is a hero; but for Arkady's father, Bazarov is a challenge. A visitor, any visitor, would be difficult at this time when the father has delicate news to break to his son; Nikolai is not only living as husband and wife with a former servant, she has had his child.

Adding to the tension is the presence of Nikolai's elder brother, Pavel, the former officer whose life has been dominated by a disastrous obsession with a married princess who not only toyed with him, she died. Pavel is cool, cynical, elegantly embittered and apparently making the best of life in the provinces as he deals with his regrets. While Nikolai is attempting in his own ramshackle way to be progressive, Pavel represents the old Russia and is well aware of the threat presented by nihilists such as the outspoken, opinionated Bazarov. The narrative is precise, atmospheric and sustained by Turgenev's elegant genius for characterisation, and most particularly, for the dynamics of relationships.

Social change is a major theme. Yet Turgenev, who was born in 1818, is drawn to the distinctions between friendship and affection; passion and sexual curiosity. Bazarov is interested in science, dissects frogs and tests everything, every remark, each expression of emotion, relentlessly. He and Arkady set off on a visit that eventually leads them to the home of a glamorous, fascinatingly world-weary widow, Madame Odintsov, now raising her younger sister Katya with a care more like that of a mother than an elder sister. Arkady decides that he is in love with Madame Odintsov; Bazarov rather peevishly fears he may also have succumbed to her allure, while the lady herself feels drawn to Bazarov's lack of affectation.

The dialogue is remarkable, particularly the exchanges between Bazarov and Madame Odintsov. Most touching of all is Bazarov's visit to his elderly parents who worship him and try so desperately hard not to suffocate him with their love. While the portrayal of Bazarov's retired army doctor father could have collapsed into caricature it instead triumphs, and would prove inspirational to Chekhov. Sophisticated and engagingly honest, Turgenev's masterful, and ultimately tragic, study of emotional ambivalence marks the emergence of one of world literature's enduring achievements, the Russian novel.

Ivan Turgenev *(1818-1883)*

He is the most European of the great nineteenth century Russian writers and the most obvious influence on Chekhov. Ivan Turgenev certainly lived the life of a character in a nineteenth century Russian novel, most probably one written by him. Born into wealth on his mother's vast estate, some three hundred miles south-west of Moscow, Turgenev was the son of a handsome young cavalry officer who had arrived at what appeared to be a self-contained kingdom of five thousand serfs, hoping to purchase horses for his regiment.

Instead, the officer married the owner, an heiress six years his senior and apparently, plain to the point of ugly. The estate had its own private orchestra and other fairytale splendours, yet Turgenev's mother was a feudal tyrant who believed in beating her children in addition to her serfs. His country childhood left Turgenev with a love of nature and a fondness for his socially misplaced father who, aware that Russian aristocrats favoured French for conversation and correspondence, urged his children to practise writing in Russian at least twice a week.

The family moved to Moscow when he was nine. At sixteen he went to university in Petersburg, and within three years, had had his first poems published. Then Turgenev made the move that set him apart from his peers and would shape his fiction; he went to study in Berlin. There he absorbed German idealism, was drawn to the writings of Goethe, and would visit Germany, particularly Baden-Baden, throughout his life. Turgenev's fiction featured disaffected, foreign-educated intellectuals not unlike himself. He was a tall, attractive, languid individual who first became famous with his prose sketches, *A Hunter's Notes* (1847-1851), also known as *The Papers of a Sportsman* in the collected edition of his work published in 1852.

Some years before this, on his twenty-fifth birthday, 28 October 1843, while out hunting, he met a middle-aged man. A few days later Turgenev was presented to his new acquaintance's wife, Pauline Viardot, a famous, and reportedly ugly, Spanish opera singer. Turgenev promptly fell in love; Viardot and her husband appeared to accept this devotion. Turgenev learned Spanish, left his civil service post, and travelled Europe as part of her entourage, openly adopting the role of unrequited lover. He sent his daughter by a servant to Paris to be raised with Viardot's children. He would never marry, becoming a familiar figure in the literary circles of France, where he died in 1883, aged sixty-five, although his body was sent home to Russia for burial.

The eponymous hero of his first novel, *Rudin* (1856), captured the Russian consciousness almost as effectively as would the title character of Goncharov's *Oblomov* (1859). *Rudin* reads somewhat like a play, possibly because by 1850, Turgenev had already written what would be his only full-length work for the stage, *A Month in the Country*. Years ahead of its time, it had been banned in Russia. Its wary reception undermined Turgenev's confidence in his dramatic talents. Eventually staged in 1872, *A Month in the Country* pre-empts Chekhov's plays and would, with Chekhov, revolutionise Russian theatre.

Turgenev's novel *Home of the Gentry* was completed on the eve of his fortieth birthday and published in early 1859. In this novel of a homecoming, the central character, Lavretsky, returns to his country estate after his marriage collapses. The story is personal, while it also looks to the wider experiences of a generation of Russians who sampled the West, only to return home to Russia. Turgenev, the cosmopolitan revolutionary and conservative traditionalist, is looking at both the old and new faces of his motherland. *Home of the Gentry* is an elegiac variation of a conflict which would also be explored in his masterpiece, *Fathers and Sons* (1861), which is dominated by the complex presence of Bazarov the anarchist.

Written in between these two novels and a third, *On the Eve* (1859), is the exquisite novella, *First Love* (1860), in which a man is asked over supper to recount his earliest romance. He agrees to do so, but insists on taking time to write it. He does and in a remarkable tale, recalls how his younger self idealised a slightly older girl only to find his rival was none other than his unhappy father. A work of devastating beauty, pitting a boy's infatuation against an older man's tormented passion, *First Love* achieves perfection. The power of this subtle, graceful work is further heightened by the knowledge that in creating the character of the father, Turgenev drew on memories of his own father, a romantic who married for money and regretted it.

A stylist who created his characters not by infiltrating their consciousness but instead by examining their behaviour, Turgenev, who outraged Dostoyevsky with his interest in German culture and

9

All Quiet on the Western Front (1929)
by Erich Maria Remarque

ALL QUIET ON THE WESTERN FRONT

Erich Maria Remarque

Several German schoolboys, all from the same class, volunteer as soldiers to fight for the fatherland in the Great War. Told in an urgent first-person voice in a continuous present tense by Paul Bäumer, a sympathetic young fellow from a poor country family, this harrowing narrative is unexpectedly beautiful, more pensive than angry. Bäumer recalls having once begun writing a play and mentions the bundle of poems he has back home. This explains and convincingly justifies the literary tone Remarque has taken.

The war, which began as an adventure, has quickly gone horribly wrong, becoming a nightmare. Food is the great distraction. Early on, the friends are faced with the death of Kemmerich who lies in the dressing station, having had his leg amputated: "He looks ghastly, yellow and wan . . . Death is working through from within." Bäumer remembers how distressed Kemmerich's mother was at the station the day the boys left for the war. Now one of them, Müller, openly covets Kemmerich's fine English leather airmen's boots.

First published in 1929, *All Quiet on the Western Front* sold two and a half million copies within eighteen months. It was immediately translated into English. This is the story of the war from the German viewpoint. There are no heroes, just humans caught up in a mindless disaster. Bäumer watches as his friends each die in turn. At one stage he goes home on leave where his mother is dying from a recurrent cancer – and all his father can do is ask him about the killing. When Bäumer goes to see Kemmerich's mother she challenges him: "why are you living then, when he is dead?"

The narrator is conscious of how quickly he and his friends have become old in experience. Above all, there is a powerful sense of waiting. As they battle the fat corpse rats swarming through the trenches, intent on eating the army bread, the men also have to contend with lice, gas, the mud, the fear, the noise. Bäumer notices that "The backs of the horses shine in the moonlight, their movements are beautiful, they toss their heads, and their eyes gleam . . . the riders in their steel helmets resemble knights of a forgotten time; it is strangely beautiful and arresting." But the horses fare badly under fire and their dying cries fill the air.

In one of the many heartbreaking set pieces, Bäumer describes lying in a shell-hole when a soldier jumps in on top of him; the narrator recalls stabbing the man repeatedly and then sitting with him as he dies "The gurgling starts again – but how slowly a man dies." Later, having been wounded, he drags his badly injured friend Kat to a field station for help. In triumph he arrives, only to be told that Kat is dead. All the while Bäumer is thinking, remembering, compiling a lasting account. He seems more philosophical than despairing. He realises what will happen to his generation: "the war will be forgotten – and the generation that has grown up after us will be strange to us and push us aside . . . the years will pass by and in the end we shall fall into ruin."

Then Remarque adds, almost by way of a footnote: "He fell in October 1918, on a day that was so quiet and still . . . that the army report confined itself to the single sentence: All quiet on the Western Front."

Humane and haunting, this is the novel that set the standard for war fiction. Ironically, by 1933, it was being burnt in Berlin, denounced by the Nazis as "defeatist".

Erich Maria Remarque (1898-1970)

Unlike Bertolt Brecht, his senior by a few months, Erich Maria Remarque had first-hand experience of what he was writing about; he had served at the Front. He was sixteen when the war began and, in November 1916, was called up for military service, directly from school. Ten days short of his nineteenth birthday, he was posted to the Arras front and fought at Passchendale. Wounded during British shelling, he recuperated in a military hospital. While he was lying in a ward, his thoughts drifting, his mother died. He would take her name, Maria, and add that to his on the publication, in 1929, of *All Quiet on the Western Front*.

Born Erich Paul Remark at Osnabruck, Hanover, in northern Germany, he grew up in the Rhineland. His family was part French. Remarque was sensitive; a dreamer and natural romantic. By the time he came to write his famous book during the 1920s he had already worked as a teacher, a businessman and a sports reporter. He was handsome and sympathetic. Although his most famous book draws heavily on his personal experiences he wanted it read as a novel, not a memoir. Nor is it a confession; Remarque wanted to give some idea of what serving at the Front like. He neither romanticised the war, nor idealised it. The young soldiers, including Bäumer, the narrator, are just that – young. One of the most shocking revelations in the quiet and impressively understated narrative is Bäumer's grave awareness of how dehumanised he and his friends have become, observing: "we are indifferent."

Although an international success, even in the US where its publication in an English translation coincided with the beginning of the Great Depression, Remarque's disturbingly beautiful and brutal book outraged the Nazi propaganda machine which by 1933 had dismissed its author as anti-patriotic. He left Germany, and initially sought exile in Switzerland. In 1938, a year after the publication of *Three Comrades*, a sequel to *All Quiet on the Western Front*, he was stripped of his German citizenship.

In common with so many German writers, Thomas Mann included, Remarque became part of the European émigré set, eventually arriving in the United States. He acquired US citizenship in 1947. In true Hollywood style, by 1956 he was a movie star, featuring in a film of his own, *A Time to Live and a Time to Die*. Always an approachable and humane witness, Remarque was often called upon to comment on war and he wrote a dozen books, including *Arch of Triumph* (1946), in which Ravic, a concentration camp survivor, hunts down his Nazi tormentor in Paris. Yet for all the truth and understated courage of his vision, he was never again to articulate the eerie, sombre beauty of *All Quiet on the Western Front*. The years passed and he divided his time between the US and Locarno, Switzerland, where he died, in 1970.

In *The Rebels* (Budapest 1930; first English translation 2007) by another European literary exile, the Hungarian Sándor Márai, a group of boys prepare for war. It offers a fascinating and sophisticated variation of *All Quiet on the Western Front*. Yet Remarque's book remains the enduring novel of war, probably because it articulates the barbarism with melancholic regret, not anger.

10 | Heart of Darkness

(1902)

by Joseph Conrad

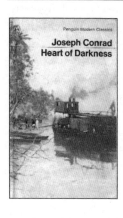

Few novels have been immortalised on the strength of a despairing exclamation: "The horror! The horror!" Joseph Conrad's most famous, and most controversial tale, first published in 1902, is based on a journey up the Congo River undertaken by him in 1890. The heat, the smells and the brooding atmosphere fester throughout with the sharpness of lived experience and prose that is as precise as a Bach score. It is a shocking yarn, an adventure which far from celebrating imperialism and colonisation, attacks the greed and cruelty of the Europeans who set out to systematically rape Africa. Nor could one claim that Conrad's central character, the enigmatic, deranged and powerfully self-loathing Mr Kurtz is presented as a hero.

Often referred to as one of the outstanding achievements of literary high modernism, *Heart of Darkness* has also had its critics. In 1973 Nigerian writer Chinua Achebe denounced the novella, by then an established classic, describing Conrad as "a bloody racist". It is difficult to grasp Achebe's objections to the narrative, as told by Marlow to four friends aboard a small boat, Nellie, anchored in the Thames estuary at sunset waiting the turn of the tide.

At no stage does Marlow attempt to either glorify or justify the events. It is a grim story and sure of his audience, the narrator does not spare the details. Conscious of being the career seaman among weekend sailors, Marlow recalls the difficulty he had securing a job on a seafaring ship, so instead he looked inland, and accepted a freshwater appointment with a continental trading company, replacing a steamboat captain who had been murdered by natives.

Marlow is a good talker with a gift for telling a story and describes setting off for his interview, not forgetting to mention that the company doctor even measured his skull. Then he is on his way and recalls his sensations. "Watching a coast as it slips by the ship is like thinking about an enigma. There it is before you – smiling, frowning, inviting, grand, mean, insipid, or savage . . ." Marlow, though in love with adventure, is perceptive and aware of the contrasts between the "starched collars and got-up shirt fronts of the company's chief accountant" and the filthy conditions of the natives.

He outlines how he first heard of the "remarkable" Mr Kurtz who is stationed, "in the true ivory-country." Some ten days later, his head already full of Kurtz's talents and mystery, Marlow leaves with a team to walk the final two hundred miles to the Central Station where his steamboat waits. On arrival he finds his boat has been sunk. Gradually he begins to realise deliberate efforts have been made to delay assistance reaching Kurtz. Marlow battles on and finally meets Kurtz.

The son of a half-English mother and a half-French father, Kurtz, who had been educated in England, is an interesting cultural mix, causing Marlow to reflect, "All Europe contributed to the making of Kurtz." It was Kurtz who had travelled into the interior with which he made his Faustian pact. His hypocrisy is vile, unforgivable. Having learned the native ways and become part of their world, he then would conclude a report urging, "Exterminate the brutes."

When Marlow finally comes face to face with Kurtz the reality is far from mythic. Borne aloft on a stretcher, Kurtz has been reduced to a fading ghost. His delusions are obvious to Marlow to whom Kurtz entrusts the papers for his "Intended". Later, on meeting her, he declines to tell her that Kurtz's last words expressed horror at the legacy of his depraved antics. Instead Marlow lies, assuring the grieving woman that the dying man's final thoughts were of her: "The last word he pronounced was – your name!"

Kurtz the anti-heroic ivory dealer symbolises hypocritical, greedy, ruthless Western man on the colonial rampage in Africa. It is a daring, strongly political book. Marlow is both witness and moral consciousness in a taut, urgent polemic that continues to shock.

George Orwell certainly looked to Conrad who was also the most profound literary influence with whom the young Graham Greene would engage. For V. S. Naipaul, *Heart of Darkness* was the inspiration for *A Bend in the River*, which was published in 1979 and wears its debt to Conrad as a badge of honour. J. G. Ballard, as a fellow outsider, shared that sensibility unique to the marginalised, and would consistently identify with the graphic strangeness of Conrad's vision.

Joseph Conrad *(1857-1924)*

His life was the stuff of a great action yarn combining elements of the thriller, seafaring adventures, romance, petulance and outright comedy, all of which would eventually settle down into that of a British literary institution. Jozef Teodor Konrad Korzenowski, who would become Joseph Conrad, enjoyed mystery not only in his writing but also as regards his personal biography which he would often further complicate, although there was no need. Born in the Polish Ukraine to honourable parents intent on their country's independence from Russia, Conrad absorbed drama as if by divine right.

His father, Apollo Korzenowski, belonged to the landed class and was a poet, a dreamer, a patriot and an intellectual with a family history of anti-Russian activity. His mother, Eva Bobrowski, came from similar, if less openly radical stock. The Russian authorities found Apollo difficult to deal with, eventually exiling him and his wife to a remote part of Russia. It was 1861, Conrad was four years old. The brutal climate soon affected Conrad's mother. The family were relocated, too late, to a milder area north-east of Kiev. Eva died. His father slid into despair, leaving the boy, then seven and sickly, to find comfort in books. Following his father's death four years later, Conrad, who had led the funeral procession, was entrusted at the age of eleven to his mother's brother, Tadeusz. The uncle was kindly, but strict. Little is known of Conrad's formal education although he often mentioned, perhaps ironically considering his travels, he had enjoyed geography.

At sixteen he set off for sea. Conrad joined a crew at Marseilles as arranged by his uncle. His first voyage was as an observer and on returning to France he socialised with the ship's owners. But suddenly it all became more serious; Conrad joined his next crew as a serving sailor. He took up gambling and soon had large debts. Suicide appeared a possible solution. But his uncle rescued him, for neither the first nor the last time.

Conrad became a British merchant seaman, and a British subject. His adventures reside somewhere between fact and fiction, according to whatever version he decided to tell. The image of him is that of a handsome, exotic depressive who read Balzac, Flaubert and Maupassant, spoke French and English, carried himself like a Polish aristocrat, was given to tantrums and tended to confuse people. Whatever about the conflicting accounts of his life, Conrad's adventures inspired his thrilling fiction and writing in his third language, English, he injected energy into the English literary novel. His presence is everywhere; in the work of Virginia Woolf, to Graham Greene, William Golding and J. G. Ballard and beyond Britain to Thomas Mann, Faulkner and Hemingway as well as T. S. Eliot. His work is diverse and, ironically, the writer who most heavily sits at his shoulder is one he consistently criticised for "being too Russian" – Dostoyevsky.

As a seaman Conrad was respected and usually popular with crews, securing his share of admittedly minor commands, no doubt because he had acquired a reputation for quitting after little, or no, warning. Of all his adventures the one that most shaped his art, and possibly his life, was his journey into the Congo. It gave him the material for *Heart of Darkness*. While there, he also met Roger Casement, whom he was initially impressed by, yet would later denounce. During leave from the sea, Conrad began writing, in English. The manuscript which survived several adventures, including being lost in a Berlin railway station, was lucky to eventually arrive with London publisher Edward Garnett and it became *Almayer's Folly* (1895).

Conrad the artist had a commitment to justice. This is powerfully evident in *Heart of Darkness*. *Lord Jim* (1900) represents the finest of

Conrad's seafaring tales and also conveys Conrad's sense of anarchy. With *Nostromo* (1904) it was obvious that an inner artistic evolution was transforming him into an ambiguous, ironic and ultimately, iconic modernist. His use of a multiple narrative device would influence Faulkner. *Nostromo*, demanding and bleak, remains Conrad's finest technical as well as artistic achievement. He shrouded its genesis in mystery, tracing it back to a story he had heard while a young seaman in the 1870s, who had newly landed in the Gulf of Mexico.

There are many sides to Joseph Conrad – including the man who married an English typist, Jessie George, sixteen years his junior, with whom he had two sons. For a while he collaborated with Ford Madox Ford who recalled him having "the gestures of a Frenchman who shrugs his shoulders frequently". Their partnership was not to last.

In another of Conrad's great novels, *The Secret Agent* (1907), a story based on an abortive anarchist plot, but concerned with larger issues of loyalty and betrayal; stability and anarchy; moral heroism and cowardice, he emulated none other than Dostoyevsky. Mann admired it, commenting on how Conrad's "Polish Russophobia" had expressed itself in English. Dostoyevsky's presence would be even more powerfully evident in *Under Western Eyes* (1911), a political novel in which a group of Russian revolutionaries in St Petersburg move on to Geneva. Conrad was drawn to revolt and ideology as impulses, and understood the dissent that would culminate in the Bolshevik Revolution of 1917.

Nigerian writer Chinua Achebe, author of *Things Fall Apart* (1958), sees *Heart of Darkness* as an imperialist text yet V. S. Naipaul reveres it as a seminal work. Conrad has often been misread, possibly because his work is so diverse, even ambivalent. For all the adventure and incident, it is fuelled by ideas and his sense of the elusive ideal. His genius is filtered through an ironic vision and four major achievements: *Heart of Darkness*, *Nostromo*, *The Secret Agent* and *Under Western Eyes*, each of which define literary modernism. This Polish dandy with a melancholic streak changed British and international fiction, bequeathing a valuable artistic legacy to novelists committed to story – and meaning.

11 | Cry, The Beloved Country
(1948)
by Alan Paton

The Reverend Stephen Kumalo is parson of a poor Zulu village community in rural South Africa. At first glance, it seems a green, beautiful place, but the earth is barren and the reality is sombre: "They are valleys of old men and old women, of mothers and children. The men are away, the young men and the girls are away. The soil can not keep them any more."

A little girl knocks at the pastor's door, intent on delivering a grubby, much-handled letter, a letter which will change his life. A fellow churchman, based in faraway Johannesburg, has written to Pastor Kumalo, telling him that he has met a young woman in difficulties, and that she is the pastor's much younger sister, Gertrude. Out of concern, not censure, the Rev. Theophilus Msimangu urges Pastor Kumalo to come to Johannesburg, where he will help him save his sister.

The pastor listens while his wife reads the letter aloud. The couple realise they must help rescue Gertrude, but the only way they can is by using the money they have been saving to give their son, Absalom, the chance to study at St Chad's College. The pastor's wife finally relinquishes the long-held fantasy that their son, who had already left home to live in Johannesburg, will one day attend St Chad's. As she points out wearily: "When people go to Johannesburg, they do not come back."

Paton's heartbreaking, yet often movingly hopeful polemic is told with near-biblical simplicity in lyrical prose that is subtle and vividly physical. The narrative unfolds through a series of dramatic experiences foisted upon the gentle, increasingly bewildered and frail Kumalo, who accepts each new blow with philosophical dignity. His sister, whom he barely knows, is some twenty-five years younger than him, has a child and is involved in prostitution. The poor old man is then faced with another sorrow; his long-missing son, Absalom, has been arrested for the murder of a white man named Jarvis who had tried to help the black majority, and whose home Absalom and his friends were planning to burgle.

Also involved in Absalom's crime is Pastor Kumalo's nephew, the son of the pastor's ruthless brother, John Kumalo, a local political force of sorts who makes sure his son is cleared. John Kumalo makes no attempt to help Absalom who is sentenced to death, while his accomplices are pardoned. Paton confronts apartheid as an evil yet also shows the efforts made by both sides to understand race. The characterisation is restrained, understated, and the dialogue has a rare, eerie grace of its own, articulating the rage and despair but also the love and forgiveness of which both sides are capable.

Kumalo, a weary, aged man at sixty, returns to the village with his son's pregnant girlfriend and his sister's child. The murdered man's father refuses to judge his son's killers, and instead helps improve the life of the villagers. Yet Paton has not written a naively idealistic fairytale. In the symbolic closing sequence, the pastor climbs a mountain before sunrise to pray on the morning of his son's execution.

This is a towering work, written with courage and abiding belief in God, as well as in human goodness. It is sustained throughout by Paton's profound love for his tormented country. Well received on publication in the United States and Great Britain in 1948, *Cry, The Beloved Country* has retained its status as not only the first major novel of South African literature in English, but also as an enduring work which may have influenced J. M. Coetzee's magnificent parable, the 1983 Booker Prize-winning *Life & Times of Michael K*.

Alan Paton (1903-1988)

Alan Paton, a one-time science teacher, was the principal of a reformatory for delinquent boys in Johannesburg, and during 1947, was sent by South Africa's Department of Education on an investigative tour of prisons and reform schools in Britain, continental Europe and the United States. While in San Francisco he was invited by an educational welfare official to stay at his home. Paton accepted, on the condition that his host would read the manuscript he had been carrying around the world in his suitcase, working on it in whatever hotel room he found himself.

The manuscript, which was handwritten, was entitled *Cry, The Beloved Country*. His American host was deeply moved by what he had read. Paton wanted to make revisions but had no time; his fixed itinerary required that he travel to Halifax in Canada, for a freighter back to Cape Town. The man's wife offered to type out the manuscript. A plan was devised; the couple were prepared to send out the first five chapters with an accompanying letter to five publishers. Paton was grateful for their help. One of the five publishers was the legendary Maxwell Perkins at Scribner in New York.

Perkins, possibly the most famous figure in US publishing and revered as the guiding presence behind F. Scott Fitzgerald, Hemingway, Ring Lardner, Edmund Wilson, Sherwood Anderson and the difficult Southerner, Thomas Wolfe, was a perfectionist, yet supportive, willing to cajole and inspire his writers to save them from personal excesses and crippling doubt. But Alan Paton's experience of Perkins was not typical. The man he met was exhausted, distracted, his concentration and stamina had finally begun to fail him.

His vague comments about *Cry, The Beloved Country* left Paton confused and unclear as to the prospective publisher's opinion of the book. Perkins's deafness didn't help matters. Paton left New York without a contract but with the American editor's goodwill and copies of Wolfe's novels which he read on the way home. Paton wrote to his hosts in San Francisco, explaining in detail the various criticisms Perkins had made and vowed to make the revisions. Before he did, however, he was sent a contract by Perkins, who, dismissing his earlier criticisms, rushed the manuscript off to the printers. *Cry, The Beloved Country*, a powerful first novel by an unknown, was published as written and unedited.

But the book made him famous and gave him a national voice within South Africa. His second novel, *Too Late the Phalarope*, was published in 1953. About this time he became deeply involved with the fledging Liberal Party of which he would become president. Eight years later the South African government disbanded the party under the Prohibition of Political Interference Bill. Paton's South African passport was revoked in 1960, on his return from New York where he had been presented with that year's Freedom Award. A short story collection, *Debbie Go Home*, was published in 1961.

His two volumes of autobiography, *Towards the Mountain* (1980) and *Journey Continued*, published shortly after his death in 1988, reveal as much about South Africa's history as they do about him. He had been born in Natal where he later attended university, taking a degree in maths and physics. Throughout his life he represented the dignified face of liberal consciousness.

Paton had an important story to tell and never told it as well as he did in *Cry, The Beloved Country*, a gracious, dignified work of subtle artistry.

12 | Wuthering Heights
(1847)
by Emily Brontë

The better elements of the Gothic and the Romantic are summoned in this strange, sophisticated, meticulously imagined and claustrophobic study of destructive passion. *Wuthering Heights*, set in the brooding Yorkshire moors, is overwhelmingly philosophical and explores the themes of morality, eternity, regeneration and ultimately, salvation. Brontë establishes a convulsive ambience by juxtaposing nature and some semblance of normal domestic life with darkness and light, storm and calm, weakness and strength, all caught between the moral and the amoral.

Emily Brontë's singular, quasi-Shakespearean novel, published in 1847, the year before her death at the age of thirty, remains one of the seminal texts of world literature for many reasons, not least because of its luminous prose, vivid characterisation, convincing dialogue and multiple ironies as well as the extraordinary technical adroitness which she brings to a compelling tale that plays with time and relies on flashback and a two-generational structure.

Sin and damnation permeate the oppressive world of the book where the characters are at the mercy of the physical environment as well as each other. Much of the behaviour in the story is extreme, often savage. None of the relationships is conventional with the exception of Catherine Earnshaw's initial affection for Edgar Linton. She marries him to the despair of Heathcliff, who is left with no option but to inflict revenge on his beloved's family while pursuing a tormented, self-destructive existence, viewing hell as his only refuge.

In the beginning, there are two children; Catherine Earnshaw and her older brother Hindley. Their father sets off for Liverpool asking them what gifts he should bring back. Hindley asks for a fiddle, while young Catherine, then six, demands a whip, an odd request from a child. Watch closely, the text is rich in symbol, metaphor and the supernatural. Mr Earnshaw returns, carrying an urchin boy, Heathcliff. As for the gifts, the fiddle is discovered to have been smashed in Mr Earnshaw's pocket, while the whip, to Catherine's fury, has been lost and she blames the newcomer.

Saving the wild boy from a life on the streets has ironic repercussions. This random act of kindness instigates the hatred that drives the metaphorical heart of the story. Heathcliff's arrival brings out the worst in the Earnshaw children; Hindley beats him but Catherine claims him as her possession. Heathcliff soon reveals terrifying qualities of stoicism and ruthlessness. Catherine Earnshaw, hysterical and wilful, is the central dynamic and is drawn to her neighbour, the gentle, upper-class Edgar Linton. Yet she also has an inexplicable bond with the enigmatic Heathcliff; it proves a dangerous obsession.

She likes Edgar well enough to marry him in the void that opens after Heathcliff disappears. However on his return, now grown mature and prosperous, Catherine's happiness with Edgar falters, incapable of withstanding the heightened passion she feels for her old soul mate. The exasperated love of Catherine and Heathcliff takes over the action, destroying them and testing the next generation.

The two narrators are well pitched; the first, and more minor figure, is the peevish Lockwood, an outsider on the run from his own failure of emotion. The second is Ellen 'Nelly' Dean, the ever-present, perceptive, candid and helpfully, from the point of driving the narrative, talkative housekeeper who having spent her life witnessing the complicated, often deranged behaviour of most of the motherless central players, is privy to their histories and their secrets. Brontë conveys Nelly's fascination with the story, which the housekeeper in turn passes on to Lockwood – and the reader.

Her pleasure in books – hence her ability to tell a good story –

makes Nelly become alive; she is sympathetic, alert and appears to almost like the thwarted, tormented Heathcliff, often directly questioning his actions, such as confronting him when he disturbs Catherine's grave. Nelly explains much of what happens; the pulsating atmosphere does the rest. Small wonder that in Lockwood, having arrived to rent Thrushcross Grange, once the home of the Lintons, she finds a willing audience.

This skilfully plotted and daring early Victorian family saga with its layered narrative exploded into being. No fey romance, it looks beyond passion to larger issues of obsession and eternity; the ordinary and the surreal.

Emily Brontë (1818-1848)

The face is that of a young girl; it is a profile, delicate with dark hair framing small features. She is pale. Her intense gaze is directed away into the distance. This is a solitary individual no one really knew, not even her siblings. Her closest relationships were with dogs and cats; she had no friends, she left few letters. Emily Brontë was about fifteen years old when she sat for the ghostly study, possibly a fragment of a larger work, painted by her brother Bramwell. The image hangs in the National Portrait Gallery in London where millions of visitors have peered closely at it, wondering at this romantic visionary, whose only novel exudes such terrifying imaginative energy.

Why did this girl, the fifth child of an Irish clergyman whose wife's death resulted in all the children being raised by his sister, a staunch Methodist, write such a powerful tale? Growing up in an isolated parsonage with siblings, all of whom were bookish and sickly, what made her think of evoking domestic tension spanning the generations? How did she create Heathcliff? What experience could have possibly helped the remote, introspective Brontë whose mother had died when she was three years old, grasp the emotional turmoil that sustains *Wuthering Heights*? Aside from her schooling, a stay in Brussels where she discovered German literature and her brief, unhappy period working as a governess, Brontë lived her short life at Haworth, on Yorkshire's brooding moors.

By thirty she was dead, dying of tuberculosis three months after Bramwell at whose funeral she had contracted a chill. Only on her last day of life did she agree to see a doctor. It was too late. Her sister, Charlotte, recorded the final hours: "She sank rapidly. She made haste to leave us. Yet, while physically she perished, mentally, she grew stronger than we had yet known her . . . I have seen nothing like it: but, indeed, I have never seen her parallel in anything. Stronger than a man, simpler than a child, her nature stood alone."

Ravaged by consumption Emily Brontë fought death like a warrior of old. On the evening before the day she died, she collapsed while feeding the dogs. The next morning, she insisted on her habitual seven o'clock rising and combed her hair by the hearth. The wooden comb slipped from her fingers. She was too weak to pick it up. She dressed and made her way downstairs, gasping for breath.

By noon, she could barely speak. She was carried upstairs and, in Charlotte's words, "turning her dying eyes reluctantly from the pleasant sun" Emily Jane Brontë, poet and loner, died at two o'clock in the afternoon of 19 December 1848. Her dog had kept vigil by the bedside. If Brontë's belief in life after death was as strong as her masterpiece suggests, her spirit no doubt continues to patrol her dark, beloved moors.

13

A Confederacy of Dunces
(1980)
by John Kennedy Toole

Society, no – make that mankind – disgusts Ignatius J. Reilly, deranged intellectual anti-hero of this exuberant comedy which makes inspired use of the lavish rhetoric of the US South. Ignatius is the idle, domineering, over-educated son of a bewildered, semi-literate mother who refers to him as having "graduated smart". They live in squalor in New Orleans. While she frets about her arthritis, he directs his invective against pretty much everything, penning churlishly bombastic tirades on a variety of subjects, and all sprawled across the yellow lined pages of Big Chief writing tablets.

Early in the narrative, Ignatius, now thirty, is accosted by Patrolman Mancuso, an eager policeman whose career depends on his succeeding in making an arrest. Mom, who had been buying cakes to appease her boy, arrives at the scene intent on rescuing Ignatius. An elderly man also intervenes, and a riot begins. Mother and child seek sanctuary in the Night of Joy bar, a dubious establishment where Mrs Reilly demonstrates her liking for hard liquor. All is far from correct in Miss Lee's strip joint where Jones, a black man with a flair for exasperated speech, appears doomed to sweep floors for the rest of time, but is all the while amassing evidence related to Miss Lee's sideline in pornography.

John Kennedy Toole's outrageously funny burlesque which was published in 1980 – eleven years after he had committed suicide – features a cast of vividly eccentric misfits who are not merely foils for the theatrical Ignatius but are three-dimensional characters in their own right.

The narrative races along on Toole's fluent and rhythmic prose, a barrage of hilarious dialogue, manically comic set pieces and our anti-hero's one-liners, which he invariably delivers with stately, often righteous, assurance. Ignatius, who plays the lute and favours a green hunting cap sporting ear flaps teamed with capacious tweed clothing, is unemployable. He attends the local movie house mainly out of a compulsion to shout abuse at the actors. It is not easy being him; his corpulent, heaving mass fills three cinema seats, while his often-mentioned "valve" frequently threatens to close at moments of crisis.

Small wonder he spends a great deal of time in bed and in the bath contemplating the sexually crazed fantasies of his erstwhile girlfriend, Myrna Minkoff, currently pursuing political excitement in New York.

On being asked to leave Lana Lee's bar, mother and son set off for the family car. Mrs Reilly crashes into another vehicle and damages a building. Patrolman Mancuso, the inept policeman so desperately in need of an arrest, is watching. The bad news for Mrs Reilly is that she is going to have to pay for all the damage. On the plus side though, she strikes up a friendship with Mancuso and his aunt, Santa Battaglia.

Suddenly, to Ignatius's horror, his formerly indulgent mother acquires a social life, takes up bowling and begins to openly challenge him. Even more upsetting is her insistence that he get a job. Fate, together with an obvious lack of other offers, brings Ignatius to Levy Pants, a defeated family clothing firm. Mr Gonzalez, the meek office manager, is so intimidated by Ignatius that he hires him as a filing clerk. Also working there is the ancient Miss Trixie, who has difficulty staying awake and resents the firm's delay in sanctioning her retirement. She takes a liking to Ignatius, and somehow decides that his name is Gloria. They immediately bond.

Ignatius settles into a routine of arriving an hour late for work, breezing in like a debutante at a ball. However when his thoughts turn to revolution, he incites the factory workers to protest against their conditions. It backfires, the workers turn on our anti-hero. He then becomes a hot dog vendor, only to eat more than he sells. His mother is in despair: "He don't care about his poor momma" she laments, "With all his education, mind you. Selling weenies out on the street in broad daylight."

All the while Ignatius is keeping a journal signed "Your Working Boy" and sustains an abusive correspondence with Myrna. Dr Talc, his former history professor, comes across some of the threatening letters, signed Zorro, that Ignatius used to send him. Ignatius J. Reilly lives off the page, as do they all; Mrs Reilly, Jones, Miss Lee, Patrolman Mancuso, Miss Trixie, Mr and Mrs Levy, the downtrodden Gonzalez and most of all, New Orleans itself, every element brilliantly fashioned by Toole's vivid combination of the colloquial, the politely old fashioned turn of phrase and the anti-hero's rhetorical impatience with lesser minds.

Posthumously awarded the 1981 Pulitzer Prize for Fiction, *A Confederacy of Dunces* is an unforgettably virtuoso comic performance, yet for all the hilarity and there is sufficient to send most readers into a state of helpless laughter, there is the sombre realisation that Ignatius, a misfit, and simply too clever to belong anywhere, is the consummate outsider.

John Kennedy Toole (1937-1969)

It is almost fitting that a talent as extreme as John Kennedy Toole's would have an extreme story. *A Confederacy of Dunces* takes its title from Swift's famous observation: "When a true genius appears in the world, you may know him by this sign, that the dunces are all in confederacy against him." Frustrated by the reluctance of the slow-witted world to recognise exactly what he was trying to do, and had in fact achieved with his comic masterpiece, Toole killed himself at the age of thirty-two. What went through his mind? Was he angry? Or defiant? Or defeated? Or all three?

Toole, by then introverted and paranoid, was very different from the happy, indulged, smartass prodigy he had been as a boy. His mother, Thelma Toole, a frustrated pianist and speech-teacher, had regarded her only, unexpected child as a miracle. He seemed to agree with her. When he was ten years old he introduced a school essay by announcing: "I have been praised so often in my life that I think this epic should speak for itself." It could almost have been uttered by Ignatius J. Reilly.

John Kennedy Toole, 'Ken' to his friends, was born in New Orleans. His father, who had no interest in books and even less in his son's battle to get his novel acknowledged, was a car salesman. He was bright and completed a master's degree in English from Columbia University and later taught at the University of Southwestern Louisiana. On completing *A Confederacy of Dunces* in the early 1960s, he was not prepared for the years of rejection. As his depression deepened, his thoughts turned to suicide on 26 March 1969, while sitting in his Chevrolet near Biloxi, Mississippi, or so the story goes. He left behind a tattered manuscript, which was, as novelist Walker Percy recalled, "a hefty, badly smeared, scarcely readable carbon". He also left a mother who was determined that her son's book would be published.

Thelma D. Toole loved her son and believed in his opus. Through either great foresight or simply good luck, she brought the manuscript to the right man, Percy, the author of *The Moviegoer* (1960) who was teaching at Loyola University at the time. As Percy would write in his foreword there were several determined phone calls put through to him. The woman caller was not making a plea on behalf of her own literary efforts; she wanted Percy to read her son's novel. Admittedly the book had been written almost a decade earlier, no one had shown any interest in it, it had had several rejections and, by the way, her son was dead, having killed himself in despair. But she still had the book and believed it could have a life. It was still in the raw and messy manuscript form, just as Toole had left it. Percy, understandably, was not too excited.

This would change once he began to read this unforgettable comic extravaganza. Percy proved a great champion and through him, the novel was finally published. A mother's belief in both her son and in his belief in his book was vindicated. His anarchic satire was awarded the 1981 Pulitzer Prize for Fiction and an American masterwork of extraordinary panache continues to be celebrated.

But, as with many literary stories, there is a footnote. John Kennedy Toole had left another book, an apprentice work, *The Neon Bible*, written when he was sixteen. Grim and sentimental, it is set in the 1940s South and just about suggests an element of promise. It tells the story of a family tragedy as seen through the eyes of a boy, sitting on a train, lost in thought. His father's death in the war had caused the boy's mother to slide into decline and young David's only comfort is his colourful Aunt Mae, a singer of limited ability. When his mother dies, David is left with the body. The local preacher arrives and David shoots him.

This early effort was quickly forgotten by Toole whose life would become dominated by *A Confederacy of Dunces*. It sustained him for a while, until its apparent failure killed him.

Irony, human greed and the legendary opportunism of publishers appeared to conspire in getting *The Neon Bible* published in May 1989, twenty years after Toole's death. Despite Thelma having stipulated in her will that the book should never be published, her husband's family, motivated by the sales of *A Confederacy of Dunces*, overturned her wishes under the Napoleonic Code which remains part of Louisiana State Law and allows the husband's side of the family equal rights to a wife's property. Reading *The Neon Bible* is about as different from reading *A Confederacy of Dunces* as night is from day, but it shows that even this obviously gifted writer was once just a boy trying to tell a story.

14

To the Lighthouse
(1927)
by Virginia Woolf

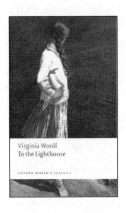

Virginia Woolf
To the Lighthouse

OXFORD WORLD'S CLASSICS

A small boy pleads to visit the lighthouse; for him it has become a personal quest. Nothing else matters. His mother attempts to bargain, "Yes, of course, if it's fine tomorrow." His philosopher father, however, is a man of science who deals in facts, not promises. "But it won't be fine," declares the older man. Small wonder the boy's response is to imagine a weapon close at hand, one capable of killing his father. Mr Ramsay prides himself on the truth; his wife favours grace, charm, imagination and the unsaid. He deals in posterity, she lives for the moment.

To the Lighthouse is Virginia Woolf's most personal lamentation; a symphonic novel in which her literary genius confronts ghosts and memories, most especially her love for her wistful, tragic mother. Summoning all her technical skill, lilting prose and inspired use of the consciousness as a conduit of powerful emotion, Woolf shapes an astute meditation on the dramatic choreography of life and death. The narrative proves an atmospheric, heartbreakingly elegiac study of a family and its close circle of intimates. At its heart shimmers Mrs Ramsay, a beautiful woman, still lovely though aging; enthusiastic, if weary; a magician preparing to vanish for all eternity.

Some two years after completing *Mrs Dalloway* (1925), itself a formidable achievement, Woolf crafted her artistic testament. In *To the Lighthouse* she draws on the physical reality of life to sustain an exploration of emotion and memory. It is as instinctive as it is analytical. The characters engage, react, observe and are in turn, observed and in the case of Mrs Ramsay, invoked, lamented.

The long opening section recreates the bustle of a ritualised family vacation. Each summer the Ramsays forsake London for the Isle of Skye. The children vary in age from young James and Cam, who is still wary of shadows at night, to Andrew, a promising mathematician, and Pru, poised for romance. Mrs Ramsay has established a household away from home where she nurtures her family and friends. Woolf allows her characters freedom to think, to muse, but it is to the aspiring artist, Lily Briscoe, a watchful, single woman, that she entrusts the vital role of observer. It is Lily, existing beyond the immediate control of Mrs Ramsay, though moulded by both her presence and her absence, who ponders late in this dreamy, exact, boldly impressionistic narrative, the meaning of life.

There is gaiety, eccentricity. There is also a prevailing male/female tension in the ramshackle if all-welcomingly chaotic holiday house. Mr Ramsay, egotistical and volatile, shouts, pontificates, quotes poetry and argues. His wife accepts him as he is; his children seethe and rebel. All the while, romances evolve, an engagement is announced and the future beckons – as does fate.

The daring middle section, Time Passes, acts as a chill wind. In a single sentence deliberately placed off stage, almost as an authorial aside, and set within square brackets, the heroine's abrupt departure is reported – "[Mr Ramsay stumbling along a passage stretched his arms out one dark morning, but, Mrs Ramsay having died rather suddenly the night before, he stretched his arms out. They remained empty.]" – Woolf boldly jolts the reader into the far- reaching significance of a narrative that not only chronicles a family's history, it also considers an England faced with social upheaval and a generation lost on the battlefields of the Great War.

Most of all there is Woolf's preoccupation with the relentlessness of time and its cruel changes. Death strikes at the family, old routines end, all the while the neglected house stands empty and forgotten: "It was left like a shell on a sandhill to fill with dry salt grains now that life had left it." A decade passes bringing with it decay, until finally the caretaker, an old local woman, is contacted; the Ramsays "might be returning for the summer."

Woolf evokes a mood of resolve in the final sequence. Surviving family members and friends return. Mr Ramsay, James and a sullen Cam, at last undertake the odyssey to the lighthouse, "the tower, stark and straight" luring them, while Lily, older, wiser, looks on and understands so much more.

Virginia Woolf *(1882-1941)*

She began as a critic; incisive, magisterial, often cruel. But before becoming the literary conscience of the Bloomsbury set, Britain's response to the Continental intelligentsia, Virginia Woolf was a second daughter in a Victorian family; that was the role that initially defined her sense of self and would determine her political analysis of society. Social class shaped her reactions to everything, not only people. Woolf was a snob, and an egoist who battled an illness that eventually defeated her. She was also a genius, a Modernist born a Victorian, who then became an Edwardian – and a writer who helped pioneer the device of continuous stream of consciousness.

The early death of her beloved mother Julia Stephen in 1895 effectively ended the future writer's childhood. She was then thirteen and already aware of the oppressive presence of her intractable father, Sir Leslie Stephen. Fifty at the time of her birth and seventy-two when he died, he was overpowering and his daughter conscious that had he lived to ninety-six "like other people one has known . . . his life would have entirely ended mine . . . no writing . . . no books . . . inconceivable."

She published her first review in 1904, the year he died. He is the domineering, egocentric Mr Ramsay in *To the Lighthouse* (1927), just as her mother is the inspiration for Mrs Ramsay whose death in the novel is a symbol of upheaval. Woolf never recovered from the loss of her mother. *To the Lighthouse*, published when Woolf was forty-five, remains her masterpiece; it is the book most central to her own, and to our, understanding of her life.

Bloomsbury, geographically situated in the heart of Georgian London, was an artistic, Bohemian revolt against the Establishment which would become an Establishment unto itself, particularly from the 1920s onwards, as it began to dominate publishing and magazine editing. By the time she married Leonard Woolf in 1912 when she was thirty, they were both central to and detached from Bloomsbury, the literary movement. In 1917 they founded the Hogarth Press.

As a critic and essayist Virginia Woolf had assessed the canon and also looked to important new voices such as Joseph Conrad and Henry James. She wrote influential pieces about Dostoyevsky as his novels became available in English editions through Constance Garnett's translations. Her literary voice, honed by her critical judgment and the extensive reading begun as a girl in her father's library, appeared initially in the *Times Literary Supplement*, and was recognised well before the publication of her first novel, *The Voyage Out*, in 1915.

That same young girl had written to James and would much later as a famous writer pay respectful visits to Thomas Hardy. She knew T. S. Eliot and initially had been sweepingly dismissive of James Joyce. Ironically, it was to him that she would be increasingly compared. Woolf was interested in fiction that looked inward and broke free of the old chronological conventions. *Jacob's Room* (1922), her third novel, was inspired by the death of her brother Thoby Stephen, and expressed her emerging form of lyrical experimentalism.

With *Mrs Dalloway* (1925) she pursued themes of loneliness and separation. Taking place like *Ulysses* over the course of a single day, it also owes something to Conrad in its evocation of London as two contrasting cities – that of Clarissa's cosmopolitan society juxtaposed with the living hell of the shell-shocked soldier. It is a novel of moments; it also shares Joyce's concept, and use, of the epiphany as a narrative device.

Woolf kept an intense diary from the age of fifteen until her death, and lived a childless, self-protective life choreographed by her metaphysical defiance to others, to existence itself. She engaged in complex, often sexual, relationships with women. Yet she and Leonard Woolf remained together. All the while, through her nine novels, literary criticism, feminist essays, volumes of diaries and letters, she was exploring the business of being alive. Her vision was both narrow and as wide as the ocean.

But Woolf's habitual simmering despair, combined with the relentlessness of the war and the bombing of London, eventually overpowered her. Filling her pockets with stones, she famously walked into the River Ouse near the Sussex country house she shared with her patient, sympathetic husband. It was 1941. She was fifty-nine.

15 | Ulysses
(1922)
by James Joyce

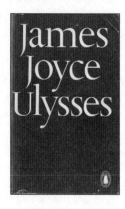

Like a thief in the night, James Joyce, the consummate self-exile, ingeniously exploded all notions of traditional fiction with his playful, earthy, rampagingly human, urban anti-epic. Intended to keep the critics busy, it has done exactly that, filling libraries and supporting a body of international scholarship that amounts to an industry, much of it preoccupied by the novel's complex textual history.

Allusive in its classical, literary, historical, political and popular cultural cross references, as well as Joyce's personal jokes, *Ulysses* is also a stylistic and linguistic tour de force which makes inspired use of interior monologue as a way of juxtaposing the richness of the imaginative life with the meanness of social intercourse.

Set in a sultry Dublin, on 16 June 1904, it is an odyssey of the ordinary. Joyce created a world by capturing the body and soul of a colonial city he mapped with all the precision of a military surveyor – and immortalised. Joyce's Dublin has defied time and the developers. *Ulysses* also debunks the myth of the heroic by taking as its central figure a mild, if opinionated, pacifist – Leopold Bloom, advertising canvasser, cuckolded husband and definitive Everyman. He is an outsider, a Dublin Jew relegated to the margins by the culturally racist nationalism that Joyce was determined to expose. He waged war on preening national vanity. *Ulysses* is a comic, often vicious, at times moving, and always inspired parody.

Above all, in Bloom, Joyce presents a man possessed of a sense of justice. Though living in a misogynistic society, Bloom, despite his lascivious musings, is sympathetic to women. Here is an Edwardian male who having done the shopping, serves his wife breakfast in bed, and laments the lack of public toilets available to ladies "caught short". Bloom is opposed to war and all forms of violence. For him, true heroism is the act of childbirth. His sexual life is confined to fantasy and speculative glances, reaching true pathos as he masturbates while watching young Gerty MacDowell's flirtatious performance, an interlude based on her doubts, fantasies and frustrations.

The chapters, moving through a sequence of city locations, reflect the episodes of Homer's *Odyssey* from which Joyce has taken themes as well as a structure of sorts. *Ulysses* has been described as being both plotless and over-plotted. In either case, it has a central theme – that of wandering. Bloom – Odysseus - wanders through a day during which he at all times is moving closer and closer to an encounter with Stephen Dedalus, the self-absorbed artist and Telemachus figure, and also symbolic son to Bloom, bereaved father of little Rudy. And then there is Molly – Penelope – a fading popular soprano who lingers in bed, thinking her confused thoughts and is involved with her caddish manager, Blazes Boylan.

Bloom's morning begins in Eccles Street preparing breakfast, defecating and tending the cat. Simultaneously, across the city, in a tower by the sea, the disgruntled Stephen has been party to Buck Mulligan's ceremonial shaving, a task that parodies church ritual.

Stephen sets off to his lowly teaching job. Having dealt with his pupils, he then collects his earnings from Mr Deasy who lectures him on the virtue of saving. Their banter culminates in Deasy, who requests some help in having a letter published, remarking to Stephen "You were not born to be a teacher, I think. Perhaps I am wrong." Stephen's reply is interesting; instead of proclaiming himself "artist" as would be expected for all his obvious conceit and intellectual pretentions, he says "a learner rather". Joyce makes it clear that Stephen also has his doubts.

Meanwhile, Bloom checks for the post he receives under the name of "Henry Flower, Esq." at the post office in Westland Row. A letter is waiting and it gives him a boost. When purchasing Molly's beauty aids at the chemist, he also buys himself a cake of lemon soap. Unintentionally, a hot tip for the Ascot Gold Cup is exchanged.

Joyce proceeds to ease his characters into one of the finest of many immortal set pieces; the carriage trip to poor Paddy Dignam's funeral during which quick-fire comic dialogue is exchanged between the mourners. Vivid characterisation, images, headlines, gossip and heated arguments are tossed in the air, apparently casually but deadly deliberate, to be invariably retrieved. Joyce remembers every detail. The hours pass; Bloom and Stephen come closer and closer. The narrative moves from realism to fantasy. Night town explodes into surreal virtuosity, before yielding to the domestic and sleep.

Is it the greatest novel of the twentieth century? Not quite. Yet *Ulysses* with its cynicism, wordplay, invention, wit and humanity lives and breathes; scratches, sings and sighs through Joyce's singular, eloquent celebration of the commonplace.

James Joyce *(1882-1941)*

It was James Joyce who decided that literature had moved on from traditional narrative and was now concerned with language and form as well as the complex deconstruction of itself. He both initiated and killed off modernism; *Finnegans Wake* (1939) is his history of the world, and it is as much a wake for modernism as it is for poor old Finnegan. Joyce, the sophisticated outsider had moved on from the intimacy of the superb short stories in *Dubliners* (1914) and the quasi-autobiographical, *A Portrait of the Artist as a Young Man* (1916) to consider Europe, its languages, its cultures and its conflicts in taking Irish writing away from protest and lamentation. Instead of composing a post-mortem on the lost Gaelic culture, he was drawn to the two major international literary movements of the 1890s, naturalism and symbolism – nostalgia did not concern him.

Peering intently at his country with the eyes of an anthropologist alert to political and cultural shifts, he neither sentimentalised nor romanticised Ireland as is obvious from his brilliant satirical creation, the Citizen, as debilitated Gaelic athlete and embittered nationalist ideologue, and the personification of the tension between myth, politics and economic reality. *Ulysses* and *The Waste Land*, both published in the same year, are twin pioneering modernist texts. When reviewing *Ulysses*, T. S. Eliot noted that Joyce was "giving a shape and a significance to the immense panorama of futility and anarchy which is contemporary history".

Joyce, who considered himself the Irish Zola, was not the first writer to attempt a big city novel. Russian symbolist Andrei Bely had already done that with *Petersburg* (1916), but Joyce's methodology was radically new. He revealed the artist's mind at work through his use of the interior monologue. His influence would shape Virginia Woolf – no matter how often she dismissed Joyce as "underbred" – and Alfred Döblin's *Berlin Alexanderplatz* (1929), while Joyce would prove vital to the young William Faulkner. *Ulysses* is also a historical novel, set at a distance of almost twenty years earlier than when it was written. It takes place not in the postwar era, but in the pre-war epoch of a European city on the fringes of Europe, with a people subjected to the twin dominion of the British crown and the Roman Catholic Church.

The period between the date the narrative takes place, 16 June 1904 and that of its publication on 2 February 1922, Joyce's fortieth birthday, was one of breathtaking revolutionary change; Europe and the world changed, as did the new, independent Irish State. Joyce's bohemian leave-taking had acquired a more serious dimension of politically determined exile. In common with the Austro-Hungarian Joseph Roth, Joyce watched the collapse of empires. *Ulysses* offers a bridge between the pre-war world and the postwar one. Joyce the middle-class boy had watched his family's fortunes decline much as Dublin's emerging working class became inflated by country people flooding the city desperate for jobs that didn't exist, and in the process over-populating already squalid slums.

Above all *Ulysses*, drawing its structure from Homer's *Odyssey* and reducing a ten-year time span to a mere eighteen hours, is the story of its own act of creation. Joyce composed it against the backdrop provided by the Irish Literary Revival. The opening scene,

Buck Mulligan's morning shave in the tower which parodies Catholic ritual, is overseen by an invisible, yet clearly very much present cast, which includes Yeats, James Stephens, George William Russell and Oliver St John Gogarty, the real-life character-about-town who inspired Buck Mulligan.

So *Ulysses* looks to two exiles, that of Odysseus and an anti-heroic counterpart, one Leopold Bloom, the wandering Jew of Hungarian origin adrift in a culturally hostile Dublin. Central to Joyce's genius is his political intelligence which has been seriously underestimated by most cultural critics. As early as *A Portrait of the Artist as a Young Man* (originally published serially in the *Egoist* between 1914 and 1915 and first published in novel form in 1916), Joyce saw himself reflected in the misinterpreted Parnell; he identified with Parnell's outsider status, absorbing part of it into his own self-myth. In *The Shade of Parnell* (1910) Joyce wrote of the fallen leader of the Irish Parliamentary Party: "In his final desperate appeal to his countrymen he begged them not to throw him as a sop to the English wolves howling around them. It redounds to their honour that they did not fail this appeal. They did not throw him to the English wolves; they tore him to pieces themselves."

James Joyce though choosing to live at a physical remove never relinquished his astute understanding of Ireland.

16 | Berlin Alexanderplatz
(1929)
by Alfred Döblin

There is a man standing alone in the street. All around him people are moving, shouting, shopping, ordering food. Trolley cars pass. The scene is busy, but the man continues to stand, staring, as if paralysed, bewildered by life itself. The scene is Weimar Berlin and the man is slowly shaking off the four years he has spent in Tegel Prison. "Yesterday in convict's garb he had been raking potatoes with the others in the fields in the back of the building, now he was walking in a tan summer top-coat; they were still raking back there, he was free." In one of the most cinematic novels ever written Alfred Döblin introduces his Everyman, Franz Biberkopf, on the day of his release from jail.

Biberkopf gathers himself and leaps on to a street car: ". . . people got on and off. Something inside him screamed in terror: Look out, look out, it's going to start now . . . He got off the car, without being noticed, and was back among people again . . . How they hustle and bustle! My brain needs oiling, it's probably dried up." He notices shoe stores and hat stores and wax figures "in the show-windows, in suits, overcoats, with skirt, with shoes and stockings. Outside everything was moving . . ."

Movement and sound take over, the man is invisible. But no, he isn't. Someone does see him. A kindly Jew speaks with him and encourages old Franz to sing out loud. Döblin's vivid, cautionary novel is an Otto Dix painting come to life. The characters have faces that may well have been captured by George Grosz, a native Berliner who knew the facial expressions of his fellow citizens. The world recreated here is that of Berlin between the two world wars, the dingy eastern part of the city near Alexanderplatz, populated by gangsters, petty crooks and weary, compliant women.

Life is relentless and everyone knows it. Biberkopf the news vendor is no saint. He had been an ordinary labourer and before that, a soldier; not a hero, just a soldier. But just when he was living his life, what did he do? Became very drunk one night, as he often did – and will again – and got angry, angry with Ida, his fiancée, so angry he killed her. Got sentenced he did, but not for murder, only for manslaughter. After all, Ida was a woman, wasn't she? And women don't do so well in this part of the city where many of them are grateful to have a man, even when he is no more than a pimp and free with his fists.

The narrative is delivered through a rhythmic, continuous present tense, as if by chanting chorus; the tone is knowing and ironic because the outcome is inevitable. The earthy language is colloquial, nothing fancy – these characters react, demand, question – they don't make speeches. It's about life, not art. Here is the story of an ordinary man who has done wrong but now has returned to the world determined to live a normal life.

Technically, it is a montage of images and scenes; the narrative is a fast-moving camera. Watch this man, this man here whose story will be told as surely as a dance will be danced, but watch everyone else as well, and listen closely.

Berlin Alexanderplatz was published in the same year as Remarque's poignant war elegy, *All Quiet on the Western Front*. These two German novels could not be more different. The influence of Joyce is obvious; Döblin is also bringing a city to life and using mythological parallels. But this is bleaker; there is less poetry, little empathy and no humour. The horrors mount up like so many blows. The style is that of John Dos Passos's *Manhattan Transfer* (1925); documentary-like, graphic. Lives are pieced together by so many incidents, all caught by Döblin's forensic lens.

Snatches of conversation are overheard; faces merge, equal measures of hope and despair. In a scene of eerie, slow-moving beauty an old man walks into the cattle market with a young calf.

"He leads it in alone by a rope; this is a huge hall in which the bulls roar . . . He lifts the delicate little calf with both arms, puts it on the bench . . . The animal is patient and still, there it lies, it does not know what is going to happen . . . it bumps its head against a stick and does not know what it is: but it is the end of the club which is standing on the ground and with which it will soon receive a blow. That will be its last encounter with the world." The little animal dies, without protest, because "that's the way it has to be". The death of the calf becomes symbolic.

Franz needs sex just as he requires food and drink; it's another fuel. A young reader may have sympathy for him but returning to this novel after many years alerts one to the daunting mindlessness of Franz. He is not really a victim of the system; he is his own human disaster, too lazy to think or feel much beyond himself and his needs. He is no Leopold Bloom; there is no fantasy, no lamentation. Bloom has a sense of justice; Franz Biberkopf does not. He slides into a doomed association with the vicious Reinhold and reluctantly becomes involved in a crime. Another young woman, Mieze, who had trusted Franz, pays the price for her loyalty. Her murder leads Franz through a quest that ends in a salvation of sorts.

Döblin's choreographed morality play, predating the camera's-eye fiction of Don DeLillo by decades, has lost none of its cautionary, operatic power.

Alfred Döblin (1878-1957)

In the most famous of his many works, *Berlin Alexanderplatz*, Alfred Döblin summoned the life and, admittedly, defeated soul of a city he had moved to as an adult. It is a huge, panoramic novel, as much a documentary moral polemic, as it is an allegorical story. Döblin the expressionist, possessed of a powerfully visual imagination, was an unusual character. He was Jewish and an outsider, born in Stettin, in Pomerania, then the extreme east of Germany.

On initially completing his medical studies in 1905, specialising in psychiatry, Döblin worked as a journalist. By then, he had already completed a first novel, *The Black Curtain*, although it would not be published until 1912, the year after he had settled in Berlin to practise as a doctor. Based in the working class area of Alexanderplatz, he became involved in the various arts circles, finding a rapport with fellow literary expressionists. About this time he had begun contributing stories and sketches to the influential weekly literary journal, *Der Sturm*. It had been founded in 1910 by gallery owner and arts impresario Herwarth Walden (1878-1941), and would be edited by him until its demise in 1932.

A collection of Döblin's fiction, *Murder of a Buttercup*, appeared in 1913. The publication two years later of a strongly religious novel, *The Three Leaps of Wang-Lun*, consolidated his reputation. Wang-Lun, is a fisherman's son who founds a sect of idealists later eradicated by the Chinese establishment. Döblin reacted against soulless materialism – in the title story of *Murder of a Buttercup*, a businessman beheads a butterfly – and in subsequent works, such as *Wadzek's Struggle with the Steam-Machine* (1918) and the futuristic *Mountains, Seas and Giants* (1924), he would pursue these themes. *Wallenstein* (1920) is a long, historical novel which pits the eponymous man of action against the passive Emperor Ferdinand, while making a subtle comment on the epoch in which Döblin was writing. He also wrote a series of political satires under a pseudonym, "Linke-Poot" – and a number of unsuccessful plays.

In the midst of all this activity his other life as a doctor gave shape to the work which would become *Berlin Alexanderplatz* – as much about Berlin's teeming underclass of crooks and prostitutes as it is about the hapless anti-heroic and all-too-convincingly human Franz Biberkopf. Döblin's experience working with patients suffering from mental breakdowns is central to the novel, which draws on a range of devices such as montage, interior monologue, the use of a cautionary narrative tone, popular songs, radio announcements and, in the style of Joyce, mythological parallels. A fellow German, movie maker Rainer Werner Fassbinder (1945-1982), identified with Döblin's novel, describing it as "a huge part of myself . . . decisive in determining the course of my life" and would make a fifteen-hour film version of it which premiered at the Venice Film Festival in 1980.

The novel is immensely political in that it is a determinedly unsentimental study of a working man at the mercy of the system, ably abetted by his many personal failings. It is interesting to consider that such is the narrative's edgy emotional drive that the full force of Döblin's polemic tends to emerge only in hindsight.

Intensified anti-Semitism in Germany caused Döblin to set off on a series of international travels bringing him to Russia, Palestine, Zurich, Paris and the United States, where he converted to Catholicism. After the war he returned to Germany, settling in the south where he edited a magazine. He continued to write until the end of his long life. On a visit to Berlin in late 1947, ten years before his death at the age of seventy-nine, he was shattered by the destruction and commented: "Nothing remains of that [Berlin] any more, none of the people, none of the buildings, the whole place is now brought to ground level. Historically, the past has been totally expunged."

Man Without Mercy (1935), set in an unspecified country, hovers uneasily between fable and realism in following the career of a hero, who becomes a capitalist, only to die during a riot. His younger brother, a kind of semi-religious revolutionary, stays put.

Döblin continued to explore the themes of religion, politics and the misplaced. *Land Without Death*, a long work about South America, came out between 1936 and 1938, while the trilogy, 'November 1918', which he began in 1939 with *The Betrayed People* (1948) and *Return From the Front* (1949), culminated in *Karl and Rosa* (1950), which chronicles the assassinations in 1919 of Rosa Luxemburg and Karl Liebknecht.

Döblin's final novel, *Hamlet* (1956), the story of a disturbed Englishman who returns home to discover his marriage in ruins, draws on the multiple-device technique he had used in *Berlin Alexanderplatz*. Times, however, had changed for him; it took ten years for that book to find a publisher, and then, only in East Germany. Much of his work is still awaiting translation and a fresh translation of *Berlin Alexanderplatz* is long overdue. Stylistically, he is a bridge in German fiction between the traditional narratives of Thomas Mann and the free-wheeling creativity of Günter Grass.

113

17 The Lord of the Rings
(1954-1955)
by J.R.R. Tolkien

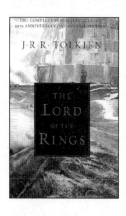

Middle-earth is facing cataclysmic upheaval. Sauron, the Dark Lord, is in possession of all but one of the Rings of Power. He needs to locate "One Ring to rule them all and in the darkness bind them." With it, he will have full domination and is massing an army of monsters. The One Ring is currently held by a most unlikely custodian, Bilbo Baggins, the now elderly hero of *The Hobbit* (1937), who is preparing to leave his home in the Shire to go on a long journey. He entrusts the Ring, which is known to do strange things to all who grasp it, to his cousin Frodo.

But for young Frodo, it is no gift. The Ring is dangerous. Frodo has accepted an immense responsibility; he must embark on a life-threatening odyssey across Middle-earth to the far Cracks of Doom in Mordor, and there destroy the Ring before it causes greater evil.

Here is a heroic quest that instead of pursuing an elusive object, is about ridding the world from one, by destroying the Ring. This is the definitive adventure, a consummate feat of the imagination, as violent as it is courtly, lyrical, often funny, strangely beautiful and ultimately, profoundly moving in its romantic pathos. The three-volume epic – *The Fellowship of the Ring*, *The Two Towers* and *The Return of the King* – which was not written as a trilogy but rather as a continuous narrative, is inspired by myth and daring. It has consistently emerged in literary polls among readers as the book of the twentieth century ahead of works by Joyce, Proust, Nabokov, Mann, Grass, Pynchon and a great many other literary heavyweights.

Critics may snarl – many of whom have never read it – but readers insist otherwise; the power of Tolkien's dense, high-speed narrative, with its detailed characterisation and complex web of racial tensions, cultures and histories, is the most seductive and complete world into which any reader could hope to wander.

Much of the genius of the tale, with its menacing Dark Riders and flashes of *Macbeth* and *Paradise Lost*, lies in Tolkien's brilliant juxtaposing of middle-class English values, as represented by the provincial hobbit citizens of a cosy Shire, alongside strongly heroic elements of the distant past. Also dominant are darker elements from the European fairytale such as trolls, goblins and dragons, as well as the austere stately grace and ethereal beauty of Elrond's generous Elven kingdom of Rivendell.

Whereas Bilbo's chance discovery of the Ring is but a subplot in *The Hobbit*, the destruction of that same golden object becomes central to *The Lord of the Rings*. Running parallel with Frodo's mission is the dwarves' pursuit of their lost treasure.

Tolkien, who was an internationally acknowledged authority on Old and Middle English literature, evoked the atmosphere of works as diverse as the Anglo Saxon epic *Beowulf* and the medieval romance *Sir Gawain and the Green Knight* when shaping the mood of his story. Also key to Tolkien's achievement was his experience of the Great War; he had spent three months on the Somme in 1916, seeing friends die in action.

The story alone is compelling, the old fashioned prose formal and descriptive, but the vividly drawn characters render it unforgettable. The hobbits – Frodo, the unlikely ring-bearer; his faithful gardener Samwise Gamgee, who gradually emerges as the unsung hero of the book; Merry and Pippin – are joined in the Fellowship forged at the Council of Elrond by Gandalf the wizard who brings his very English irony and logic to the tale; Legolas the elf archer; Gimli the dwarf; Boromir a man of Gondor, and Aragorn, the heir to Isildur, who had first entered the story as Strider, a Ranger of the North back at the Inn of the Prancing Pony.

Most memorably of all is the grotesque, ambivalent creature Gollum, a crazed, fallen hobbit who lured by the Ring, which he once owned and still calls "my precious", stalks Frodo and Sam, pursuing Frodo and his deadly burden to the very Crack of Doom. It is Gollum, more Caliban than Lucifer, who has a central role in the outcome. "But for him, Sam", admits Frodo, "I could never have destroyed the Ring. The Quest would have been in vain, even at the bitter end." Man is ultimately presented as the most vulnerable player in the action. Aragorn's romance with Arwen, daughter of Elrond, the Elf Lord, symbolises the tension between mortality and immortality. It is easy to see it as a battle between good and evil but Frodo the ring-bearer is not a Christ figure, as has been suggested by some commentators. *The Lord of the Rings* is an adventure, not an allegory.

Rich in symbolism and allusion, Tolkien insisted his tale was a test of storytelling. It's more than that; it is a literary masterwork, once experienced impossible to forget and is invariably re-read, sustaining generations of Middle-earth geeks, myself included.

J. R. R. Tolkien *(1892-1973)*

Jokes were made about Humphrey Carpenter's difficulties when writing his biography of J. R. R. Tolkien, which was published in 1977. No politics, no scandals, no strange habits; was Tolkien's life really so uneventful that the day the professor cycled off to buy sausages only to leave them on the butcher's counter merited inclusion? Tolkien lived in his imagination but he had also experienced life at its most intense, on the battlefield during the Great War.

Long before that though, while still a child, he had been tested. John Ronald Reuel Tolkien was born on 3 January 1892 in Bloemfontein, South Africa, to English parents. The family returned to England when Tolkien was three years old; his father died the following year. His mother's death when he was twelve left him an orphan. He was sent to live with relatives in and around Birmingham. Despite his foreign birth and his German-sounding name, Tolkien considered himself deeply rooted in the English midlands, which would influence his creation of the Shire homeland beloved of his hobbit heroes.

At sixteen he met his future wife, who was three years his senior. His guardians were strict and forbade him to see, or even write to her, until he was twenty-one. Tolkien's quiet determination was already apparent. Deferring to his guardians he applied himself to his studies. On his twenty-first birthday he wrote to her, proposing marriage. They married while he was at Oxford. In 1915, he took up a commission with the Lancashire Fusiliers and was sent to the Front.

During his three months on the Somme, from July to October 1916, he saw two of his closest friends, and many others, die. He was later invalided out, suffering from trench fever. It is not fanciful to describe Tolkien, so often presented as a cosily eccentric fantasy writer, as a member of the Great War's literary generation, many of whom perished. His fiction could as convincingly be interpreted as a response to experiencing war as is that of Kurt Vonnegut (1922-2007). As a veteran of the Somme Tolkien had witnessed horrors, horrors that may well have inspired the many battle scenes in *The Lord of the Rings*, particularly in the second volume, *The Two Towers*. He never forgot the war. He knew all he needed to know about violence and evil.

On Tolkien's return to civilian life he worked briefly for the *Oxford English Dictionary* before receiving a readership, and later, a chair at Leeds University. Then, in 1925, he was appointed to the chair of Anglo-Saxon at Oxford. He was thirty-three years old and would remain there until retiring as Merton Professor of English Language and Literature in 1959, a position he accepted in 1945. His life would become shared between scholarship and imaginary worlds from the time he returned to Oxford as a professor – and he enjoyed both.

Tolkien was a Christian and a Catholic, the religion to which his mother had converted but is often inaccurately described as a religious writer. He is more of a moral storyteller. His faith is not overtly reflected in his work, unlike that of his friend C. S. Lewis, author of the Narnia chronicles.

While inventing Middle-earth, Tolkien, a talented artist and illustrator, was also engaged in academic work such as co-editing, with E. V. Gordon, an edition of the medieval romance, *Sir Gawain and the Green Knight* (1925). Tolkien's 1936 British Academy lecture on *Beowulf* remains the defining essay on the great eighth-century Anglo-Saxon poem. Within a year of delivering that lecture Tolkien had published *The Hobbit*, which he had written for his children. It has a wonderful lightness of touch and in Bilbo Baggins, a reluctant hero. Less than twenty years later, his children grown, he would complete *The Lord of the Rings*, a continuous panoramic narrative. In common with *The Hobbit*, it also features a reluctant, if courageous hero, Frodo.

Undoubtedly his life as a career academic may appear staid to most onlookers, yet Tolkien's imagination must have raced at twice the speed of light when creating his complex and heroic tales.

18 | A Handful of Dust
(1934)
by Evelyn Waugh

Life at Hetton Abbey is sufficiently content for most of the London set to envy the Lasts; Tony Last is devoted to the family seat, a large country estate which is very grand – if frightfully expensive to run. He is considered "madly feudal" by his wife, Brenda, a lovely and obviously shallow socialite. The couple sweet-talk each other, while their only child, little John Andrew, is taught to horse ride – and swear – by the colourful Ben, a former farm worker.

Brenda, married seven years, is bored and pokes fun at Tony's pomposity and dogged belief in the old social order. The arrival of an unexpected weekend guest changes their lives. The guest is John Beaver, hopeless, irredeemably idle son of a mother who runs a frenetic décor business. Mrs Beaver is the universal provider of everything from cushion covers to entire flats. She indulges her boy, while he takes whatever he can get through random invitations secured through his usefulness as a single man available for escort duties on the dinner-party circuit. Beaver's arrival at Hetton causes Tony to leave Brenda to play hostess. She is heroic. Not only does she entertain the boring, self-absorbed and, as she says herself "pathetic" Beaver, she decides to fall in love with him.

On the publication of his first novel, *Decline and Fall* in 1928, Waugh had emerged as a gifted comic writer with a flair for brilliant caricature and crisp, class-nuanced dialogue, capable of replicating the pace and witty crackle of Wilde's comedies. Society and human behaviour intrigued Waugh and with *A Handful of Dust*, possibly his finest book, second only to the 'Sword of Honour' trilogy, he revealed a forensically astute moral sense.

Brenda's infatuation with Beaver feeds the gossips, yet Waugh is more than playing for laughs, and shrewdly conveys the lowliness of Brenda's deceit which quickly extends to requiring a London flat. Soon she announces to Tony that she *really* should enrol in an economics course, in order to help him run Hetton. All the while, Brenda remains well aware that Beaver has no interest in her.

At the time of Beaver's visit to Hetton, Brenda remarks: "Beaver isn't so bad. He's quite like us in some ways." To which Tony immediately retorts: "He's not like me." In this he is correct. Beaver is not like him; Tony is an old-school product of the upper classes. Waugh is not unsympathetic to Tony Last and chronicles his increasing bewilderment as Brenda distances herself from their marriage, refusing even to speak to him when he travels to London to visit her at her new flat.

The loss of their son, John Andrew, in a hunting accident, is the climax of the book. On being told of John's death, Brenda at first thinks that her lover has been killed, and appears relieved on realising her son is the victim. It is a chilling moment and clear evidence of Waugh's darker genius. For all the comedy, particularly when Tony sets out in the company of a woman and her child to provide evidence of infidelity to a pair of detectives working for divorce lawyers, the tone blackens. More is to follow as this social satire develops into the darkest of morality plays and Tony asserts himself, rejecting Brenda's selfish divorce demands.

Aware that "A whole Gothic world had come to grief . . . there was now no armour glittering through the forest glades, no embroidered feet on the green sward: the cream and dappled unicorns had fled" he travels to Brazil and joins an expedition. Delirious and experiencing bizarre hallucinations, he is rescued by Mr Todd, an insane recluse who insists Tony read the works of Dickens aloud to him, apparently forever. In exposing the cynical hypocrisy of the post-first World War generation, Waugh may well be suggesting that re-reading Dickens in the Brazilian jungle throughout eternity is not the worst of fates.

Evelyn Waugh *(1903-1966)*

A monster or a maligned romantic? Very funny or merely vicious? Opinions vary about the most stylish of twentieth century English satirists, Evelyn Waugh. His wit was as sharp as his life was unhappy. To consider his novels lightweight entertainments about bright young society things spiralling out of control is to miss a great deal about this hurt, angry individual. Waugh could be cranky, often vindictive but was possessed of a well-defined notion of right and wrong; his fiction is moral and strangely honest. Tony Last may be a bore and snob, but his instincts are good. There is also an element of Waugh in Last the betrayed husband. Waugh liked to think of himself as a lover but social class, education and intelligence can only get one so far in life – as Waugh was to discover to his cost.

He was born into the literary set; his father was a publisher and a literary critic. Books and writers were part of Waugh's experience from the very beginning. Unfortunately, so was his elder brother, Alec, the family favourite. Evelyn Waugh spent his childhood in his brother's shadow. On leaving public school, Waugh opted for Hertford, a less fashionable Oxford college in order to take up a modest scholarship. He read modern history. Much as he would have loved to convey a careful debonair ease, Waugh worked hard at life. He was a craftsman, an artist who decided to study cabinet-making because he believed in honouring the way things are made.

His disastrous first marriage to Evelyn Gardner, whom he could well have invented himself, so similar was she to some of his characters, damaged him for life. Waugh's ego was brittle, his self-loathing central to his personality. Although he did not shine at Oxford, he had by the age of twenty-four published his first book, a study of the poet Dante Gabriel Rossetti. He also wrote a life of the Elizabethan Jesuit martyr, Edmund Campion. Waugh's autobiographical first novel, *Decline and Fall* (1928), was based on his undistinguished teaching career. It immediately won an audience and it is hilarious. Yet even at that early stage Waugh's melancholic side was evident, as was something of his romantic feeling for Oxford, an affection which would surface dramatically in *Brideshead Revisited* (1945).

Before that, though, the younger Waugh was enjoying popularity. *Vile Bodies* (1930) kept the readers laughing and the reviewers impressed. The pattern continued with *Black Mischief* (1932), in which two very different former Oxford students set out to reform the African kingdom, one of them, Seth, has inherited. It is very funny, as is his Fleet Street satire, *Scoop* (1938). Yet, Waugh had already achieved a major breakthrough with *A Handful of Dust* (1934). It is about many things including society in free fall, but at the centre of the novel is an abuse of trust. In Brenda Last, bored wife and uncaring mother, he may have been settling scores, but by far the most interesting theme is the death of the old values in which Tony Last believes.

The popular image of Waugh is as the self-invented country squire and father of six living in the West Country. He had settled into a second, less traumatic marriage to a cousin of his first wife. His military service through which he travelled extensively in Europe, Africa and Asia tends to be forgotten. There is a real sense of army life in several of his novels, and it is life as lived on the military base; the routine and the boredom, not the heroics. This mood would grow darker in *Officers and Gentlemen* (1955), the second part of his superb trilogy, 'The Sword of Honour', which follows Guy Crouchback from larks in the army as described in the opening volume, *Men at Arms* (1952), to an injury and a compromise marriage, and the concluding volume, *Unconditional Surrender* (1961).

On the publication of *Brideshead Revisited*, attention was deflected away from the nostalgia and the lyric prose of a softer, more reflective Waugh, by the speculation as to how closely the novel drew on his association with the Lygon family on which the Marchmain clan was based. In Charles Ryder, the narrator, Waugh was dealing with among other things, an intense relationship between a middle-class history student and the despairing, alcoholic son of a marquis. Ryder's fascination with Lord Sebastian Flyte, his home and ultimately Flyte's sister Julia, is played out against a backdrop of class and religious doubt. Ryder, the artist with an interest in architecture and beautiful things, takes to life in the great house at a cost. He is the Waugh figure, albeit glamorised.

His melancholy was balanced by humour, which is invariably sharp, at times didactic. *The Loved One* (1948) is an inspired satire about the funeral business California-style. It is an unusual subject for Waugh, luxury undertakers at work in the US. Yet at Whispering Glades Memorial Park, conveniently near Hollywood's movie studios, death is approached as if it were the ultimate screen test. Mr Joyboy the mortician regards himself as an artist. This sharp, tightly-written comedy about contrasting cultural attitudes, European versus American, is as wry as it is grotesque, very funny and, as always with Waugh, its apparent flippancy is buttressed by sombre reality.

His humour assumed a strangely personal tone in *The Ordeal of Gilbert Pinford* (1957), in which a fat, Catholic, heavy-drinking and unhappy famous novelist, not unlike Waugh, sets off on a cruise. Too obviously based on its author, who had famously converted to Catholicism in 1930, it leaves one feeling that Waugh was profoundly tragic, and knew it.

Few writers shape a sentence as elegantly as he did. He saw social class as a life-defining reality. Despite the revival it occasioned there is far more to Evelyn Waugh than a superb television dramatisation.

19 | So Long, See You Tomorrow (1980)
by William Maxwell

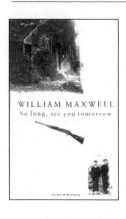

WILLIAM MAXWELL
So long, see you tomorrow

An elderly man describes a series of family tragedies that dominated his childhood and shaped his life. Yet of even greater importance than these personal losses, including the death of his mother, is the painful recollection of a chance encounter in a high school corridor with a boy who had once been his friend.

Winner of the US National Book Award in 1980, this calm, reflective and extraordinarily skilful short novel displays American fiction at its finest. It inspired Alice Munro and, in particular, Richard Ford, who said of it: "what a model to take on! Easier to bottle the wind" and describes his novel, *Wildlife* (1990), as a response to it. Maxwell, a Midwesterner, together with Southerner Peter Taylor, represents the writers who predate Ford, sharing a quiet, sensitive tone and graceful prose. *So Long, See You Tomorrow*, possessing the subtle insistence *Le Grand Meaulnes* (1913), another story about boyhood, is a wise, beautiful, at times brutal, meditation on the past. Once read, it is never forgotten.

The theme of Maxwell's story is loneliness, and it was mutual loneliness which once brought together the bookish young narrator, obviously Maxwell, and another boy in small-town Illinois, to play in a half-built house due to become the narrator's new home. The novel is also concerned with various levels of upheaval. The narrator's real life began with the sudden death of his mother when he was ten years old; her absence forces him into accepting change. Far more vividly described than her death is the gruesome murder of a tenant farmer. It is this event which has remained in the narrator's memory for more than fifty years. He would not have kept the murder of this man he never met, alive for so long if "(1) the murderer had not been the father of somebody I knew, and (2) I hadn't later on done something I was ashamed of afterward. This memoir – if that's the right name for it – is a roundabout futile way of making amends."

The narrator regrets that people spoke of his mother in generalities: ". . . her wonderful qualities, her gift for making those around her happy, and so on – that didn't tell me anything I didn't know before. It was as if they couldn't see her clearly for what had happened to her. And to us." He remembers his father's attempt to capture a lasting image of his dead wife by having a photographer retouch a picture which had been taken of her as a girl, to simulate an image of her face at thirty-eight, her age when she died. The project failed, "The result" recalls the narrator, "was something I was quite sure my mother had never looked like – vague and idealised and as if she might not even remember who we were . . . The retouched photograph came between me and the face I remembered, and it got harder and harder to recall my mother as she really was."

The narrative voice sustains this precise intensity and heartbreaking longing. It is as if Maxwell is endeavouring to recreate a lost world by reliving past experience. Much of the novel's gentle power rests in the narrator's efforts to understand a life, and lives, which have long since disappeared. Although the narrator's tone is deliberate, the story is neither detached nor remote.

He describes being invited to stay at the home of a woman who had been friendly with his mother. His hostess also had a son. "Without any experience to go on, I tried to be a good guest. Most of the time he [the boy] was friendly, and then suddenly he would mutter something under his breath that I could not quite hear and that I knew from a heaviness in my heart was the word 'sissy' . . . he was exactly the kind of boy I would have liked to be."

At the heart of the story, beyond the death of the narrator's mother, is the vicious killing in the barn. The unlikely murderer is a husband whose unhappy wife has fallen in love with his closest friend; the killer is also the father of Cletus, the young boy the lonely narrator had played with on the building site. It is at this point, when the narrator begins to focus on the disruptive build-up to the crime and the aftermath of the killing, that Maxwell's astonishing technical skill asserts itself.

Even while reflecting on his boyhood and gradual acceptance of his father's kindly new young wife and the goodwill which existed between them – "there was enough self-control in the household for six families" – he constantly alludes to the crime, and then begins to concentrate fully on it and its impact on several people, including a bewildered farm dog. In his meticulous piecing together of a sequence of events long past, the narrator constructs various flashbacks, including imagined scenes from the respective marriages of the tenant farmers. It all fits together like a Greek tragedy, leading to the moment of moral cowardice which has haunted the narrator all his life: "I saw Cletus Smith coming toward me. It was as if he had risen from the dead. He didn't speak. I didn't speak. We just kept on walking until we had passed."

William Maxwell *(1908-2000)*

In the summer of 2000, the American writer Richard Ford greeted me in the lobby of a Kilkenny hotel with an expression of kindly sorrow and the following words delivered in his softly menacing Mississippi drawl: "Well, there's poor Bill Maxwell gone and died, just a week after his wife." "Bill" was William Maxwell, the revered fiction editor of *The New Yorker* magazine and an author of subtle genius, as typified by his magnificent late short novel, *So Long, See You Tomorrow*.

Maxwell, who had been born in 1908, died just short of his ninety-second birthday and for anyone who read his work, or benefited from his editorial genius, he was already an immortal. Ford's announcement carried that familiar hint of wonder, when the living have only just discovered that someone they knew well has joined the newly dead. Here was one great American writer lamenting the loss of another. And Maxwell, from Lincoln, Illinois, was great – his reputation resting on a small body of autobiographical fiction that includes, *They Came Like Swallows* (1937), *The Folded Leaf* (1945), *Time Will Darken It* (1948), *The Chateau* (1961) and *So Long, See You Tomorrow* (1980), as well as many short stories, such as 'Over by the River', 'The Thistles in Sweden', the Billie Dyer stories, and 'The Front and the Back Parts of the House' – collected in *All The Days and Nights* (1997).

Decades of working with writers such as John Cheever, John Updike, Frank O'Connor, Eudora Welty, Maeve Brennan and J. D. Salinger, helping them, and writing himself, left him fulfilled, not weary. Maxwell, though tested as a child by his adored mother's early death, the depression which led to his suicide attempt as a young man, and his loneliness before, in his mid-thirties meeting Emily Noyes, to whom he would be married to for fifty-five years. For him, the smallest moments created history. His fiction was exclusively autobiographical; he saw human experience as the ultimate source and writing it all down was a way of ensuring that people he knew and loved lived on. "The novelist," he said in 1995, "works with what life has given him. It was no small gift that I was allowed to lead my boyhood in a small town in Illinois where the elm trees cast a mixture of light and shade over the pavements. And also that, at a fairly early age, I was made aware of the fragility of human happiness."

For all the understatement of his craft Maxwell's approach could be deceptively daring, such as his handling of the theme of a young male friendship in his third novel, *The Folded Leaf* – based on his experience of a love triangle culminating in a suicide attempt. The tone is gentle, considered and reflective yet the themes include murder, possible adultery and passion as well as loss. Although a Midwesterner, Maxwell's comedy possesses Southern flair. The gestation of *The Folded Leaf* was slow. It took about seven years, partly because of the increasing demands of Maxwell's editorial role at *The New Yorker*. During this period, 1938-1945, the war years, he was far from happy. Ill health had prevented him going to war, but his despair went deeper; he battled incapacitating self-doubt.

The tragedy of the sudden death of Blossom Maxwell, his mother, during the influenza epidemic of 1918, when the future writer was ten, never left him, or his fiction. The theme of a mother's death is a constant in his work. His openness encouraged candour in others; Maxwell, an inveterate letter writer, understood the art of friendship. This is well illustrated in *The Happiness of Getting It Down Right* (1996), the correspondence between Frank O'Connor and William Maxwell, edited by Michael Steinman. For John Updike, "he had a gift for affection, and another – or was it the same gift? – for paying attention."

Reading Woolf's *To the Lighthouse* (1927) as a student proved hugely significant for Maxwell, who immediately identified with its emotional resonance; he could relate to Woolf's sense of loss. He recognised Mrs Ramsay, the mother figure, as the abiding presence of that novel and understood what Woolf was doing. In an interview with George Plimpton, Maxwell said, "How close Mrs Ramsay is to my own idea of mother . . . both of them gone, both leaving the family unable to navigate very well. It couldn't have failed to have a profound effect on me."

Emotion defines his vision, as does a prevailing sense of justice. At the heart of *So Long, See You Tomorrow* is the older Maxwell's regret at his boyhood self's failure to speak to his friend after the boy's father had committed a crime of passion. That guilt – not the narrator's grief for his dead mother – dominates the story. For all its stylistic grace and elegance there is an edge to Maxwell's work as well as a sense of social history and racial awareness. The quiet Maxwell shaped great writers because he was one.

20 | Thérèse Raquin
(1867)
by Émile Zola

Madame Raquin had devoted her life to keeping her sickly son, Camille, alive. From birth it was a struggle; just when it seemed he would surely die, she always saved him. "For fifteen years Madame Raquin had waged war against this succession of terrible ills trying to snatch her boy from her. And she beat them all by patience, loving care and adoration." Not only did she tend her boy from infancy to manhood and beyond, Madame Raquin also raised her soldier brother's child, a strange little girl, Thérèse, who was entrusted to her by him when the child's mother, a beautiful Algerian exotic, died.

In this, his first major novel, the young Zola, created an intense family unit. Madame Raquin treated Thérèse as if she were as sickly as Camille. When her husband died, Madame Raquin gave up her haberdashery business, and moved to a pleasant house on the river. Camille grows up and threatens to move to Paris. In order to keep her boy, the devoted mother acquires a premises with accommodation in a grim little corridor of shops in Paris.

Written in snatches when he was in his mid-twenties, this is the work, condemned by some critics as pornographic, which introduced Zola as a daring pioneer of French Naturalism.

In contrast with the indulged Camille, Thérèse is "coldly apathetic". Having shared a bed with her cousin Camille since childhood, she had, in accordance with Madame Raquin's plans, become his wife. Their marriage is farcical; Camille has no sexual interest in Thérèse, while she merely exists, expressionless.

Thérèse, who had enjoyed living quietly in the house by the river, is shocked by the dirty Paris laneway. She helps run the shop.

Madame Raquin begins holding evening gatherings. One of Camille's workmates, Laurent, who had been at school with him, joins the Raquin social circle. He is the son of a farmer who disinherited him because he had no interest in the land. So Laurent, having already tried his mediocre hand at painting and having experienced the easy sexuality of studio life, is now working in an office. Zola claws down deeply to the very souls of his characters; Laurent is charming, lazy, selfish and confident he can seduce his friend's sullen wife. But does he want to? His first sexual advance is welcomed with raw hunger. Thérèse immediately discovers she is her mother's daughter.

The couple's obsessive passion takes over. Laurent's employers notice the amount of time he spends out of the office. The threat to their daily encounters in her bed above the shop inspires desperation in Laurent and Thérèse. Camille must die. The murder is staged as a boating accident. Zola conducts the narrative as if it were an opera. The couple feign heartbreak at Camille's death, the social circle, keen on sustaining the weekly gatherings, sympathise, while the mother laments. Laurent frequents the city morgue until he sees Camille's decaying body on a slab.

Time passes. Their passion is dead. It is pointless now for Laurent and Thérèse to marry. But they do. They can no longer endure each other. Camille's ghostly presence prevails. Neither can sleep. Eventually the heartbroken old mother, crushed by grief and a stroke, becomes the silent witness to their guilt, accusations and mutual destruction. Henry James would explore a similar, if far less hysterical, situation in his chilling novel, *The Wings of the Dove* (1902). The triumph of Zola's devastating portrait of sexual passion, which became a bestseller on publication, is the transformation of Laurent's character. This once-indolent loafer absorbs and replicates not only the intensity of Thérèse, but also her passionate frenzy and remorse.

Zola's powerful debut confirmed his relentless realism. Within a decade, he would publish his finest work, *L'Assommoir*, and consolidate his place as the supreme chronicler of nineteenth-century Parisian street life.

Émile Zola (1840-1902)

Nowhere do the squalor, passion and bustling crowds of mid-nineteenth century France come as relentlessly to life as in the fiction of arch-polemicist Émile Zola. For all the extreme behaviour of his characters and the unabashed melodrama of the situations which develop, the reader is left with a vivid, almost panoramic sense of French social history.

In common with Victor Hugo (1802-1885), if even more forensically, Zola was a chronicler of Paris. But there was a difference; Hugo was a central figure of French literary Romanticism, Zola, who died at sixty-two, set out to be a realist, devoted to Naturalism and advocated what he saw as a scientific approach. He regarded family, and inherited traits such as excessive behaviour, drinking and madness, as well as one's immediate environment, as the prevailing influences in determining character. These are the themes that dominate his powerfully earthy narratives which mark the birth of the modern French novel. Between 1894 and 1898 the Vatican added all of his books to the Index Librorum Prohibitorum, the list of banned books.

Zola had been born in Paris but the family moved south, to Aix-en-Provence, where a childhood friend was the future painter, Cézanne. The sudden death of Zola's father, an Italian engineer, when Zola was seven years old, introduced the family to desperate poverty. Having been educated locally, he was then sent to the Lycee Saint-Louis in Paris where he failed his baccalauréat. Zola wanted to be a writer; nothing was going to stop him. His deliberate intent, self-belief and ability to ridicule his critics would sustain him throughout a whirlwind career that appeared to have exposed the lower middle classes and particularly the working and peasant classes, unmercifully. Far more meaningful, though, is Zola's wayward yet persuasive celebration of humanity.

The young Zola who wrote *Thérèse Raquin* as a daring thriller was also busily at work on a sprawling pot-boiler serial *Les Mystères de Marseille* while he made a living from book reviewing and art criticism. *Madame Bovary* (1857), which had brought Flaubert to court on charges of offending public morality, had been published ten years earlier. *Thérèse Raquin* introduced Zola as a serious talent and, in turn, also caused moral outrage. Then twenty-seven, Zola, was accused of writing pornography. Such accusations, however, did not deter the public from reading it. Zola caused readers to look at life as lived by the poor, and to acknowledge the realities of alcoholism, sexual disease and prostitution.

Zola had a plan; his 'Rougon-Macquart' series. Over the course of twenty novels, he followed the grim lives of individual members of a large family enduring the social conditions of the Second Empire. It was not quite on the scale of Balzac's defining 'Comédie humaine' series which comprises ninety-one interconnected novels and stories, published between 1827 and 1847. More than two thousand characters are involved, many of them appearing in several of the works. Zola avoided the supernatural and comic elements favoured by Balzac but his novels were also closely linked and cross-referenced.

He was a tireless researcher and this approach gives his fiction a visual and visceral quality. The reader can almost smell the world he evokes, the dark alleys and damp houses. *L'Assommoir* (1877), the seventh in the series, is the story of the doomed Gervaise and her desperate passage from villain to villain, only to find – too late – true love with Goujet the gentle blacksmith. Most of the action takes place within a small district between the Gare du Nord and Montmartre. Zola then follows the exploitative career of Gervaise's daughter in *Nana* (1880). He places his likeable anti-heroine, a courtesan, who is at once consuming of, and consumed by, the society she inhabits, initially in the world of theatre and then, directly as a prostitute. It is a shocking book. The entire first edition of 55,000 copies sold out on publication day – remarkable sales figures for the time.

Germinal (1885), the thirteenth novel in the series, takes the saga out of Paris and into a mining community in northern France. Again, Zola had done his research well; and the political right feared the description of a strike would incite revolution. Just as he had brought to life the hardship of mines, he would turn to the peasant world of a village in his sombre epic, *La Terre* (*The Earth*) (1887), his favourite novel, in which an aged father sets out, Lear-like, to divide his farm among his children. The land itself emerges as a central character.

Zola's outspoken realism resulted in the imprisonment of his English publisher. Yet it was his famous J'accusé defence of the wronged officer, Alfred Dreyfus, not his fiction, that earned Zola imprisonment for libel – a sentence he avoided by spending almost a year in England. Zola saw the reader as a witness to important, often sordid reality. His work brought urban realism to the centre stage of French fiction as life confronted art, often with shocking candour. Dispensing with pathos and romance in favour of dangerous, often violent passion, he saw himself as a truth teller, dealing in the harshest of truths.

21

We
(1921)
by Yevgeny Zamyatin

D-503 is a mathematician engaged in an important project, the construction of the Integral. He has regulated sexual encounters with O-90. Bedtime is 22.30. His life is organised, as are his thoughts and the diligent entries he writes in his journal.

He wonders about the past: "I have had occasion to read and hear many incredible things concerning those times when people were still living in a free – i.e. an unorganised, savage – state. But the one thing that has always struck me as the most improbable was precisely this: How could the governing power (let us say even a rudimentary one) allow the people to live without anything resembling our tables of Hourly Commandments, without obligatory walks, without exact regulation of mealtimes – how could it allow them to get up and go to bed whenever they got the notion to do so? Certain historians even assert that, apparently, in those times the streets were lit all through the night – that, all through the night, people walked and drove through the streets?" D-503 is aware that he is recording his thoughts for his ancestors, not his descendants. Through this oblique use of an alternative time frame Zamyatin is confirming that D-503's present is our future.

This terrifyingly perceptive portrait of an anti-Utopian future is pitch-perfect satire, written with cryptic elegance. D-503 may be a number wearing a uniform but he is not a machine and his observations suggest flickering traces of imagination, which at times hint at a lyric sensibility.

It is spring. D-503 notices the beautiful blue sky "unmarred by a single cloud" and then adds, "how extremely primitive in matters of taste were the ancients, since their poets could find inspiration in those absurd, sloppily shaped, foolishly jostling masses of vapour." Although a programmed number he is capable of using a word such as love: "I love – I am sure I do not err if I say that we all love – only such a sky as the present one, sterile, irreproachable. On days such as this the whole universe is moulded out of the same immovable, eternal glass as our Green wall, as are all our structures. On days such as this, one sees the blue depths of things, one sees certain of their questions, amazing and unknown until that moment – one sees them in something that may be ever so ordinary, ever so prosaic."

Into D-503's ordered existence comes E-330, a disturbing female subversive with sharp white teeth and dangerous individuality. She wants to have sex with D-503 and applies to the authorities for permission. She also sets about opening his mind. Her influence is disturbing, her tactics lethally effective, she addresses him as "Thou." D-503 is confronted by a novel sensation – passion. This new experience inflicts immense pain on his established sexual partner O-90 who, though mild and not particularly intelligent, is sufficiently territorial to advise E-330 that the narrator is registered to her. O-90 also wants a baby. She may be programmed but she is human – Zamyatin orchestrates deft touches, a little human weakness here, a slight flash of anger there, in suggesting the tension between the authorised and the instinctive; the dehumanised and the imaginative.

His vision is as angry as that of Swift's Gulliver and as subtle as a chess match being played in secret; his thesis is the dehumanisation inflicted by totalitarianism. D-503 is faced with having an operation for the removal of his imagination. He is tested, given the chance of something different, but his courage fails. Influenced by all things English and an admirer of H. G. Wells, whom he translated, Zamyatin, a marine engineer, was drawn to fiction as if by duty, a divine vocation. It is interesting if not surprising that when reading this most original of narratives the writer who most immediately stands before us is the great J. G. Ballard.

We is both inspired science fiction and barbed allegory. It remains a sophisticated and timeless work; edgy, angular and disturbingly beautiful. Although widely read in the West, this astonishingly original book was not published in Russia until 1988. George Orwell, who first read it in French, acknowledged Zamyatin's influence on his anti-Utopian fantasy, *Nineteen Eighty-Four* (1949), while Aldous Huxley, whose burlesque and inferior *Brave New World* (1932) falters into parody in comparison, denied ever having read *We* – his loss.

Yevgeny Zamyatin *(1884-1937)*

Yevgeny Zamyatin was a force with which to be reckoned. Outspoken in his opinions and unafraid to make them known, he was unusually candid in dangerous times. By profession a marine engineer, he was a writer slightly at a remove from his peers. Although political he did not eulogise revolution; he was deliberate, practical and to the point.

He had spent some months in solitary confinement in 1905 for his political views. "Real literature can be created only by madmen, hermits, heretics, dreamers, rebels and sceptics not by diligent and trustworthy functionaries," he once declared. It is a challenging quote for anyone to make at any time, not just in a Russia torn between tsardom in its death throes and violent revolution. Encountering that quote somewhere when I was at school put me on the trail of Zamyatin, a trail that led to *We* (1921), a laconic anti-Utopian fantasy, written with savage elegance modified by a lingering trace of nostalgia.

He was born in 1884 in Lebedyan, Tambov Province, the very heart of rural Russia's fertile black earth. Communism appealed to him and although he was then very young, he was twice arrested and exiled under the Tsar. Years later, he would also fall foul of the Soviets. In 1922 he was again arrested and spent more time in the same cell he had occupied in 1905. His life was like that and ultimately he died in exile in Paris. But in between, for all his innovative and experimental similarities with Nikolai Gogol, his fellow Symbolist Andrei Bely and to some extent Mikhail Bulgakov,

Zamyatin's experiences were completely unlike any other major Russian writer.

For almost two years, between 1916 and 1917, he was based in an English shipyard in Newcastle-on-Tyne where he supervised the construction of ice-breakers which had been ordered by the tsarist government. Even before he arrived in England he had been interested in English literature. He spoke fluent English and identified a literary kindred spirit in H. G. Wells, whose work Zamyatin translated into Russian.

Favouring English tweed he was teased about his "Englishness." He was also interested in American writing, enjoyed Shaw and had also translated the works of an earlier Irish playwright, Richard Brinsley Sheridan. When he now looked to Russia as the October Revolution was poised to write its own chapter of history, Zamyatin realised there would be no more shipbuilding in Russia, at least until relative peace resumed and none for him ever again.

He now looked to literature with a renewed intensity. He was, by then, a published writer; he had a short novel published in 1908 while his first significant work, *A Provincial Tale*, appeared in 1913, and was followed within a year by a novella, *At the World's End*, in which a group of army officers enjoys life in a remote garrison town. Its satire was not appreciated and all copies of the magazine which had published it were confiscated. Zamyatin was charged with maligning officers but was eventually acquitted.

All of this may have been in his mind prior to the publication of his well-received novel *The Islanders* (1918), which was based on his experiences in Newcastle-on-Tyne.

Somewhat more explosive was the attention he attracted for his role in the House of the Arts where he conducted creative writing classes. It was during this time that he wrote *We*. While Zamyatin, an incurable Anglophile, acknowledged the influence English writers had had on him, he would certainly influence them. To read *We* calls to mind Orwell and even more obviously Ballard, although he was never to adopt futuristic devices.

By 1924, *We* had been translated into English and was being read throughout the world, but not in Russia. Zamyatin's life in Russia became more difficult due to the controversial impact of a Czech edition. Just as he had been caught by the old order, he was endangered by the new. Increasingly ostracised as a writer, the one-time Bolshevik wrote a dignified plea to Stalin, requesting permission to leave Russia. But it did not secure his right to leave. A fellow writer, Maxim Gorky, who was at that time lionised, although this would change, pleaded on his behalf. In 1932 an already ailing Zamyatin was allowed to take flight.

Highly sophisticated and years ahead of his time as a writer and a thinker, he died in exile in Paris in 1937, still at work on a novel, *The Scourge of God*, which was published the following year. He believed that the most destructive threat facing man is the death of the imagination. Fifty years after Zamayatin's death *We* was finally published in Russia; his novel remains as shocking, as bleak and as real as it was on publication.

22 | The Great Gatsby
(1925)
by F. Scott Fitzgerald

A poor boy falls in love with a rich girl. He heads off to war and she, impatient with waiting for someone to organise her idle life, marries a more forceful suitor. That heartbroken boy may be a dreamer, but he is also insanely tenacious and convinced that with hard work, deceit and material trappings he can regain his lost love.

Romantic fantasy and cynical realism shape the atmospheric masterpiece that is F. Scott Fitzgerald's defining achievement. Although the quest for the Great American Novel continues, many critics have long since decided that the search ended here.

Set amid the boredom and the lurid vulgarity of the Jazz Age, a traumatised, frenetic period of "miracles, art and excess" intent on forgetting all the old rules as well as the then recent Great War, *The Great Gatsby* chronicles the collapse of the American Dream. The more traditional values of the Midwest confront the assured sophistication of the knowing and merciless East. Fitzgerald achieved high art through the cool beauty of his elegant, graceful prose with its effortless, subtle lyricism and above all, the inspired use of a wry, reflective narrative voice in what could have been merely a tale of one man's extravagant ambitions.

Instead, *The Great Gatsby* is a modern tragedy balancing symbolism and reality. Its genius lies in the narrator's bewilderment, disgust and genuine regret. Nick Carraway not only tells the story, he lives through most of it, piecing together the rest. He is a shrewd, somewhat righteous, intelligent and often ironic Midwesterner, ever conscious of the lessons learned from his father, such as "a sense of the fundamental decencies is parcelled out unequally at birth".

Arriving in New York to try his hand at bond dealing, Carraway visits his distant cousin, Daisy, now married to Tom Buchanan, a brash former college football star. They live in restless Long Island splendour. As Nick remarks: "I had no sight into Daisy's heart, but I felt Tom would drift on forever seeking, a little wistfully, for the dramatic turbulence of some irrecoverable football game."

Daisy reclines on a sofa. With her is another, slightly younger woman, Jordan Baker, a lady golfer. Fitzgerald conveys their vapid ease, particularly the jaunty indolence of Baker, obviously an intimate of the Buchanan circle, and about whom there clings a half-remembered whiff of scandal; something about cheating at a tournament.

Within moments, Tom is called to the phone. Jordan informs Carraway that Buchanan has a mistress. The revelation seems to transform Daisy into a victim. Carraway is aware that the mysterious Jay Gatsby, who owns the mansion next door to his rented house, is completely overshadowed by the lavish parties he hosts. Many of the guests speculate about Gatsby's alleged involvement in crime. Carraway finally meets him and is struck by his smile. For all his misgivings he can't help liking the edgy, distracted, restless Gatsby who may or may not have gone to Oxford.

Gatsby is obsessed with winning back Daisy. Through Jordan, he asks Nick to invite Daisy to tea. The tense meeting between the former lovers is brilliantly handled by Fitzgerald, as Nick reports: "Gatsby, pale as death, with his hands plunged like weights in his coat pockets, was standing in a puddle of water glaring tragically into my eyes." There are sentences in this novel capable of stopping one's breath. Carraway, the moral filter, having witnessed Gatsby's night-long vigil outside Daisy's house, reports: "So I walked away and left him standing there in the moonlight – watching over nothing."

Despite his affair with Myrtle, the determinedly alive, eager wife of George Wilson, the defeated local garage owner, Tom is outraged on realising Gatsby's intentions towards Daisy. A wild excursion to a humid New York through the Valley of Ashes under the huge surreal, all-seeing eyes of Doctor T. J. Eckleburg, a billboard advertising optical services, ends in the Myrtle's death. She is killed attempting to flag down Tom's car – which is being driven by Daisy.

The Buchanans, content for Gatsby to take the blame, retreat as Carraway reports, "into their money or their vast carelessness, or whatever it was that kept them together . . ." After he is gunned down by Wilson, only one of the many guests who enjoyed Gatsby's hospitality attends his funeral. When his father, an obviously poor man, arrives, his pride in his son's self-invention and success appears to outweigh his grief. Carraway, having witnessed so much, and learned even more, mourns Gatsby and returns to the Midwest.

The more closely one examines this story concerned with surfaces, the more closely one grasps the depth of Fitzgerald's wasteland symbolism and the ironic use he makes of a billboard optician in a narrative in which so few of the characters see all that clearly.

F. Scott Fitzgerald (1896-1940)

Dominant among the transplanted misfit idealists of the Jazz Age was F. Scott Fitzgerald, a big dreamer, a big talker and a romantic with a gift for lyric pathos. Capable of understanding human nature, he had no insight into his own complex misery. He had been born into a wealthy Minnesota family in 1896 and privilege was something he absorbed as a divine right. He duly went on to Princeton with spoiled peers who were just like him and he did well at football. He left without a degree and joined the US army, although he did not serve in the Great War. He married a lovely Southern belle, Zelda Sayre. Off they went to Europe to set up court.

Fitzgerald became famous, though not rich, with his first novel, *The Side of Paradise*. Published in 1920, it is heavily autobiographical and proved that Fitzgerald had the talent to match his ambitions. He also had the immense good luck to secure the advice, support and friendship of the Scribner editor, Maxwell Perkins, who was then at the beginning of his career. There was never any doubt that Fitzgerald could write; his prose is graceful, rhythmic and beautifully served by his subtle imagery, his glittering intelligence and acute social observation. His second novel, *The Beautiful and the Damned* (1922), supported his growing reputation.

Meanwhile, Fitzgerald's drinking and wild antics were drawing attention to his life. He tended to exist somewhere between crazed optimism and helpless despair. Fitzgerald was no Gatsby; he was wayward, demanding, impatient, self-destructive and dependent on Perkins, who regarded him as a son.

So how did Fitzgerald create a work as near perfect as *The Great Gatsby*? In it, Gatsby the ruthless dreamer, perverted hero, liar and fantasist is juxtaposed against Carraway, a fellow Midwesterner, but a realist with his feet on the ground and well-developed moral values. Every suggestion Perkins made to Fitzgerald about the manuscript caused him to think and draw further artistry from within his mind, his soul and place it in the text. The result is a seminal blend of realist satire and symbolism, the definitive lament for the American Dream.

Published on 10 April 1925, it was considered a commercial failure. When Fitzgerald died fifteen years later, unsold copies remained stacked in his publisher's warehouse. Between 1941 and 1949 seventeen new editions and reprints appeared. *The Great Gatsby* was on course for acquiring as complex a textual history as *Ulysses*.

Fitzgerald was becoming, and remains, revered as a seer, not only of the Jazz Age and its aftermath, but of humanity. Yet before that he wrote *Tender is the Night* (1934), a hauntingly gorgeous if formless love story which draws heavily on Zelda's personal tragedy. It is his most autobiographical novel and took him nine years to write. But by then, Fitzgerald's star had crashed to earth; he was producing often hasty stories for small fees. In 1938, *This Side of Paradise* went out of print. Zelda, ever-sliding towards madness, was institutionalised, and would die in a fire eight years after his death.

Well aware that he was experiencing the rise and fall of his career, Fitzgerald struggled as a hack screenwriter in Hollywood. He had high hopes for a novel which would become *The Last Tycoon*. On 20 December 1940 he worked on chapter six, and that evening told journalist Sheilah Graham with whom he was then living: "I've been able to fix it. Baby, this book will be good. It might even make enough money for us both to leave Hollywood." The following day he was dead, killed by a heart attack. He was forty-four. Having written the definitive lament to the American Dream, he appears to have acted out his own American tragedy.

23 | Coming Up For Air
(1939)
by George Orwell

George Bowling, fat, forty-five and far from stupid, pauses to consider his existence in suburban London: "The idea really came to me the day I got my new false teeth." He wants a brief escape from his dreary wife Hilda and their two whining children, in the form of a private visit to Lower Binfield, the Oxfordshire village where he grew up. From the opening line, Orwell establishes in Bowling a likeable, Everyman narrator who tells his story with candour and a relaxed sense of humour.

Bowling sells insurance and has few illusions about anything, least of all himself: "I was trying to shave with a bluntish razor-blade while the water ran into the bath. My face looked back at me out of the mirror, and underneath, in a tumbler of water on the little shelf over the washbasin, the teeth that belonged in the face."

Coming Up for Air, Orwell's strangely buoyant fourth novel, was written in the shadow of the threat of war. Bowling is also aware of this; after all he had served in the Great War. He is conscious of the smallness of his life, his garden, the very rooms in his house. A chance win concealed from his wife encourages him to do something different.

The narrator is wry, far from depressed whatever about the grim reality of his marriage and dull job, and is sustained by nostalgia. He is also an optimist: "In almost all circumstances I'd manage to make a living – always a living and never a fortune – and even in war, revolution, plague and famine, I'd back myself to stay alive longer than most people."

Partial to asides, Bowling does his fair share of thinking. "The past is a curious thing. It's with you all the time, I suppose an hour never passes without your thinking of things that happened ten or twenty years ago, and yet most of the time it's got no reality, it's just a set of facts that you've learned, like a lot of stuff in a history book." Walking through London's Strand to fetch his new dentures he recalls his childhood self, the son of a struggling seed merchant and a mother who was always rolling pastry. He had an elder brother as well, a wild fellow who eventually ran off leaving a trail of misdeeds.

Bowling had been a clever lad, but left school early to support the household. There is no bitterness. Instead his memories recall days of fishing, particularly the magical ones spent at a pool "ringed completely round by the enormous beech trees, which in one place came down to the edge and were reflected in the water"; that pond, as he remembers it, was always swarming with bream and pike.

His conversational tone and good nature ensure that his anecdotal narrative draws the reader into the thoughts of a man who is almost philosophical. "Well, Hilda and I were married, and right from the start it was a flop. 'Why did you marry her?' You say . . . I wonder whether you'll believe that during the first two or three years I had serious thoughts of killing Hilda . . . One gets used to everything in time."

On returning to a village he barely recognises, Bowling becomes engagingly vulnerable. Noting that the vicar is about sixty-five, he realises that twenty years earlier when he considered Rev. Betterton old, "he'd have been forty-five – my own present age."

The new war is approaching as a rogue bomb makes clear. George Bowling, fat and forty-five, recognises the threat and also the impending demise of the England he once knew.

Coming Up for Air is one of those rich, definitively human novels which triumph because of a narrator so convincing you feel as if he has sat down specifically to tell you, and you alone, his story of his life.

George Orwell *(1903-1950)*

Eric Arthur Blair, a lower middle-class Etonian, wanted to be a writer and so became George Orwell. Repressed bully? Or saintly prophet? Or both? Who knows? Encased by contradictions, Orwell, widely regarded as an inspired polemicist, social commentator and essayist who also wrote novels, is probably the most underrated novelist of the major twentieth century British writers. His literary reputation is dominated by his political satires, the cleverly allegorical *Animal Farm* (1945) and his futuristic parable, *Nineteen Eighty-Four* (1949), yet he wrote other novels, each evoking the defeated atmosphere of 1930s Britain.

For all the passion of his Swiftian polemic and his sense of social justice equal to that of Dickens – about whom he wrote an extraordinary twenty-five-thousand-word essay – Orwell was much more than a commentator. Blessed with a natural, almost colloquial prose style, he *understood* the essential grief of the individual crushed by totalitarianism and the tyranny of government.

His humanity often surfaces in his non-fiction. "She looked up as the train passed", he writes in a famous passage from *The Road to Wigan Pier* (1937), "and I was almost near enough to catch her eye. She had a round pale face, the usual exhausted face of the slum girl who is 25 and looks 40 . . . She knew well enough what was happening to her – understood as well as I did how dreadful a destiny it was to be kneeling there in the bitter cold, on the slimy stones of a slum backyard, poking a stick up a foul drainpipe."

Nineteen Eighty-Four is a polemic defined by Orwell's concern for the individual; it is also a love story. When Winston Smith who has lost his personality and Julia have sex, it is not only escape, but a desperate attempt to reassert each other as human beings. Any discussion of Orwell invariably turns to it and the caustic allegory, *Animal Farm*, yet *Homage to Catalonia* (1937) is equally major. For many readers, Orwell's eye-witness testament remains the most influential account of the Spanish Civil War. His first novel, *Burmese Days* (1934), which chronicles the life of Flory, a frustrated police officer anti-hero, is a daring expose of British imperialism.

Born in India in 1903, the same year as Evelyn Waugh, a superior stylist with comic flair, Orwell's range is wider than Waugh's; his work achieves a weightier political and social content. *A Clergyman's Daughter* (1935) made an honourable stab at a Joycean narrative yet, admittedly, is far closer to the Victorian naturalist fiction of George Gissing (1857-1903). Central to appreciating Orwell the novelist is *Coming Up For Air,* published only days before his father's death in the summer of 1939. Its appeal rests in its central character, George Bowling's wonderfully wry first-person narrative alive with his memories, his observations, his nostalgia.

While Orwell had already explored this personalised territory in *Keep the Aspidistra Flying* (1936) featuring the ineffectual Gordon Comstock, *Coming Up For Air* took it to a higher artistic level. Comstock is not George Orwell; nor is Bowling. Winston Smith is the character most like Orwell, the son of a Victorian father who believed in empire and many of the things his son would oppose in his writings.

In 1922, Orwell, then still Eric Blair, joined the Indian Imperial Police and spent five years in Burma. On leave back in England he decided not to return and resigned. He was a hop picker in Kent and washed dishes in Paris – experiences which were to inspire *Down and Out in Paris and London* (1933). His health was never good, yet he volunteered to fight in Spain where he was shot in the throat. Rejected by the British Army in 1939, at the outbreak of war, he enlisted in the Home Guard. Near the end of the war he reported from Europe for the *Observer.*

Orwell claimed that the physical effort of writing *Nineteen Eighty-Four* was enough to kill him. It probably did. Six months after its publication in June 1949 – a couple of weeks before his forty-sixth birthday – Orwell died. It was January 1950, and he left Richard, his adored adopted son an orphan.

Scarcely a day passes without a reference to Orwell's cautionary vision about a futuristic dehumanisation that has become dangerously real.

24 | L'Étranger
(1942)
by Albert Camus

A young man's mother dies. On hearing the bad news, he wonders whether she had actually died the previous day. For Meursault, a clerk in an office, the death comes as more of an inconvenience than a personal loss. He is young and single, when he doesn't feel like cooking, which appears to be often, he dines at a local restaurant where he is greeted as a regular. Meursault enjoys the sun and the sea, and lives the life of an ordinary French-Algerian, a citizen of France adrift in the shimmering heat of Algiers, earning sufficient money to support an easy social routine dominated by the beach.

The laconic, self-absorbed anti-hero of Camus's taut first novel, *L'Étranger* (*The Outsider*), remains a symbol of youthful defiance. No one can tell him how to display his feelings. Nor will he feign emotion. His noncommittal attitude to his mother's passing shocks the staff at the nursing home where he had sent her three years earlier. As he travels there by bus to attend her funeral, he is more aware of the heat than grief. ". . . during the past year, I seldom went to see her", he recalls, "it would have meant losing my Sunday – not to mention . . . going to the bus, getting my ticket, and spending two hours on the journey, each way."

His indifference, although apparently casual, is disturbing. When asked by the mortuary porter if he wishes to see his mother's body, Meursault declines. He remains detached at the funeral service and admits to not knowing his mother's age. After the burial, during which he had been alert to the bright sunlight, his abiding sensation is of fatigue.

Back in Algiers he wakes to his Saturday morning and decides to go for a swim. At the beach he meets up with Marie, a girl who had previously worked at his office. After swimming and sunbathing together, he invites her to the cinema to see the comedy of the moment. She accepts and then notices his black mourning tie. When he explains about his mother's death, he recalls: "She made no remark, though I thought she shrank away a little."

Marie recovers sufficiently to go the movie and spend the night with him. He wakes alone and prepares some food. He then settles down to watching life pass beneath his window. By evening he is ready to eat again, realising that "Mother was now buried, and tomorrow I'd be going back to work as usual. Really, nothing in my life had changed."

Having established his central character's personality, Camus sustains Meursault's non-committal tone, even to the manner in which he shrugs off a promotion. When Marie asks him if he loves her, he recalls saying "that sort of question had no meaning, really; but I suppose I didn't. She looked sad for a bit . . ." He does not even get involved when a friend of his, Raymond, hits an Arab woman. The following weekend, Meursault and Marie join Raymond on a trip to another friend's beach house. The Arab woman's brother pursues Raymond and a skirmish takes place. The police step in.

There is a further episode, and Meursault, in possession of Raymond's gun, murders one of the Arabs, his only excuse being the relentless sun: ". . . all I had to do was to turn, walk away, and think no more about it. But the whole beach, pulsing with heat, was pressing on my back . . . Every nerve in my body was a steel spring, and my grip closed on the revolver."

His crime is serious. Yet during the trial that takes place it is Meursault's emotional indifference, not his killing of the Arab, which condemns him. He appears to forget that he is the criminal. People remember his attitude to his mother's death, his failure to linger at her grave, his smoking, the coffee he drank. Aware that he will be sentenced to death, all he can wonder at is his passive acceptance of his fate, and his apparent relief.

The bleak beauty of the prose conveys the bizarre apathy of an intense, pioneering existentialist narrative which continues to unsettle. Selfish and detached Meursault is terrifyingly real; he is a part of all of us.

Albert Camus (1913-1960)

At the time of his death in a motor accident the 1957 Nobel Literature Laureate, Albert Camus, then forty-seven, was working on a novel. The unfinished manuscript, consisting of 144 hand-written pages, was found in the wreckage in which Camus's publisher, Michel Gallimard, also died. The writer's family decided against publishing the work. *The First Man* was finally published in 1995, thirty-five years after his death.

Not surprisingly, Camus's forthright political views as a critic of totalitarianism in the Soviet Union and as a supporter of a multi-cultural Algeria played a major role in the wary suspension of what is a moving, extremely beautiful autobiographical work of unexpected charm. According to Catherine Camus, her father, "in denouncing totalitarianism and in advocating a multi-cultural Algeria where both communities would enjoy the same rights . . . antagonised both the right and the left. At the time of his death he was very much isolated and subject to attacks from all sides designed to destroy the man and the artist so that his ideas would have no impact."

Catherine Camus and her twin brother were fourteen when Camus died. He was a glamorous, romantic figure, the revered author of *L'Étranger* (1942), *La Peste* (1947), *L'Homme révolté* (1951) and *La Chute* (1956). For years the manuscript remained untouched. But when his widow, Francine, died in 1979, the writer's children assumed responsibility for the unpublished text in what had become the changing France of the 1980s. The family could either destroy the manuscript, causing it to be lost forever, or publish. Conscious of the autobiographical nature and value of the work, Catherine decided to go ahead.

Considering the disadvantages associated with having an unfinished draft text prepared by others for publication, *The First*

Man is enthralling, personalised autobiography, albeit carefully distanced. Whereas so much of his work tends towards philosophical abstraction and the exploration of existentialist ideas, this final book, by coming so much closer to the man himself, alludes to an important stage of Camus's artistic maturity, and a possible shedding of his previous reticence. The central character, Jacques Cormery, *is* Albert Camus. The narrative opens with a dramatic account of a couple travelling by wagon at dusk along a stony road in Algeria. It is 1913. A storm threatens but there is an additional urgency: the woman is about to give birth. The sequence works well as an independent, self-contained, if melodramatic episode touched by echoes of the Holy Family en route to Bethlehem.

By the next chapter, the baby born in the storm is now a man searching for his father's grave in a French war cemetery. Conscious that he never knew his father, who died on the Marne, Cormery is aware of being emotionally detached: "he could not muster a filial devotion he did not feel." To him, his father is no more than "a dead stranger". It is only when he notices the dates on the headstone, "1885-1914", and realises his father died at twenty-nine, that he experiences a human response. "Suddenly he was struck by an idea that shook his very body. He was forty years old. The man buried under that slab, who had been his father, was younger than he." The detached investigator now becomes a son aware that the cemetery is full of young men whose own sons are now middle aged, having lived longer than their fathers.

Throughout the cemetery sequence, Camus portrays Cormery as divided, suddenly aware that many of the answers he has been seeking are "intimately linked with this dead man, this younger father". Also central to Cormery's displacement is being part of a family "where they spoke little, where no-one read or wrote, with an unhappy and listless mother" so there was no one to tell him about his long-dead father. Initially the tone is dark and melancholic, but intense emotion begins to surface as Camus explores the despairing love Jacques feels towards his mother. Partially deaf and poorly educated; he remembers her gazing through the window at the life passing on the street beneath.

Although there are flashes of anger as the man recalls his boyhood self suffering the injustice of his grandmother's absolute power in the two-roomed flat where he and his brother are raised, the narrative is neither angry, nor sentimental, but thoughtful and full of life. The boy observes without being a watcher; his memories are of his own activities. He is a French boy to whom France is a foreign country as he has grown up in Algeria.

Understandably uneven, *The First Man* reveals a different, more personal Camus. This final, unfinished novel is not only a powerful personal testament of odd beauty, and a telling portrait of a particular place and a time, it helps complete the story of this most exciting and elusive European visionary.

25 | The Picture of Dorian Gray
(1890/1891)
by Oscar Wilde

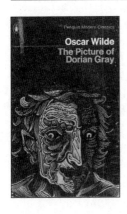

A young man gazes at a portrait, mesmerised by its ethereal beauty. The painting is of his face. His pleasure quickly turns to wistful sorrow, then despair. "How sad it is! I shall grow old, and horrible, and dreadful. But this picture will remain always young. It will never be older than this particular day of June . . . If it were only the other way! If it were I who was to be always young, and the picture that was to grow old! For that – for that – I would give everything! Yes, there is nothing in the whole world I would not give! I would give my soul for that!"

Dorian Gray's Faustian pact has been struck, although he is yet to realise it. This extraordinary Gothic parable, exploring the triumph of art over life and honour, reveals the dark side of Wilde's instinctive genius. The story, with its echoes of Baudelaire and Poe, is shocking and ironic. It evokes the opulent decadence of the 1890s, the society which was about to feed upon Wilde's heart; yet his novel's defining power lies in the brilliance of the stately prose and rich imagery.

Throughout the narrative Wilde sustains a precise balance between the languid wit of the bored aristocrat, Lord Henry Wotton, whose sardonic observations introduce the sinister twist the story will take, and the increasing hell of Gray's cursed existence, which is described with a precise detachment.

Wotton first encounters Gray at the studio of an artist, Basil Hallward, who has not only recognised young Gray's dangerous allure, he has captured it on canvas. Wilde, who always suffered for love, well understood the vulnerability of the lover. Wotton

153

immediately seizes on Dorian Gray as a potential plaything, but Hallward is reluctant to share him, and his unease is obvious. The painter sees what he calls "a fatality about all physical and intellectual distinction" and in the course of the conversation, Hallward emerges as a remarkable individual, the artist figure destined for tragedy.

"I turned halfway round, and saw Dorian Gray for the first time" recalls Hallward. "When our eyes met, I felt I was growing pale. A curious sensation of terror came over me . . ." His candid remarks have little effect on the thoughtless Wotton, who delights in drawing the young man away from the painter who is clearly fascinated with Gray.

Meanwhile, Gray, for his part, has become obsessed with a lovely young actress who nightly performs scenes from Shakespeare's plays. He wants to marry her and persuades Wotton and Hallward to accompany him to the theatre. That evening, before their eyes, her acting lacks its usual skill. She has decided that now she is loved, she no longer needs to perform other roles. Her symbolic gesture eludes Gray who, furious that she has embarrassed him, denounces her. Having adored the actress, he rejects the real girl. Later that night he detects the first signs of change in his portrait. Alarmed, he plans to seek her forgiveness. It is too late; she has already killed herself. Gray's fate is also decided.

Having begun life with a sweetness of nature, Gray becomes increasingly remote and depraved sampling each evil he is offered or seeks out. For all the horror of the tale, Wilde exerts impressive restraint in the telling. Gray's reputation descends to such depths that Hallward, en route to Paris, attempts to warn him of the offence Gray's conduct is causing. On seeing the changes in the painting, the artist is shocked. Gray reacts violently, commits a terrible act and then demands help from a former friend, who fearing blackmail, assists Gray in concealing the crime.

In a final act of madness, the tormented anti-hero attacks the by-now-hideous painting, which has become the record of his life. The portrait regains its original beauty, while its master and victim lies dead, his sins irrefutably evident in his ravaged features.

First published to some scandal in *Lippincott's Magazine* in 1890, this crafted, astutely paced melodrama is as technically accomplished as it is imaginative, atmospheric and daring.

Oscar Wilde *(1854-1900)*

Flamboyance, theatricality, arch playfulness, a bizarre innocence and dazzling self-belief all share a role in the tragedy of Oscar Wilde. Central to his marvellous rise and squalid fall is his genius and his ego, as well as his apparent confidence that everything was his for the taking. The stage Irishman who went on to become the consummate stage Englishman dealt in excess combined with extreme behaviour and mercurial wit. Personifying the artificiality of the 1890s, he took immense pleasure in parading Englishness to the English. Yet Wilde remained consciously Irish, and enjoyed satirising English class snobbery. Ever the creative artist he was capable of conferring glamour on the large body and plain face inherited from his overpowering mother.

His parentage helps explain the phenomenon that is Oscar Wilde. His father, Sir William Wilde, was a distinguished surgeon with a bluntly colourful personality shadowed by sexual scandal, yet he was generous and committed to the poor. He was also a pioneering gentleman antiquarian and, confident of his meticulous organisational skills, took on and completed the three-volume cataloguing of the Royal Irish Academy's archaeological collection in a remarkable five months, as it was obvious that the well-intentioned but hopelessly disorganised antiquarian, musician and painter, George Petrie (1790-1866), would never complete the task. Sir William was also a talented writer, the author of material ranging from travelogues to a study of Swift's final years, surgical texts and, of course, antiquarian topics.

Wilde's mother; Jane Francesca Elgee, Lady Wilde, known to history mainly by her pen name "Speranza", was no shrinking violet. She was the daughter of a solicitor and the granddaughter of Archdeacon Elgee. On attending the funeral in 1845 of Young

Irelander Thomas Davis, a co-founder of *The Nation*, Jane Elgee, then nineteen, read his poetry and promptly became an ardent nationalist. It was as Speranza that she began contributing poems and articles to *The Nation*.

In 1851 she married Dr Wilde, whose services to the census would earn him his knighthood in 1864. In that same year Wilde senior, by then Sir William, featured in a trial bought by one of his former female patients, Mary Travers, who had accused him of rape. Speranza complicated matters by writing a libellous letter about Travers, whose defence lawyer was Isaac Butt. Ms Travers emerged as deranged, but Sir William, in an eerie foreshadowing of his younger son's fate in a very different, if also nasty, case, left the court with a damaged reputation.

Oscar Wilde grew up in a household full of rhetoric, books, folklore and interesting personalities. From Trinity College, he set off to Magdalen College, Oxford, winning the Newdigate Prize for Poetry. His wit got him noticed as did his "art for art's sake" philosophy. He married Constance Lloyd in 1884 and proved an affectionate if distracted husband. By then, he had already lectured throughout North America on aesthetics. Returning to London he established himself as a reviewer. Wilde's insatiable appetite for books matched his needs in other areas. His restlessness may have been fed by his desire, half-insecure, half-egotistical, for idealised love.

His literary career began with *The Happy Prince* (1888), a beautiful collection of fairy stories. His only novel, *The Picture of Dorian Gray*, was poorly received on publication in a magazine in 1890, and in novel form the following year. In it Wilde articulates the restlessness and ambivalence which undercuts his life and his work, played out as they were amidst the cynically jaundiced sexuality of the 1890s. His comedies, culminating in *The Importance of Being Earnest* (1895), exemplify his epigrammatic humour despatched by high-speed dialogue.

Yet Wilde was essentially serious; *A Woman of No Importance* (1893), although not as dark as *The Picture of Dorian Gray*, is nonetheless a sombre work. Wilde believed he was an artist writing for posterity. This self-image dominates his most powerful literary utterance, *De Profundis*, a long letter written in prison between January and March 1897 and addressed to Wilde's treacherous lover, Lord Alfred Douglas, degenerate son of the Marquis of Queensberry.

Published posthumously in 1905, *De Profundis* is an angry manifesto which details the greed of Douglas, his vicious slights and most of all, his ingratitude. "While you were with me", writes Wilde, "you were the absolute ruin of my art." The relationship – which as Wilde stresses throughout he repeatedly attempted to end – drained him emotionally, artistically and financially. Wilde's tone is formal and dramatic. Written, a page a day, on prison notepaper, the letter looks beyond a destructive affair, and reveals Wilde reaching an understanding about life, his response to it and his awareness of the time and gifts he had wasted. He was aware, and history agrees, that he could have achieved far more had he lived longer. His heartfelt letter also serves as a metaphysical meditation about the role of the artist.

"I was a man who stood in symbolic relations to the art and culture of my age . . . Few men hold such a position in their own lifetime, and have it so acknowledged. It is usually discerned, if discerned at all, by the historian, or the critic, long after both the man and his age have passed away. With me it was different. I felt it myself, and made others feel it . . . The gods had given me almost everything. I had genius, a distinguished name, high social position, brilliancy, intellectual daring; I made art a philosophy and philosophy an art; I altered the minds of men and the colours of things . . . to truth itself I gave what is false no less than what is true as its rightful province, and showed that the false and the true are merely forms of intellectual existence. I treated art as the supreme reality and life as a mere mode of fiction."

26 | The Radetzky March
(1932)
by Joseph Roth

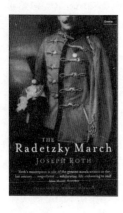

A jaunty marching tune, the very symbol of Hapsburg military might, marks time through the pages of Joseph Roth's stylish lamentation chronicling the chaotic end of empire. The melody, composed by Johann Strauss senior, ebbs and flows, conferring a polite defiance on a narrative in which the characters collectively stumble about. Life, it appears, is haphazardly overseen by the increasingly ancient presence of Emperor Franz Joseph, and by the ubiquitous portrait of his more youthful self.

This dark, disturbing novel of eccentric beauty does far more than follow the experiences of assorted dreamers and misfits; it evokes the disintegration of a complex, ailing world order – a disintegration speeded up by an assassin's bullet which would ultimately redraw the map of Europe.

Roth, who was an inspired journalist, observed, listened and understood more clearly than any of his contemporaries the havoc the empire's imminent collapse would have on the contrasting cultures of that labyrinthine Hapsburg world – with its national identities, respective histories and geographies. As a gifted novelist he was alert to the dynamics of men and women; fathers and sons; the powerful and the powerless. He also genuinely mourned the collapse of the Austro-Hungarian Empire, a vast central European kingdom stretching from Hapsburg Austria to Tsarist Russia.

Published in 1932, fittingly between the wars, *The Radetzky March* is a twentieth-century novel with roots deep in the nineteenth. It is poignant yet never settles into a nostalgic celebration of the past – there is far too much irony.

The lives of three generations of the Trotta family provide the fabric. Only F. Scott Fitzgerald succeeded in evoking the mood and atmosphere of a specific epoch as exactly as Roth has here. It is his longest, richest work and was one of his first to be translated into English. While he was writing *The Radetzky March* in one Berlin café, his rival Robert Musil (1880-1942), was sitting in another, busily at work on his massive, though unfinished opus, *The Man Without Qualities* (1930-1932).

Entrapped by a chance act of heroism that changed their family's destiny are two of the Trotta men, the aging widower chief district commissioner Trotta von Sipolje, a study in repression, and his hapless son Carl Joseph, later Lieutenant Trotta, a reluctant cavalry officer who loathes riding. Years earlier, in 1859, during the Battle of Solferino, the district commissioner's father, then a mere infantry lieutenant, had, in a moment's panic, impulsively saved the emperor's life.

That unexpected, unintentional good deed – this is not a novel about heroes; heroics never much interested Roth, who was fascinated by struggling, flawed humanity – was to change everything for the family. "The Trottas were not an old family. Their founder had been ennobled . . . Fate had singled him out for a particular deed. He subsequently did everything he could to return himself to obscurity. He was an infantry lieutenant . . . The battle had been in progress for half and hour or so. Three paces in front of him, he saw the white-clad backs of his men . . . A lull came in the fighting . . . Suddenly the Emperor appeared. He was in the process of raising a field-glass handed to him by one of his escort, to his eye . . . Trotta's heart was in his mouth. Fear of the unimaginable, the boundless catastrophe that would destroy himself, the regiment, the army, the state, the whole world, sent a burning chill through him . . . With both hands he reached for the monarch's shoulder's to pull him down."

The years pass; the emperor, now so ancient he is barely certain of his own age, half-remembers most things: "The Emperor was an old man. He was the oldest emperor in the world. All around him, Death was drawing his circles, mowing and mowing. Already the whole field was bare, and only the emperor, like a forgotten silver stalk, still stood and waited. His hard and bright eyes had been looking confusedly into a confused distance for many years . . . The creases in his face were a tangled shrubbery where the decades lived . . . At home he walked around with short pattering little steps. But as soon as he set foot on the street outside, he tried to make his thighs sinewy, his knees supple, his feet light, his back straight . . . his eyes remained fixed on the fine line that marks the border between life and death . . . People believed that Franz Joseph knew less than they did, because he was so much older than they were. But it was possible that he knew more. He saw the sun go down on his kingdom, but he didn't say anything. He knew he would die even before it went down. Sometimes he feigned ignorance, and was glad to be enlightened about things he understood perfectly well. For with the cunning of small children and the old, he loved to mislead people." Roth paints an extraordinary study of the emperor, but then, all of the characters in this wonderful novel are shaped with artistic precision.

"Of course, taken literally, it [the monarchy] still exists. We still have an army . . . and we have an officialdom . . . But it's falling as we speak", observes Chojnicki, an outspoken landowner and the prophetic voice of the novel: "As we speak, it's falling apart, it's already falling apart! An old man [Emperor Franz Josef] with not long to go, a head cold could finish him off, he keeps his throne by the simple miracle that he's still able to sit on it. But how much longer, how much longer? The age doesn't want us anymore! This age wants to establish autonomous nation states! People have stopped believing in God. Nationalism is the new religion." The speech, delivered with some exasperation, is a crucial moment in the narrative. It is also presents the understated, always subtle and ironic Roth at his most openly polemical.

Roth, ever alert to nuance, creates a group of officers, most of whom are in love with the allure of army life, particularly the cavalry, with its dashing uniforms, magnificent horses and readily available women. These are career military men who enjoy drinking, gambling, preening themselves and bantering loudly. Dying for the fatherland is not exactly a priority – war for them is an abstract concept.

Chance plays its part throughout the narrative. Lieutenant Trotta – whose carelessness causes the death in a duel of honour of his only friend, the tragic idealist Dr Demant – is aware that, despite his hatred of the army, his uniform is his sole expression of self. Roth meticulously sustains the irony to the final curtain. When news of the assassination of the emperor's nephew finally reaches their camp at the most easterly edge of the empire, the officers reckon that it is merely a rumour. Little do they realise that their world has begun to die; Roth, a romantic at heart, more than anything longed for its return.

Joseph Roth (1894-1939)

The supreme chronicler of the Austro-Hungarian Empire, Joseph Roth examined the chaos of change. As an Austrian Jew who had served with the Austrian-Hungarian army on the Western front during the first World War – possibly as a solider, more probably as a reporter – he knew where his loyalty lay, later recalling: "My strongest experience was the War and the destruction of my Fatherland, the only one I ever had, the Dual Monarchy of Austria-Hungary." Shortly before his death in 1939, Roth, still believing in the old world wrote of his desire for "the return of the Empire".

Yet this longing never compromised his fiction. As early as his atmospheric novella, *Hotel Savoy* (1924), Roth was very much aware of an emerging outsider; the displaced returning solider who no longer belongs anywhere. Gabriel Dan, the son of Russian Jews, is the first of Roth's many narrators to confront statelessness: "I am on my way back from three years as a prisoner of war, having lived in a Siberian camp . . . After five years I stand again at the gates of Europe . . . I look back upon a soldier, a murderer, a man almost murdered, a man resurrected, a prisoner, a wanderer."

Whether describing life in a remote military outpost, or a Berlin boarding house, or a drab café in Vienna, Roth remains humane and objective. Simple, kindly Andreas Pum, a Great War veteran in the wonderful early work, *Rebellion* (1924), "who had lost a leg and been given a medal", is destroyed by fate, tested by life, and finally earns a token moral grandeur, is very different from Alfred Döblin's later creation, Franz Biberkopf.

Roth is concerned with people; our fears and mistakes, our botched love affairs, our crazy dreams, the essential smallness of us all. His characterisation is forensically detailed; his prose is elegant, at times lyric with vivid descriptions of the countryside. Dialogue falls true to the ear, and he is often, very, very funny. In the context of twentieth century German-language literature, Roth's melancholic, candid oeuvre stands equal to that of Robert Musil, Franz Kafka, Hermann Broch, Thomas Mann and Robert Walser.

Assignments took Roth all over Europe; from Berlin to Vienna and revolutionary Russia, producing quality reportage such as *The Wandering Jews*, a cultural study of the Jewish experience across Europe, and on to the US in the early to mid-1920s. At the heart of the book is the plight of the Eastern European Jew, particularly when transplanted to the West. Roth rarely imposes himself yet his humour prevails: "In a true Jewish café you will walk in with your head under your shoulder and no one will notice". *What I Saw: Reports from Berlin 1920-33* and *The White Cities: Reports from France 1925-39*, two outstanding volumes of collected journalism, testify to his rare gifts.

His frenetic life was never easy. His father left his mother before his birth in Brody, Galicia, in 1894 – then the extreme east of the Hapsburg Empire – to eventually die in a Dutch lunatic asylum. Roth never met him. Raised by his mother and her family, he was educated in Brody before entering the University of Lvov (also known as Limburg), later transferring to the University of Vienna. After the Great War, he returned to Vienna, quickly establishing himself as a journalist. He also began to write fiction. By 1920, he was in Berlin. Roth's first novel, *The Spider's Web* (1923), notes the rise of Nazism and mentions Hitler by name. *Zipper and his Father* (also 1923), in which the narrator begins: "I had no father – at least I never knew my father – but Zipper had one", before evoking the world of the boyhood he shared with Zipper and beyond this, the fall of the monarchy. *Hotel Savoy* and *Rebellion* soon followed, each sustained by subtle rage.

Job – the Story of a Simple Man (1930), a beautiful account of loss of faith, gives a sense of his life, while *The Legend of a Holy Drinker* (1939), his eerily unintentionally autobiographical novella written during his final months, is bizarrely optimistic, even hopeful. Berlin-born Irmgard Keun who had criss-crossed Europe with him during two hectic years from 1936 used Roth as the model for her young heroine's journalist father in *Child of All Nations* (1938).

Near Roth's end, his career faltered; he became an alcoholic and suffered a crippling heart attack in 1938. Having abandoned Berlin in disgust in 1933, he settled in a Paris hotel. *Tarabas – A Guest on Earth* (1935) followed. Its eponymous central character, an angry sinner, seeks redemption. Set in the 1920s, it portrays the deconstructed German world in limbo. As with Roth's early novel, *Rebellion*, *Tarabas* is fascinating to look at in relation to Döblin's *Berlin Alexanderplatz* (1929).

The Emperor's Tomb (1938), an elegiac if cryptic sequel to *The Radetzky March*, was followed by *The String of Pearls* (1939), an initially comic skit which celebrates Vienna yet quickly acquires a tragic pathos, becoming languid and sombre.

Roth, a Central European Orwell, was elusive, mercurial, a teller of tales, a wanderer, an exile, a prophet of sorts and chief mourner of the passing of the Hapsburg Empire. He died poor and alone, not yet forty-five, in a Paris hospital.

27 | As I Lay Dying
(1930)
by William Faulkner

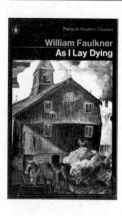

The banging is loud; the sound carries over the air. Addie Bundren, waiting for death, listens to Cash, her first-born busily at work making her coffin. Another of her sons, Darl, has faith in his brother and is certain his mother "could not want a better box to lie in. It will give her confidence and comfort". Faulkner, a skilled exponent of the interior monologue, assembles his speakers with the flair and authority of a theatre director arranging a pageant. The Bundren clan is poor white Mississippi farming stock, led by the appalling Anse. He and Addie shared scant joy but did produce four children – she, a fifth following her secret passion with the Rev. Whitfield. Anse is intent on keeping one promise; he will bury Addie in Jefferson, hauling her body on a mule-drawn cart over poor roads and across a river.

Cora, a kindly, bewildered neighbour has observed the unhappy Addie in life and now has overseen the three weeks of her dying. "She lived, a lonely woman, lonely with her pride, trying to make folks believe different, hiding the act that they just suffered her, because she was not cold in the coffin before they were carting her forty miles away to bury her, flouting the will of God to do it." Cora's husband, Mr Tull, sets her straight. "But she wanted to go. It was her own wish to die among her own people."

Addie's daughter, Dewey Dell, kneels by her mother's death bed and finally rises, as imagined by her brother Darl. "She looks down at the face. It is like a casting of fading bronze upon the pillow, the hands alone still with any semblance of life: a curled, gnarled inertness; a spent yet alert quality from which weariness, exhaustion, travail has not yet departed, as though they doubted even yet the actuality of rest, guarding with horned and penurious alertness the cessation which they know cannot last."

Faulkner took his title from Homer's *Odyssey*, Book Eleven, when Agamemnon tells Odysseus: "As I lay dying the woman with the dog's eyes would not close my eyelids for me as I descended into Hades." The narrative unfolds through fifty-nine vivid speeches, most of them delivered by Darl, who is so like his mother. He is sensitive, his observations shaped by wonder and a poet's response to all that happens. He imagines brilliantly, and is, perhaps, intended to represent Faulkner's idea of the mad artist as truth teller. But Darl is also disturbed, possibly, ultimately, insane – or at least judged to be so. It is he who knows that his sister, Dewey Dell, is pregnant. So much is festering in his thoughts, that the grief will turn his mind, and he begins to laugh, loudly, and increasingly hysterically.

Each of the characters harbours preoccupations. Jewel, Adie's wayward son by the Rev. Whitfield, only cares about his horse. Anse the widower is intent on new teeth – and a replacement wife. He feels aggrieved at the inconvenience, reflecting to himself "it's just like him to marry a woman born a hard day's ride away and have her die on him." Dewey Dell seeks medical intervention for her predicament. The funeral journey to Jefferson becomes an ordeal beset by problems; bridges are broken and the river is swollen.

Faulkner's characters emerge fully formed through their individual thoughts and utterances. Even Addie has her say, and explains why she married Anse; she was miserable teaching school. Worse would follow, marriage and motherhood were not the answer. It is a dark, bitter sequence in a novel of secrets, lies and regrets.

Cash, his leg broken by his brother's horse, travels most of the distance lying on top of his mother's coffin. As the days pass and the corpse begins to rot, vultures take up their vigil. The people encountered along the way are wary of the smell, horror-stricken and none too welcoming. Still the Bundren procession blunders on, leaving drowned mules and upset in its wake, sustained by a manic urgency that has moved far beyond Addie's final needs.

It is a human comedy but also a tragedy of sorts as Addie's dying, death and prolonged funeral procession mirrors the last gasps of the old South. For all the beauty of the prose, Faulkner wrests tremendous life from the vernacular speech and the earthy humour. Written in six weeks during the summer of 1929 when Faulkner worked the night shift in a power station, this is the novel in which he achieved not only technical perfection but full artistic expression, confidently establishing his menacingly imaginative voice.

William Faulkner *(1897-1962)*

Given to lying, given to silences, a committed boozer and a philandering husband, William Faulkner, sixth-grade drop-out and 1949 Nobel Literature Laureate is one of the greatest novelists of the twentieth century. He was, in truth, strange and difficult. Born in Albany, Mississippi, and raised in nearby Oxford, the eldest son of cold, non-demonstrative parents, he was bored at school and felt haunted by the past and by history. That same history of the South and its many legends and secrets would inspire his layered fictions.

No one ever claimed to have really got to know him, least of all himself. For the brooding Faulkner, life was a tussle; he struggled to write, yet it was writing that gave him a purpose. Whatever his inner demons, he knew the value of distancing his life from his work. Vital to any understanding of Faulkner is to grasp that he wrote best in the midst of a personal crisis, of which he had many.

Rejected by the US army because of failing to meet the height requirements – a restriction he took personally, allowing it to fuel his paranoia – Faulkner instead became a pilot in the Canadian Air Corps. Once demobbed, he briefly attended the University of Mississippi. A series of odd jobs finally led him to a stint as a reporter in New Orleans. There he had the luck to strike up a rapport with novelist Sherwood Anderson (1876-1941), by then famous for *Winesburg, Ohio* (1919), who encouraged Faulkner to write. Faulkner's response was emphatic and he wrote his first novel,

Soldier's Pay, published in 1926, followed a year later by *Mosquitoes*, and in 1929 by *Sartoris*.

By the late 1920s Faulkner had returned to Oxford to devote his imagination to life as lived in a place he created, Yoknapatawpha County. Madness and doom, as well as complex family histories pulsating with dark secrets, sustain his vision of the South. Faulkner portrayed family as a source of repression and emotional turmoil.

The Sound and the Fury (1929) sees the Compson family, former gentry already introduced in *Sartoris* earlier in the same year, in an irreversible state of disintegration. The forceful narrative unfolds through the consciousness of three family members; the tormented Quentin who kills himself because of his passion for his sister, Candace; the cruel, evil Jason, a monster to rival Richard III; and then there is Benjy, the thirty-three-year-old idiot and truth teller. A closing sequence centres on a black servant, Dilsey, whose goodness contrasts with the behaviour of the family. It is an extraordinary novel on many levels, particularly as a consolidation of Faulkner's commitment to the interior monologue. *The Sound and the Fury* was followed by the tragic-comedy, *As I Lay Dying*, the final journey of old Addie Bundren, accompanied by her husband, her sons and her pregnant daughter, all on the way to her home place, Jefferson. It is a road novel with a difference. Faulkner would never again quite strike such a perfect balance between realism and symbolism. *Light in August* (1932), the tragic story of Joe Christmas, is defiantly human. In it, Faulkner looks at the white destroyed by his inhuman treatment of the black. *As I Lay Dying* and *Light in August* are rewarding books, offering contrasting aspects of Faulkner's sophisticated, stylistic, and, at times, earthy, genius.

Absalom, Absalom! (1936) tells of another family hell being acted out in the doomed South. Thomas Sutpen, a poor white, has notions of grandeur and will stop at nothing to secure this. He marries a planter's daughter and they have a son, Charles, but he deserts them on discovering his wife has black blood. He marries again and fathers another son, Henry, and a daughter, Judith. Years pass, and Henry, unaware of the connection, meets Charles at college and admires him. Charles in turn falls in love with his half-sister, Judith. Henry, on discovering the truth about Charles, kills him – and the family's evil fortune does not end here.

The long, sweeping sentences and the hypnotic energy of his storytelling makes Faulkner irresistible. Even a tale as ill-served by a polemical narrator as is *Intruder in the Dust* (1948) has its allure. Faulkner set out to chronicle the death of the Old South and did, with staggering assurance and technical panache.

28 | The Heart of the Matter (1948)
by Graham Greene

Relentless humidity, suspicion, malaria, religious doubt, despair, cultural tensions and multiple betrayals, particularly of self; no one grasps the post-colonial legacy and the tragedy of the human condition as well as Graham Greene. His tightly written, somewhat practical fiction, which makes such effective use of the combined elements of nuanced social class, melodrama, suspense and political thriller, revolves upon one defining element – belief.

Acknowledged as a master psychologist, he is a storyteller who never forgot the importance of convincingly human characterisation. This confirmed leftist who was drawn to danger and whose ambivalent relationship with his adopted Catholicism came to dominate his taut narratives, created his own universe, an instantly recognisable and unsettling place.

Greene favours the displaced outsider, the burnt-out case, man in a supreme mess invariably of his own making. In Scobie, the laconic, battered hero of *The Heart of the Matter* (1948), which is set in wartime Sierra Leone, Greene offers a sympathetic portrait of a good man in torment. Already past fifty, Scobie, a senior officer, has served as deputy to the police commissioner who is about to retire, and has been passed over for promotion. He possesses sufficient irony to absorb the humiliation. His wife, Louise, does not. Brittle, depressed and unpopular within their small colonial set, she is desperate to leave but realises Scobie is intent on staying.

Scobie may not like Louise, but he pities her, even cares for her as one would a wounded stranger. Their only child is dead. In order to fund a trip away for Louise, he needs a loan. He approaches the local bank manager, Robinson, who spends his working day counting his steps as he walks across his office floor. But Robinson can't help with finance. When not marching about his office, the bank manager consults his collection of medical dictionaries. Health and disease, his health in particular, preoccupy Robinson, who is one of several wonderful minor characters and provides a cleverly ironic plot twist of his own.

Daily life consistently pits the hot, sweaty Englishmen against the natives, but also against each other, and particularly themselves, in a climate that undermines their social rituals. Throughout his work, and very obviously in this atmospheric narrative, Greene demonstrates not only the extent to which he was influenced by Conrad, but also the way in which he developed the Conradian vision, bringing it the next step on from early twentieth century colonialism to the wartime and postwar era of corrupt, native dictatorships sustained by international political self-interest.

As Scobie goes about his daily tasks of routine searches and half-hearted interrogations, he not only has to contend with Yusef, a cunningly charming if sinister Syrian trader intent on his friendship, he is also being watched by a new colleague, Wilson, an edgy, furtive poet who somehow manages to fall in love with Louise. Wilson's personal resentment of Scobie becomes increasingly relevant to the narrative; Greene allows the reader to see Louise through the eyes of others as well as Scobie's. For Scobie, love has become something closely bound with pity and guilt. The dialogue is often witty, many of the characters are brisk, exasperated. Greene is so deliberate; the reader "hears" the exchanges and shares the draining heat, the clammy darkness, the menace.

The same empathy that binds Scobie to Louise attracts him to Helen, a young widow, who is one of the few survivors from a stricken ship. Their romance proves impossible. Its discovery makes Scobie more vulnerable and costs the life of Ali, his devoted servant. Scobie's moral dilemma, compounded by his burden of pity, love, guilt and belief, is resolved by an ungodly act of all-too-human daring. This is why the likeable, beleaguered and human Scobie is his most memorable creation.

The Heart of the Matter is not only one of Greene's finest achievements, it stands tall among the most compelling of twentieth century morality plays.

Graham Greene *(1904-1991)*

The great novelist of escape, betrayal, failure and guilt may well have spent his long life on the run from an abiding dislike of himself. This desire for flight drew Graham Greene to some of the most dangerous trouble zones in the world, particularly Central America and parts of Africa. He set out to become a man of action through his writing.

In addition to his novels, he produced impressive, well-observed travelogues, reportage and comment pieces; Greene was always an enigma, freely admitting that his famous conversion to Catholicism had been more about wooing a reluctant woman than booking his place in heaven. Later in life, he would come to describe himself as a Catholic agnostic.

He was born in 1904, into North London middle-class comfort, the fourth of six children, to a schoolmaster father who never approved of sex. His mother was equally undemonstrative. Greene's early life was complicated by having to live at, and attend Berkhamsted School, where his father taught, and ultimately ruled, for close on forty years. The future writer was unpopular at school, where his classmates refused to allow the nervous, sickly boy to forget that he was the headmaster's son and therefore – suspect.

After several messily inept attempts at schoolboy suicide, Greene was sent off to extensive psychoanalysis. On his return, he displayed a healthy rebelliousness, so the treatment was considered successful. Greene's first short story, 'The Tick of the Clock' was published by a London newspaper before his arrived at Balliol College, Oxford. Although never a member of Evelyn Waugh's sophisticated college smart set, Greene did discover the escapist thrills of Russian roulette and took a lower second in modern History.

While at Oxford, he met Vivien Dayrell Browning, a devout Catholic. Greene was to become obsessed with her. Browning had her own problems; she was terrified of sex and very religious. Not only did Greene convert to Catholicism in order to marry her, he also agreed to a celibate union. In 1927 he was accepted into the Catholic Church. Meanwhile his beloved wondered should she become a nun. They married, neither wanted children, yet somehow pregnancies occurred and childbirth followed.

Restlessness, the defining quality of Greene's remote, for a time, manic-depressive personality, surfaced when he set off to Liberia. His experiences almost cost him his life and produced a fine book, *Journey Without Maps* (1936). His first novel, *The Man Within*, had been published in 1929. It success encouraged him to resign from his job with *The Times*. His next two novels flopped. The success of *The Stamboul Train* in 1932 was overshadowed by two subsequent libel cases; one raised by the writer J. B. Priestly, the other involving disparaging comments made by Greene about Hollywood child star Shirley Temple.

Greene, who sustained a life-long hatred of the United States, supported various causes, including communism. His life and his work were grounded in faith, loyalty, betrayal, stoicism and doubt. His fictional universe is populated by whisky priests, lost souls, weary romantics and the hunted – all at the mercy of good and evil. In person, he had the demeanour of a retired civil servant or, possibly, an exiled spy. His marriage to the hyper-devout Browning eventually faltered to a close after twenty years. Content to settle into a solitary, increasingly reclusive life, Greene enjoyed occasional visits from a long-time girlfriend whose husband indulged the relationship.

Greene died in April 1991, leaving a powerful body of atmospheric fiction as well as an exhausted but determined biographer, Norman Sherry, at work on the second volume of the writer's life, it was published in 1994. The concluding volume followed in 2004. Greene's particular genius rests in combining the tension of the best thrillers, a feel for place, understated irony, and an overwhelming understanding of how people think. Among the finest of his novels are *Brighton Rock* (1938), a wonderful point of entry into his abiding interest in man's flair for self-destruction; *The Power and the Glory* (1940); *The Third Man* (1950), which was originally written as the screenplay for Carol Reed's iconic film of the same name; *The Heart of The Matter* (1948); *The End of the Affair* (1951); *The Quiet American* (1955); *Our Man in Havana* (1958); *The Comedians* (1966) – a novel worthy to stand beside *The Heart of the Matter* – and the masterful, if often overlooked, novella, *A Burnt-Out Case* (1961).

Born the year after Orwell, Greene has a great deal in common with him, as he does with a later original, the pioneering surreal futurist, J. G. Ballard.

The Expedition of Humphry Clinker (1771)
by Tobias Smollett

It is a family holiday like no other. Squire Matthew Bramble, righteous, possibly inclined to hypochondria, and incontestably human, is intent on visiting old friends. He sets off from his home, Brambleton Hall in Wales, on a hectic and lengthy odyssey through England and northwards to Scotland. With him are his appalling, somewhat desperate spinster sister Tabitha and the squire's grown wards, nephew Jery and niece Lydia (often referred to as Liddy) Melford, fond siblings endowed with independent minds of their own.

Luckily each member of the squire's party prove keen correspondents, despatching vivid, if contrasting accounts of their travels, and at times their personal woes, to their respective friends. Accompanying the party is Aunt Tabitha's illiterate maid servant, Winifred Jenkins, who is given to wild affections and even wilder bouts of misspelling. As one of the earliest examples of a road novel – and the gifted Scot Tobias Smollett does make several nods to an even earlier road novel, *Don Quixote* (1605 and 1615) – *Humphry Clinker* is not only insightful Georgian social history, it also remains screamingly, insanely funny.

Samuel Richardson (1689-1761) and Henry Fielding (1707-1754) had pioneered the epistolary form, but it was Smollett who really opened it out by increasing the number of letter writers – and with this extended cast of scribblers, ever increasing the comic potential of juxtaposing contrasting, overlapping versions of the same events. The squire's detailed twenty-seven letters to his friend and doctor

Dick Lewis dominate the narrative and provide the fullest, most opinionated account of the places visited.

Young Liddy, however, caught up in a romantic dilemma of some ambivalence, is understandably, distracted. Her determined swain pursues her across the country and, indifferent to the scenery and much else besides, Liddy breathlessly reports to a school pal every sigh pertaining to her secret romance. Meanwhile, her brother Jery sustains a running commentary, spanning twenty-eight letters, to his college friend Phillips. Wry and ironic, Jery is a witty, often merciless observer who is particularly amused by his Aunt Tabitha's grotesque efforts to secure a man. Mindful of his sister's honour, Jery challenges Lydia's admirer to a duel.

Smollett shrewdly establishes and sustains the individual voices, allowing each character to emerge fully formed through the respective ways in which they express themselves to their intimates. The squire, initially preoccupied with supplying quality intellectual discourse to Lewis, enjoys interludes of philosophical awareness. He is alert to his surroundings and remarks on the changes relentless time had made on places he has not seen for years.

Jery is different. Here is a young man living in the moment. The squire's voice is reflective, even nostalgic; while his nephew's tone confidently conveys the impression of an individual laughing so hard that he can barely keep his pen steady. Aunt Tabitha, owner of Chowder, a vicious dog, despatches sharp missives to her housekeeper back at Brambleton, and Winifred, drawing on her ramshackle use of English, keeps her fellow servant Molly informed of developments.

Travelling through the eighteenth century Britain of George III has its physical perils; horses fall lame or throw a shoe; carriages break down, become stuck in mud, slide into rivers and overturn. Unexpected drama frequently overtakes the travelogue. The party chances upon an unfortunate victim of a miscarriage of justice – one Humphry Clinker.

Fate "intervenes". Thomas, the postilion, is bitten by Aunt Tabitha's savage pet and rendered unfit for his duties. The Bramble party need a replacement and find it in Clinker, initially described as "about twenty years of age, of a middling size, with bandy legs, stooping shoulders, high forehead, sandy locks, pinking eyes, flat nose and long chin". He quickly confirms his loyalty, even to the point of "rescuing" the squire while swimming, as well as saving him from more serious plights. Interestingly, Clinker, a Methodist and an enigma of near-saintly simplicity and many talents – from shoeing horses to preaching – never takes pen to paper. Nor are any of the eighty-two letters written by Lismahago, the eccentric Scottish soldier who eventually weds Tabitha, and in common with the squire, represents aspects of the author's varied life.

Revelations and marriages abound in this picaresque romp of exuberant genius completed by an ailing Smollett in 1771, only months before his death in Italy at the age of fifty.

Tobias Smollett *(1721-1771)*

It's not easy being a natural satirist; particularly should you also have a polemical streak. Tobias Smollett suffered in comparison with Samuel Richardson, who was serious and openly moralistic. Richardson was in fact so given to darkly psychological investigations that by the nineteenth century readers tended to shun him. Yet Richardson's reputation did recover. Then there was Henry Fielding, a comic writer whose moral values seemed able to satisfy everyone. All too often Smollett was dismissed as an eccentric journalist who habitually ranted to the point of libelling his victims. This tendency once landed him in prison. But Smollett the novelist was an original with much in common with a singular pioneering subversive, Laurence Sterne (1713-1768), who with *The Life and Opinions of Tristram Shandy* (1759-1757) had deconstructed the novel form in its infancy.

Nothing was simple for Smollett; not least the fact that religious works dominated eighteenth century publishing sales. Yet this was changing, and the rise of the novel form had begun with the emergence of Daniel Defoe (1660-1731), who produced a steady output of work including *Robinson Crusoe* (1719), *Moll Flanders* (1722) and *A Journal of the Plague Year* (also 1722). "Nobody reads sermons but Methodists and Dissenters," declares Henry Davis, the London bookseller in *The Expedition of Humphry Clinker*.

Born in Dunbartonshire, Scotland, in 1721, Smollett studied at the University of Glasgow and was then apprenticed to a surgeon. By the age of eighteen, however, our hero was on his way to London with the script of *The Regicide* in his fist. It was never staged. Smollett, true to his volatile nature, took this setback personally. At twenty he set sail for the West Indies on H.M.S Chichester, serving as a surgeon's mate. He spent three years in Jamaica before returning to London to practise as a doctor. This didn't go overly well either.

But Smollett for all his touchiness was possessed of strong, at times courageous, opinions. Interested in violence as a phenomenon, he began drawing on his personal experiences and attitudes in a new career, journalism. He also tried his hand at translation. Most importantly of all, his first novel, *The Adventures of Roderick Random* (1748), was published when he was twenty-seven. About this time his only child, Elizabeth, was born.

Random's picaresque adventures were based largely on his creator's experiences and hint at what would prove one of the strengths of *The Expedition of Humphry Clinker*, Smollett's knowledge of contemporary politics. *The Adventures of Peregrine Pickle*, alive with comic grotesquery, followed in 1751.

Smollett co-founded *The Critical Review* in 1756 which he would edit brilliantly – if outrageously – until its collapse seven years later. His travel writings, such as the epistolary *Travels through France and Italy* (1766), also attracted eager readers. Smollett had a fierce and mercurial mind; his work bristled with intrigue, astute insight and digressions. His political writings invariably caused trouble. These same political criticisms run through his Clinker picaresque, mainly in the form of opinions expressed by the squire and his nephew, Jery. Don't be misled, it may appear simple fun, and it is vastly entertaining, but *The Expedition of Humphry Clinker* is also dauntingly well-informed and reflects the prevailing tensions between England and Scotland.

Smollett would finally enjoy success on the stage in 1757 when his naval farce, *The Reprisal*, opened at Drury Lane. By then he had also launched *The British Magazine*, a political-cum-literary review which included among its contributors Oliver Goldsmith (1728-1774). It would survive until 1767. By then Smollett's health had already begun to fail.

A few years earlier, after his daughter's death in 1763, just short of her sixteenth birthday, Smollett and his wife had travelled to France and Italy. A brief return to England after a couple of years in Europe convinced them to settle permanently in Italy. When an anonymous, viciously outspoken attack on British politics, *The Adventures of an Atom*, was published in 1769, it was assumed, though never proven, that Smollett was the author.

Although he had abandoned Britain with its diverse social and cultural idiosyncratic traits, his homeland would provide him with the ideal theatre for his final, most successful work, *The Expedition of Humphry Clinker*.

30 Black Beauty
(1877)
by Anna Sewell

Peaceful days passed in the meadow with his wise mother, followed by livelier sessions playing with the other colts, provide the narrator with a happy early life. There is also the confidence of being the handsome, well-bred grandson of a racehorse twice victorious at Newmarket. Black Beauty seems destined for a pampered future as a gentleman's accessory. At the age of four he is purchased by the local squire and is fortunate in that his loving first master, who bred him, undertakes the breaking.

Although he recalls the gentle hands that introduced a bit to his mouth and first placed a saddle on his back, Black Beauty is honest and admits to feeling pain: "Those who have never had a bit in their mouths, cannot think how bad it feels; a great piece of cold hard steel as thick as a man's finger to be pushed into one's mouth, between one's teeth and over one's tongue, with the ends coming out at the corner of your mouth, and held fast there by straps over your head, under your throat, round your nose, and under your chin . . ."

Anna Sewell's immortal classic gives an account of one horse's progress from ease and affection to suffering through a series of harsh experiences which become steadily worse.

It is an important book – it is also a great one. Man is the source of all of the grief and cruelty experienced by her narrator and the other horses. Sewell became an invalid when she was fourteen and remained so until her death at fifty-eight, a few months after the publication of this, her only book. She loved horses – and justice.

Her love of horses had a practical dimension. She was painfully aware of the abuse horses suffered at all levels of Victorian society, from the careless antics of the gentry at play on the hunting field, to the impossible labour demanded of working horses. This most moving of stories told by an innocent, increasingly despairing hero is, for all its appeal, graphic polemic. It is also a vivid social history and illustrates how essential horses were to daily life.

Black Beauty quickly settles at Birtwick, the squire's comfortable home. The horse has a good temperament, having from birth only known kindness. There is a dramatic new difference to his life. Instead of playing in the fields, he is now expected to stand in a stable, waiting to serve as both riding mount and carriage horse. He makes friends with Ginger, a chestnut mare who has become soured by harsh treatment. She is destined for tragedy and after many twists of fate, is again seen by Black Beauty who describes watching as he, by chance, notices her dead body being carted away from the cab rank.

Sewell makes many welfare points, condemning in particular the vicious bearing rein which was widely used to keep the heads of carriage and haulage horses held unnaturally high, even when confronted by steep hills and hauling heavy loads.

In one of the strongest set pieces, the narrator recalls slowly waking up to a new sensation – fear – as fire tears through the stables at an inn where his master is staying. Black Beauty's world changes when the squire's wife becomes seriously ill and the family decide to leave England, causing the horses to be sold.

His new owner is a lord whose wife, a fashionable lady, insists on the use of bearing reins. Further problems emerge through the carelessness of an alcoholic stableman who whips Black Beauty to gallop despite the horse having thrown a shoe. This causes him to stumble and damage his knees while the drunkard dies in the fall. Sewell's prose is plain, direct and meticulously detailed. She evokes the intelligence of the animal without faltering into whimsy or fantasy.

His scarred knees result in Black Beauty being sold off. He begins a career of desperate hardship which includes being rented as a "job-horse." One such client drives him hard despite the lameness caused by a stone in his foot. By the time the narrator arrives at a horse fair, he accepts his days as a valued animal are over. Yet he is bought by a kindly London cabbie. The work is demanding, but Jerry the cabman and his family love "Jack" as they name him. In Jerry's yard he meets Captain, an old former army horse who had survived the horrors of the Crimean War.

Black Beauty enjoys living with Jerry but when the cabbie becomes dangerously ill, the horse is again sold and is soon hauling massive loads. Just when Black Beauty sees death as his only release, a miracle happens.

Anna Sewell set out to change attitudes to the treatment of horses and created in her narrator a mild mannered, unforgettable hero, who though weary by much of what he has endured, remains convincingly philosophical in a story of hard fact and profound emotion.

Anna Sewell *(1820-1878)*

Anna Sewell was fated to write only one novel, but that lone work, *Black Beauty*, has proved a remarkable testament. Although never intended as the children's book some feel is has become, this brave polemic has endured as a literary classic beloved by readers of all ages.

It is the story of a black horse born into ease and privilege who unfortunately suffers a change of circumstances which heralds a life of hardship. Sewell was open about her intentions; she wanted "to induce kindness, sympathy, and an understanding treatment of horses."

She was the elder of two children born in Great Yarmouth, Norfolk, to a Quaker couple, Isaac and Mary Wright Sewell, both of whom would survive her. Sewell's mother was an independently minded woman and an established writer of children's books. Her views on education decided her on educating Anna and her younger brother at home. Initially the Quaker ethos had a significant role in this educational regime. Issac Sewell's keen pursuit of available work caused the family to often move house. When Anna was twelve, the family settled in Stoke Newington.

There she was finally allowed to experience conventional

schooling and was introduced to maths and foreign languages. Her pleasure in this was to end abruptly. Within two years, her life changed dramatically. A simple fall when walking home from school resulted in a serous illness. What had appeared to be a sprained ankle that never healed, or possibly because of the long bed rest involved, ended in a chronic mystery illness. At fourteen, the girl who had had a normal childhood, always being part of whatever community that her family had settled within, suddenly became an invalid.

In 1836, when she was sixteen, her father took a job in Brighton, hopeful that the sea air would restore her health. It didn't. Recent research suggests that Sewell had been misdiagnosed and that it appears likely that she was suffering from a severe form of lupus. She was no longer able to walk and could rarely even stand without assistance. Although her mother and Sewell would abandon Quakerism, they never forsook their faith in God. Her parents consulted a range of doctors and healers, using herbal potions as well as conventional medicines. They also sent her to various health spas in England and abroad.

While taking a water cure Sewell met the poet Tennyson. As the daughter of a writer Anna Sewell was well read and enjoyed poetry. She had an affinity with animals, particularly horses. When well enough she rode and also became a skilled driver. This knowledge gave her insight into the plight of carriage horses which frequently suffered as much through the use of the fashionable but cruel bearing rein, as did haulage animals pulling heavy loads. Sewell stresses that the gentry at play inflicted as much pain on horses as did desperate working men pushing them beyond humane limits.

Horses were a crucial element in the nineteenth century English society and would remain so until the second World War when improvements in mechanised transport resulted in the slaughter of hundreds of thousands of working equines. By Sewell's time horses already had a long history in battle. Old Captain, the white horse Black Beauty meets in Jerry's yard, had served in the Crimean war.

When she began writing *Black Beauty*, Sewell was fifty-one, with only seven years left to live. Then living in Old Catton, near Norwich, she was increasingly bedridden and dictated much of the book to her mother.

In November 1877 Sewell sold the manuscript to local publishers. Thousands of copies were soon being distributed free by animal welfare groups to yard owners, drivers and stable hands.

Now believed to be the sixth highest-selling English-language book of all time, *Black Beauty* remains a powerful tract that is also loved, and invariably recalled by adults as the most enduring story of their childhood. Anna Sewell died in April 1878, within a month of celebrating her fifty-eighth birthday and is buried in the Quaker cemetery at Lammas, near Buxton, Norfolk. It is ironic that one of literature's most famous novels is the work of an author who, as the daughter of a writer, never saw herself as one.

31

Malone Dies
(1951)
by Samuel Beckett

"I shall soon be quite dead at last in spite of all. Perhaps next month. Then it will be the month of April or of May. For the year is still young, a thousand little signs tell me so. Perhaps I am wrong, perhaps I shall survive Saint John the Baptist's Day and even the Fourteenth of July, festival of freedom. Indeed I would not put it past me to pant on to the Transfiguration, not to speak of the Assumption." Laconic and precise, the unforgettable Everyman narrator establishes his wry voice and jaunty wit from the opening sentences, in this the magnificent, and most cohesive, second volume of arguably Beckett's finest achievement, his incomparable prose trilogy.

Attend closely to the death-bed soliloquy of an old man waiting for the end, his world reduced to the now largely impersonal business of eating and excreting. A trolley arrives with a pot containing soup, the same, or possibly another materialises, to depart bearing waste. Armed with two pencils, an exercise book and his memories, Malone shares many of the thoughts preoccupying Molloy, one of the two narrators delivering the comic burlesque of *Molloy* (also published in 1951), but Malone soon reveals a more deliberate poetic grandeur.

As he lies in bed he notes: "In a flicker of my lids whole days have flown", and he asks, "Does anything remain to be said?" Having given up on his body – "There is virtually nothing it can do. Sometimes I miss not being able to crawl around anymore" – he instead demonstrates a spectacular strength of mind. His reveries wander through a maze of memory and anecdote, much of it bleak, even caustic; a great deal more of it is dominated by Beckett's singular comic genius and his ability to expose the horrors of existence as an absurd sideshow.

Yet along with the comic asides – "Let me say before I go any further that I forgive nobody. I wish them all an atrocious life and then the fires and ice of hell . . ." – there is immense despair and Beckett's extraordinarily perceptive grasp of what it means to be human. There is also the shimmering musicality of the prose: "I hear the wind. I close my eyes and it mingles with my breath. Words and images run riot in my head, pursuing, flying, clashing, merging endlessly."

Fragments of Malone's earlier life and several existences filter through his thoughts. He recalls a phrase: "Nothing is more real than nothing." Although trapped in his bed, his search for a pencil lost among his bedclothes becomes an epic quest. "What a misfortune, the pencil must have slipped from my fingers, for I have only just succeeded in recovering it after forty-eight hours of intermittent efforts." Ever the optimist, Malone decides: "I should really lose my pencil more often, it might do me good."

His bed heaves with the rigours of a battlefield, his imagination continually defying his physical confinement. Pondering his chances of moving his bed towards possible flight, he imagines: "To be off and away" only to shrewdly reflect: "And then, who knows, the physical effort may polish me off."

The narrator's moods shift from the snappily exasperated, to the philosophical, the bleak and, most movingly, to the tender. At one time, he had been cared for by Moll, an ancient toothless woman; it was she who brought his food, she who emptied his bed pan. They embark on an unlikely romance; their passion igniting their ancient bodies. It is funny yet desperately heartbreaking.

She begins to rot and one day she dies, leaving him to the mercies of the malevolent Lemuel who rounds up the inmates for a memorable outing with Lady Pedal. She is the chatelaine of the local manor and enjoys occasional bouts of largesse. "One morning Lemuel, putting in the prescribed appearance in the great hall before setting out on his rounds, found pinned to the board a notice concerning him. Group Lemuel, excursion to the islands, weather permitting, with Lady Pedal, leaving one p.m." It ends rather badly.

Written in French shortly after *Molloy* and followed within two years by the darker agonies endured by the bewildered narrator of *The Unnameable, Malone Dies* is a huge work contained within a slim volume. It soars, beckons and beguiles throughout with the unparalleled vision of the defining genius of literary modernism.

Samuel Beckett *(1906-1989)*

Bleakly, blackly comic, Samuel Beckett's unrelenting pessimism soars on the strangest blend of hoping against hope whether you are stuck up to the neck in sand or sitting in a trash can. While his one-time friend James Joyce put everything in, Beckett, the quiet Irishman who lived in France and wrote in French, took out as much as possible. Educated at Earlsfort House School, Dublin; Portora Royal School, Enniskillen; and at Trinity College Dublin, he was the son of an affectionate, sports-loving quantity surveyor father and a strange, remote woman given to sudden anger followed by depression. Beckett famously said of his mother: "I am what her savage loving had made me."

He was a successful scholar and sportsman. His father had wanted him to become a professor, as Beckett ruefully recalled, yet he never found happiness in Ireland. His restlessness led him to London and on to Europe. As the narrator says in the fragment *From an Abandoned Work*: "I have never in my life been on my way anywhere, but simply on my way."

He first visited France in 1926 as a student and enjoyed a cycling holiday in the Lôire Valley. Paris became his home and French his artistic medium, yet Beckett would never forget the Irish idiom which remained ever-present in his work.

By the time he joined the Resistance he had already published a collection of stories, *More Pricks than Kicks* (1934), and *Murphy* (1938) – both of which he wrote in English, as he would the much later *Watt* (1953). Involved in translating into English reports filed from

Resistance agents all over France and then preparing them for transmission to London, Beckett and his wife Suzanne were forced into hiding after an informer had betrayed them to the Gestapo. He made little of his Resistance efforts, but in 1945 President de Gaulle presented him with the Croix de Guerre.

When Beckett had recovered from a serious illness in 1947 during which he suspected he was dying of cancer, he wrote *Waiting for Godot* in French and worked on the great prose trilogy, *Molloy* (1951), *Malone Dies* (the same year) and *The Unnamable* (1953). Each of the three, intense, bleak and often funny, monologue-like works were written in French. Beckett translated *Malone Dies* into English in 1958.

Following the first production of *Waiting for Godot*, Beckett became famous. It was 1953. The success changed his life; it had an equally dramatic impact on modern drama, the theatrical revolution known as the Theatre of the Absurd had been born. No one sustained it better, with a little help from Eugène Ionesco and Harold Pinter, than Beckett with works such as *Endgame* (1957), *Krapp's Last Tape* (1958), *Happy Days* (1961) and *Not I* (1973). A few years earlier, in 1969, Beckett had become the third Irish man to win the Nobel Prize for literature. Although pleased to be honoured, he did not attend the ceremony.

Despair was his theme, and memory his canvas. The influence of the trilogy lingered, and would inspire *How It Is* (1961), a narrative which takes the form of a journey. It unfolds in three stages. Beckett wrote it in French and published an English translation in 1964. The plays dominate the legacy, and yet the trilogy could well, and should, emerge as his greatest achievement. Late in his career he wrote the remarkable *Ill Seen, Ill Said* (1981), the haunting, philosophical middle section of a trilogy including *Company* and *Worstward Ho*. It describes an old woman, alone in her little house in an empty landscape, aware of morning and evening skies. Her life has become a ritual of visiting a nearby grave: "Winter evening in the pastures. The snow has ceased. Her steps so light they barely leave a trace." His beautiful final work, *Stirrings Still*, is a stark, graceful study of loneliness.

In conversation he was more likely to discuss cricket than debate the meaning of existence. The many actors he worked with enjoyed his humour and admired his discipline. He never wasted words and could charm with a one liner or intimidate with a distant glance. Samuel Beckett conveys in a sentence what it would take others a book, no, a lifetime, to attempt to explain. He certainly has left far more than "a stain upon the silence."

32 | Great Expectations
(1860-1861)
by Charles Dickens

The local churchyard may seem an unlikely sanctuary for a young boy but when your tyrannical sister, some twenty years your elder, has grudgingly reared you "by hand", there is some comfort to be had from looking at the tombstones that confirm your father and mother did indeed once walk among men. Pip Pirrip has a wonderfully bewildering story to tell and no one could tell it as vividly and as excitingly as the master storyteller, Charles Dickens. A chance encounter with a dangerous and desperate convict named Magwitch in that very churchyard changes Pip's life for ever. The grown Pip, a candid, thoughtful narrator alert to his own snobbery and errors of judgment, looks back and recalls his younger self, reliving his earlier terror.

Once the convict realises that the boy's sister is married to a blacksmith, he knows the problem of his ball and chain is about to be solved. "You get me a file", he demands, "And you get me wittles . . . Or I'll have your heart and liver out." Pip flees back to his home where he enjoys the kindness of Joe Gargery, a gentle individual always endeavouring to soften the harshness of his wife, Pip's sister. Young Pip supplies the convict's needs. The law eventually steps in and the convict is recaptured but not before Pip sees him again, albeit from the safety of Joe's shoulder.

Some time later, the boy is summoned by the local rich lady, an eccentric recluse who though "done with men and women" wishes to watch him play. So Pip arrives at Satis House and, having been greeted by the beautiful if cold Estella, meets Miss Havisham.

"She was dressed in rich materials – satins, and lace, and silks –

all of white. Her shoes were white . . . But, I saw that everything within my view which ought to be white, had been white long ago, and had lost its lustre, and was faded and yellow. I saw that the bride within the bridal dress had withered like the dress, and like the flowers, and had no brightness left but the brightness of her sunken eyes . . . I should have cried out, if I could."

By the time Dickens began writing *Great Expectations*, he was famous and adored by a public eager for his high-speed, yet detailed, cliff-hanger instalments. He was also sufficiently shrewd to have re-read his earlier, autobiographical masterwork, *David Copperfield* (1846-1850), for fear of replicating himself. *Great Expectations* has a similar theme; that of a young boy overcoming early hardship, but it is a darker, more mature work with less of the familiar exuberant comedy and all of the perception, sensitivity, moral outrage and narrative twists that makes reading any Dickens novel a living, breathing and unforgettable experience.

Elevated in social rank thanks to an anonymous benefactor whose identity he wrongly assumes he knows, Pip believes he is being groomed to wed Estella who in fact has been shaped into an icy breaker of hearts, intended to avenge Miss Havisham's ruined life in the aftermath of a wedding that never happened.

Once settled into London life, our narrator finds himself in the company of Mr Jaggers, Miss Havisham's dour lawyer. Pip becomes increasingly friendly with Wemmick, whose robotic law office persona contrasts with the loving son he becomes when at home with "Aged Parent". Somewhere in the back of Pip's mind lingers an awareness of how deeply he has hurt his former protector, the ever-faithful Joe Gargery, to whom he had been apprenticed before fortune beckoned.

Pip comes to know himself, particularly when he begins to unravel the several knots that bind the major characters. He also discovers the unlikely source of his wealth and ultimately his hard-won happiness.

It is a sustained drama. Dickens's prose is visual, rich and physical; his characters real, their aspirations understandable.

Whether set in the marshes where we first met Pip and he encounters the convict; or in a dank London street, or with a group of frenzied policemen engaged in a boat chase down the Thames, or when describing moments of menace or pathos, his prose compels because of his feel for story. To read Dickens is to share his frenetic, singular imagination, his extravagant playfulness, his grief and his humanity. Small wonder that so many, when asked by aspiring readers which English-language writer they should begin with, reply "Dickens".

Charles Dickens *(1812-1870)*

Sentimental, melodramatic and sensationalist Charles Dickens comes complete with sufficient faults to scupper a lesser writer. His female characters were either doomed innocents or monsters and no other novelist could as brazenly toss in a coincidence – or several – as Dickens frequently does with such abandon. He wrote as if possessed, not just because of the pressure of deadlines, but also to meet his bills. His method of plotting was determined by the then practice of publishing novels in instalments.

Serialisation was the way novels were read in his day; the luxury of sitting up all night was not familiar to readers who waited a week, or no, good grief, an entire month, in between reading, or hearing, the latest instalment of the story that happened to be gripping their imagination. Broadsheets and magazines, not leather-bound books, were the reading matter of the majority; and Dickens, showman supreme, master storyteller, social commentator and by thirty, the most famous writer in the world, knew his public. And how they loved him – and his humour, the comic dialogue, the descriptions, the eccentric names and all the characters, the put-upon Everymen, the grotesques, the villains, who once encountered live forever.

No other storyteller has captured the popular and critical vote quite as conclusively as Dickens, whose childhood experiences not only prepared him for life, they provided him with a heaving mass of material. Dostoyevsky admired him and interestingly, they share that trademark manic energy. Queen Victoria was also a fan. But

191

then Dickens who had famously seen his father disgraced in a debtor's prison and had been sent at the age of twelve to work in Warren's Blacking, a rat-infested factory where he spent more than a year pasting labels on to jars of boot polish, understood poverty, humiliation and above all, humanity.

Having escaped his childhood, he never forgot it. It would prove valuable and would surface again and again – vividly, terrifyingly, tenderly. The young Dickens learned shorthand and became a parliamentary reporter. Then he invented Mr Pickwick and the rest is history. Dickens created a world of the imagination, but he also chronicled the one he lived in, that of Victorian London, a city where the poor suffered for simply being alive.

The Posthumous Papers of the Pickwick Club was published in 1837, when Dickens was only twenty-five. It was the beginning of probably, in terms of showmanship, the greatest literary career of all time. *Oliver Twist* (1837) followed in which Dickens demonstrated he had absolutely no difficulty with portraying violence and brutality. Quick as a flash, he was busy with *Nicholas Nickleby* (1840), *The Old Curiosity Shop* (1840-1841), *Barnaby Rudge* (1841) and *Martin Chuzzlewit* (1843-1844). When *Martin Chuzzlewit* did badly, all was saved that same year by the success of *A Christmas Carol*, the inspiring account of Ebenezer Scrooge's journey towards understanding.

In 1846 Dickens travelled to Switzerland to write *Dombey and Son* (1848) but realised he needed London's bustle in order to create. He returned to England and still the torrent continued, he wrote on; producing a masterpiece in *Bleak House* (1852-1853). Next came the blunt polemic of *Hard Times* (1854), followed in quick succession by several contrasting works; *Little Dorrit* (1855-1857), *A Tale of Two Cities* (1859), *Great Expectations* (1860-1861) and *Our Mutual Friend* (1864-1865).

In the midst of all this writing Dickens, a husband and father, became obsessed with actress Ellen Ternan, with whom he may have begun a passionate affair. Either way, he defied the gossip by continuing to produce stories and give public readings of his books which were more like dramatic performances. On return from another visit to America, the exhausted Dickens dropped dead – he was only fifty-eight. *The Mystery of Edwin Drood* was left unfinished.

If one were limited to only one writer, Dickens, with his infinite variety and linguistic energy, offers a vaudevillian lifetime of entertainment and story. For him, writing was breathing. In addition to the novels, he produced short stories, travelogues, reportage, essays, speeches, polemical rants and an estimated 15,000 letters. Probably no one has written as many words in English. He broke all the rules with his excess, his use of coincidence, melodrama and blatant sentimentality. If genius exists, it does in Charles Dickens. Novels such as his, populated by unforgettable characters, are independent and enduring worlds.

33 | The Magic Mountain
(1924)
by Thomas Mann

Orphaned by his parents and then by his grandfather, and about to make his way in the world, young Hans Castorp first sets out from Hamburg to a Swiss mountain village. His plan is to visit his cousin, Joachim, an aspiring soldier who is recuperating at the Sanatorium Berghof before joining the war.

Hans, the consummate civilian, also reckons a three-week vacation should prove restful preparation for his new job as an engineer in a shipyard. He is of steady, *burgher* stock, a cautious, innocent lad of twenty-three. Those three weeks turn into seven years.

Thomas Mann's calmly epic study of the mystery of time also considers the major themes of life and death and love, all within the setting of a somewhat eccentric sanatorium inhabited by an international cross-section of patients conducting themselves more like guests staying at an exclusive hotel.

For all the philosophy, irony, the preoccupation with the nature of time, and the extraordinary, lengthy, often adversarial debates about faith and humanism – largely fought out between the angry, fatalistic Naphta, a Jesuit who had been born Jewish, and Settembrini, a Freemason with literary tendencies – this is a strongly historical tale of transition. It is also a European novel of ideas marked by the influence of two giants – Goethe, Mann's favourite writer, and Nietzsche.

Hans is the ideal central character; mild, ordinary, oblivious to the personal and intellectual odyssey he is about to begin. Most importantly, he is not an artist. Mann, who began the novel in 1912 following the completion of *Death in Venice*, appeared to have set out with a loose plan. He was confident, famous by then due to the success of his first novel, *Buddenbrooks* (1901), which would later be banned by Hitler and publicly burned – as were all Mann's books.

Published in 1924 between the two world wars, *The Magic Mountain* is many things, including a burlesque human comedy, as well as being a supreme example of a traditional German literary genre, the Bildungsroman, a story in which a character reaches self-understanding. It is also a heartfelt response to the political upheaval facing Europe, in the aftermath of one war and the threat of another acquiring shape. Deliberately set earlier than Mann's immediate period, the narrative is the story of the collapse of a civilisation, the end of an epoch. The disease killing the patients is a metaphor for the insanity of the Great War, the global war which would follow and the emergence of twin menaces – fascism and communism.

In the opening sections Mann presents Hans as the healthy, detached visitor who quickly feels unwell. The symbolism is established; Hans has exchanged Prussian order for chaotic thought. He has also left the flat lands; and has entered the uplands, a mountain haven.

Despite the eccentricity of life in the sanatorium, it is here that Hans Castorp discovers self-knowledge and has encounters which are philosophical, political, intellectual, sexual and ultimately, moral. Memories return as troubling dreams begin to stimulate his consciousness. One of the patients, Clavdia, an intriguingly awkward Russian, irritates Hans because she habitually slams the glass door of the dining room. He falls in love with her. His devotion means that when she leaves the sanatorium, he decides to stay because she will return – most of the patients do come back, still uncured.

Even before his initial three-week visit is over, Hans becomes unwell. The months pass. His love for Clavdia consolidates his attachment to the sanatorium. An X-ray causes him to reflect: "for the first time in his life he understood that he would die." In another outstanding set piece, Hans, the unlikely athlete, goes skiing and is caught in a vicious snowstorm.

All the while, his former complacency is yielding to curiosity and a new interest in knowledge. Joachim goes off to war but obviously not cured, soon returns to die. Naphta and Settembrini are not only battling for the soul of Hans – they represent the conflict between liberal reason and totalitarianism. Hans Castorp eventually leaves the sanctuary of the mountain-top sanatorium, a place in which he has learned and experienced so much and he too heads for the war. We last see him singing Schubert's 'The Linden Tree' as he stumbles in the mud.

Thomas Mann made the transition from late-nineteenth-century writer to modernist. Balanced between humour and horror, rooted in its own world and beyond that world, *The Magic Mountain* is an ambiguous tragic comedy; it remains a book of its time as well as being a defining text for our time, all time. Literature would have to wait until 1955, and William Gaddis's *The Recognitions*, for a magnum opus as rich in ideas.

Thomas Mann (1875-1955)

He was a modernist whose creative heart remained rooted in nineteenth-century traditionalism. Thomas Mann, cosmopolitan and intellectual, loved his country and believed in Germany, although not in the way the Nazis did. He came from classic *burgher* stock. He honoured Goethe, not Hitler. Born in the Baltic city-port of Lübeck in 1875, he was the violin-playing son of a wealthy merchant whose family records were traceable back to 1644. However, after his father's death, the family discovered the fortune was gone. Mann's widowed mother moved to Munich in 1893, taking her children with her. Thomas Mann briefly worked as an insurance clerk before going to the University of Munich to study arts and decided, as had his elder brother Heinrich, to become a writer.

After completing some short stories, he moved on to bigger things, literally, and wrote *Buddenbrooks: The Decline of a Family*. It is a realist family saga spanning four generations in the style of Tolstoy with elements of Zola. Plotting the rise and fall of a Lübeck merchant clan, it is the story of Mann's family. Yet along with the portrait of society, there is a second theme; that of the emergence of the artist searching for a sense of self as expressed through art. Hanno, the last

Buddenbrook, is an artist, vulnerable, individualistic and doomed. *Buddenbrooks* was published in 1901 and was a major success, praised by Rilke among others. It established Mann at the age of twenty-six. Not only did he become a famous writer, he was quickly accepted as a public figure whose opinions would be heeded.

The conflict between the creative consciousness and society, as well as the inner turmoil of the artist attempting to balance concepts of reason and order with the quest for dangerous knowledge, dominate Mann's unexpectedly autobiographical fiction. As always in Mann, there is also the element of the erotic. In all things his ironic detachment was defined by the nineteenth-century legacy of literature and philosophy, and his admiration for Goethe. In both *Tonio Kröger* (1903) and the novella, *Death in Venice* (1912), in which a famous German writer, Gustave von Aschenbach, defies a lifetime of discipline to travel to the decadent city of Venice, Mann explored the conflict of the artist and society. *Death in Venice* sees the thesis pitched at its most extreme; Aschenbach becomes obsessed with a beautiful boy he notices on the beach. Plague breaks out in the resort, but Aschenbach refuses to leave as he sees death as the natural fulfilment of his romantic self.

Soon after completing *Death in Venice*, Mann began work on *The Magic Mountain*. Ironically, it was partly inspired by a stay at a sanatorium. In 1912, Mann's wife was diagnosed with a lung condition and she went to the Swiss Alps to recover. Mann visited her and developed a bronchial infection. In common with Hans Castorp he was advised by the doctors that he should become a patient for at least six months. Unlike his fictional character, Mann rejected the advice. But one thing he brought away with him from the sanatorium in Davos was a powerful sense of time as experienced there, high in the mountains. Of all the great modernists, Mann, the most accessible, is consistently preoccupied with this notion of time as history and as part of the ever-moving present. At the beginning of chapter seven he describes time as the medium of narration as well as the medium of life.

The writing of *The Magic Mountain* would be delayed by the war which had a terrible effect on him. He supported it, while his brother denounced Mann's views as conservative and anti-democratic. This criticism caused Thomas Mann to reconsider his opinions in *Reflections of a Non-Political Man* (1918), in which he attempted to separate the Germany of literature and music from its emerging political entity. There is no doubt that he was, and would remain, a *burgher*, though not a bourgeois, defender of the old ways. *Buddenbrooks* was far more than a novel he wrote; it was his life.

Mann's personal dilemma, this conflict of ideas and his wartime crisis of belief in how he viewed his country influenced *The Magic Mountain*, which he had conceived as a comic satire. And it is very funny. Yet just as the ordinary Hans Castorp begins a journey of self-discovery, the novel looks at the results of historical transition, and acquires far darker implications. Mann had begun it in 1912; he concluded it in the early 1920s and it was published in 1924, in a very troubled Germany, in a different Europe. Mann was then famous and would be awarded the Nobel Prize in 1929. Interestingly, his conservatism had evolved into humanism. He would be no figurehead for the new administration and quickly fell out of favour with the Nazis. Mann's books, once revered in his homeland, were publicly burned.

In 1933 Thomas Mann, then fifty-eight years old, and caught, as his biographer Ronald Hayman describes it, "between melancholy and panic", left Germany. This was not easy. "It was a deep cleavage and gulf that divided his present from the past – it was the grave," he wrote at the beginning of *Joseph in Egypt*, the first of the four 'Joseph' books (1933-1943). ". . . His vital forces collected themselves quickly and easily, which did not prevent him from distinguishing sharply between his present existence and the earlier one, which had led to the grave, or from regarding himself no longer as the old Joseph, but a new one. If to be dead and gone means to be bound irreversibly to a condition that permits no backward signal or greeting, not the slightest resumption of contact with one's former life, if it means to have vanished from that former life . . . then Joseph was dead."

At first Mann and his family lived in Switzerland. He made several visits to the US, before settling at Princeton, New Jersey, where he finally completed *Lotte in Weimar* (1939), an imagined re-creation of a meeting between the aged Goethe and a former lover. Eventually, Mann moved to California, where he wrote *Doctor Faustus*. Published in 1947, it is a major achievement and Mann's definitive statement about the history of his time. Through the life of a composer, Adrian Leverkühun, he follows the costly evolution of genius as overseen by the composer's friend, the narrator Zeitblom. Although the novel was enthusiastically received, Mann had angered Arnold Schoenberg (1874-1951), who felt his music and theories had been used without acknowledgement. Schoenberg went so far as to write an imaginary dictionary entry in which Thomas Mann, at some future date, would be accredited with the pioneering of twelve-tonal music.

The dispute became bitter, yet Mann would face far more serious problems. His second son, Klaus (1906-1949), also a writer and a one-time prodigy, who at the age of eleven had written a play about a suicidal schoolboy, made several suicide attempts.

In 1936, while living in Amsterdam, Klaus had written *Mephisto*. A flamboyantly barbed political satire in its own right, it was based on the career of his then former brother-in-law, actor Gustaf Gründgens, who had enjoyed the favour of Hermann Göring, despite having had a communist past. It was well received across Europe. When it was finally published in Germany in the early 1960s, it caused the longest lawsuit in German publishing history.

Mephisto was translated into English in 1977. But Klaus Mann was, by then, long-dead, having killed himself in Cannes in 1949.

The living embodiment of the tensions between art and reality, Thomas Mann wrote in the present, always looking back to the past. He visited Germany in 1949 and eventually returned to Europe to live in Switzerland, where he finally wrote the picaresque novel that had dogged him for years, *Confessions of Felix Krull, Confidence Man* (1954).

The rich cultural legacy of Germany and his awareness of how life had once been, not only kept his political concerns in perspective, it guided him through a career in which he always looked to the tensions of art and reality, while nodding warily at his many demons.

34 | The Optimist's Daughter
(1972)
by Eudora Welty

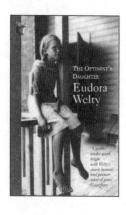

A middle-aged daughter, on learning that her father is worried about difficulties with his sight, hurries to New Orleans to join him as he consults an eye specialist. Some eighteen months earlier, the father, Judge McKelva, who still lives in the old family home in Mississippi, had remarried. His new wife, many years younger than him – in fact younger than Laurel, the judge's daughter – is also at his side. The ghost of Laurel's mother remains a palpable presence and the antagonism between the daughter, herself a war widow, and Fay, her unlikely stepmother, is obvious. Equally apparent is Fay's additional irritation; being trapped inside a doctor's office is not her idea of visiting New Orleans, especially during carnival time.

Initially written in 1969 as a story for *The New Yorker*, this perceptive tale was brilliantly revised and extended by Welty and went on to win the 1973 Pulitzer Prize. Although there are abundant flourishes of her characteristic social comedy and feel for Southern speech, the story is also rich in festering resentments. Many of the exchanges are as sharp and punchy as a stage play. Deceptively replete with Jamesian symbolism, particularly of restraint, it is a darkly ironic study about what happens when a grown child begins to look beyond the known surface of the marriage that had produced her.

The narrative begins in the doctor's examination room, a room without windows. The specialist knows the judge and Laurel, but has had to be introduced to judge's new wife. Beneath the friendly banter there is also an emerging doctor-patient relationship. It appears that the judge may have scratched his eye while pruning his late wife's roses. But it is more serious; the damage is within the eye.

While the doctor is discussing treatments, impatient, pushy Fay wails from the sidelines, intent on having no further time wasted on an injury that she believes will heal itself. Welty establishes Fay's petulant nature before looking more closely at the other characters. Fay, half-child, half-monster, has infiltrated a closed society. Early in the story when asked by Laurel about her family, she retorts, "None of 'em living. That's why I ever left Texas and came to Mississippi. We may not have had much, out in Texas, but we were always so close. Never had any secrets from each other, like some families." Implicit in her remarks is her hostility towards Laurel. Fay remains abrasive and wary.

Throughout the narrative Welty sets up a series of surprises. Having heartily opted for surgery, the judge, the self-proclaimed optimist of the title, slides into an unexpected passivity. His daughter and wife take turns at his hospital bedside but he withdraws further into a paralysing lassitude. Shrieking "it's my birthday", Fay loses patience and beats him until he rises from the bed. Her attack has fatal results.

Back in Mississippi, family and friends gather in the newly dead judge's home and attempt to re-instate Laurel in their old circle. Further layers of truth filter through the small talk. The wake and funeral sequences allow Welty to balance the drama with comedy. The arrival of Fay's allegedly dead clan members, including little Wendell whose curiosity is impossible to contain, not only exposes Fay, it also consolidates Welty's theme that nothing is what it seems. Meanwhile, mourners recall Judge McKelva as a man bearing little resemblance to the father Laurel thought she knew.

In the closing pages an already outstanding, fluidly written narrative acquires a heightened artistry. Left alone in her childhood home, a home soon to be claimed by Fay, Laurel attempts to retrieve the past, remembering her mother's courageous girlhood and the sorrows that followed. She recalls her father lighting a fire, and reflects of that moment: "Then he was young and could do anything." Another ghost is that of Laurel's dead soldier husband.

Into an atmosphere of emotional collapse enters a bird, whose frenzied flight through the house terrifies Laurel before releasing her, if not quite fully, from a past clouded by ambivalence.

Eudora Welty *(1909-2001)*

She was the last of a special breed of US Southern writers: Eudora Welty stands shoulder to shoulder with Flannery O'Connor, Carson McCullers, William Faulkner, and the great, seriously under-celebrated Peter Taylor, author of *A Summons to Memphis* (1986) and *In the Tennessee Country* (1992). Unlike O'Connor and McCullers, Welty was not overly drawn to grotesque Southern Gothic. Her art is more subtle; it celebrates family and place.

She could also summon immense comic power, as evident in *The Ponder Heart* (1953), and throughout the often burlesque domestic saga, *Losing Battles* (1970). Welty understood the singularity of people. A natural storyteller with a flair for Southern speech, particularly at its most colourfully vernacular, she could portray eccentrics, such as the post mistress in 'Why I Live at the P.O.', wryly and compassionately without resorting to stock grotesque devices. Jane Austen was her literary heroine, while Chekhov was an influence; she admired the way he described people talking, with apparently, no one listening.

Despite her travels in Europe and New York, including a year at Columbia School of Business studying advertising, Welty decided to claim the South as her chosen literary terrain. Before that, she had enrolled at the Mississippi State College for Women when she was sixteen, and had spent a further two years studying at the University of Wisconsin.

Born in Jackson, Mississippi, in 1909, Eudora Alice was the eldest of three and years later would dedicate *Losing Battles* to her brothers, both of whom were dead before it was published. A job in an insurance company had attracted Welty's father, a former school teacher from Ohio, to Jackson. Her mother, originally from West Virginia, had also been a teacher.

Welty grew up in a household where books were loved, the Bible was revered. Her father died before she had returned home from her studies. But return she did, living with her mother until the old lady's death in 1966. Welty never married, and had no children.

A singular perceptive intelligence shines through her work. Welty's humour may be earthy and often spins on the skilful use of coincidence and mistaken identities, as in *The Ponder Heart* featuring the self-destructive Uncle Daniel falsely accused of killing his hysterical wife.

Welty at one time wrote a social column in a newspaper. Photographs she took for a series of interviews she conducted during her travels through poverty-stricken Mississippi were exhibited in New York in 1936, and eventually the interviews and pictures were published in 1971 as *One Time. One Place: Mississippi in the Depression, A Snapshot Album.*

About the time of those travels during the 1930s she began writing fiction; her first published story, 'Death of a Travelling Salesman', appeared in the *Southern Review*. A debut collection of short stories, *A Curtain of Green*, was published in 1941 and the following year saw her first novel, *The Robber Bridegroom*, an inventive variation of the European fairytale. British writer Angela Carter (1940-1992) is often credited as the pioneering experimentalist in the genre – but Welty was there decades earlier, already exploring the sexual undertones of female fear when confronted by male sexuality.

Delta Wedding, published in 1946 and set in 1923, is a graceful and nuanced portrait of Southern life seen through the eyes of Laura, a nine-year-old guest. This novel could be viewed, and has been, as a celebration of the traditional sphere of women's lives, and as a pastoral hymn to fertility. But the narrative transcends gender-based literary criticism and is, I believe, intended to depict a family anxious to seek a retreat from the modern world by looking to the past.

Welty was a personal rather than autobiographical writer, committed to character, whether it is the hilariously fluid and unreliable narrator Edna Earle of *The Ponder Heart* or the brutal monologue allegedly delivered by the crazed white killer in the terrifying story, 'Where is the Voice Coming From?'

Losing Battles, which spans a two-day family reunion and years of memories, triumphs because Welty writes such convincing dialogue. It is a big, comic novel of voices revelling in her impressive technical virtuosity. She published five collections of short stories and invariably features in anthologies. Her masterpiece is *The Optimist's Daughter*, which began life as short story for *The New Yorker*, and having been extended into a novel, won the Pulitzer Prize. Few writers have matched Welty's intensely exact depiction of the pain experienced by Laurel, the widowed daughter of the title, as she finally confronts the story of her parents and their marriage.

Her autobiography, *One Writer's Beginnings* (1984), opens the door towards explaining her literary consciousness. Never concerned about having the "regionalist" label affixed to her, Eudora Welty refused to make a mystery of either her art or her life, and remains an unforgettable voice.

35 December Bride

(1951)

by Sam Hanna Bell

Andrew Echlin and his two grown sons face domestic confusion when his wife dies. The only solution is to find help. The widow Gomartin and her daughter, Sarah, are recruited for the task. The women assess the situation and move to the farm, efficiently restoring order.

Little comment is passed on the arrangements. In a tough Presbyterian farming community scattered across the magnificent landscape of Strangford Lough in County Down, there is scant time for nonsense. The locals work hard, heed nature, attend their church and abide by the rules. Yet gradually many of those rules begin to be challenged by Sarah, whose determination to defy her destiny shapes her every thought and gesture.

It is no coincidence that Sam Hanna Bell prefaces his dramatic narrative with a quote from Thomas Hardy's poem 'Honeymoon-Time'. If ever a literary presence were seen to grace the telling of a tale, it is that of Hardy, whose bleak, lyric genius presides over this powerful novel.

Andrew Echlin proves a kindly patriarch, and to young Sarah Gomartin, well used to hard work since childhood, the securing of his favour is all important for her future.

Although she is aware of the interested glances directed at her by Frank, the attractive younger son, Sarah knows that real power lies with the father. What begins as a treat, the granting of a boat trip, ends in tragedy. Andrew gives up his life to save his sons and the girl. From that point on Sarah, long convinced she has no need of God, having reminded Martha Gomartin, her mother – "My father died on the roads, and ever since I can mind my life has been nothing else but slaving for other folk" – is confident she can handle the sons. She does.

Bell was born in Glasgow in 1909 to an Ulster-Scots family and worked at many jobs before turning to writing. He was lucky in the support of Louis MacNeice, but there was more than luck to it – Bell's descriptive, austerely rhythmic prose lives off the page. The characterisation is exact; here are plain-speaking Ulster farming people caught in an unnatural dilemma. Ceaselessly simmering in the background are the realities of religious bigotry, tribal loyalties and sexual jealousy. The story is set in the early years of the twentieth century, yet not only does *December Bride* preview McGahern's Ireland, it could as easily take place in the France of Balzac or Zola.

Sarah soon attracts a suitor, Pentland, a local man of property; but she gambles on securing the Echlin household and defies her mother who returns to their family home without Sarah. Pentland gradually detects the sexual tension between Sarah and Frank, and abandons his quest. The stark potency of the narrative rests in the astute characterisation of the secretive, calculating Sarah, who engages sexually but never emotionally with the brothers. "She shared herself between them both, in body and in mind, and so disarmed the younger brother."

Frank's urgent desire is balanced against the less complex needs of Hamilton, his older brother. Sarah manipulates them both and Bell carefully plots the power shifts within the household. When a baby boy is born his paternity is questioned. The local rector becomes involved and takes flight on discovering his confused sexual interest in Sarah. All the while she watches. Just when she feels she has control, Frank begins to look elsewhere for romance, causing Sarah to identify a potential threat to her position – the possibility of his taking a wife.

Resentments grow. Frank's bid for freedom ends in disaster. The Echlin farm expands and Sarah sees off the local Catholic woman tenant who never approved of her. Lives end. Sarah loses her mother, and then old Agnes, her only friend. Agnes's death leaves her husband, Petie, increasingly helpless and destined to a nightmare end in a Belfast alley.

Time passes, a second baby is born to Sarah, who, never relaxing her watch, retains control. When an accident results in yet another death, she realises who she really loved during those long years.

This is an intensely humane morality play about desires sought and ambitions snatched. Situations become part of local history and regrets linger as major decisions are reduced to logical outcomes. Sarah Gomartin emerges as a shrewd, dauntingly human survivor in Bell's grim masterpiece that ranks high among Ireland's finest novels.

Sam Hanna Bell *(1909-1990)*

By the time of his retirement from the BBC in 1969, Sam Hanna Bell had made more than six hundred radio documentary features, including the classic, 'This Is Northern Ireland'. He had a singular flair for broadcasting, even at a time of great radio performers. Yet before revealing his radio talents, he had already published *December Bride* (1951), the first, and the finest, of his four novels.

Bell's arrival at the BBC had not come easily; he had had his share of hardship which included working as a labourer in Belfast's docks. There had also been a spell grading potatoes. He had been a lab technician conducting postmortems on diary cows, and a desk clerk, but made the time to enrol at the Belfast School of Art as a night student because of his interest in cartoons. Bell, a natural raconteur, had a gift as a communicator, a talent poet Louis MacNeice noted on hearing a documentary Bell had made about rural depopulation.

There was an additional strand to his programme-making; Bell possessed an astute understanding of social history and was aware of the changes that make a society and confer an identity on it. He was the eldest son of a journalist, James Hanna Bell, who came from just outside Larne and worked on the *Glasgow Herald*. Hanna Bell senior had married his cousin Jane McIlveen from the townland of Raffrey, a village about four miles from the shores Strangford Lough. Sam Hanna Bell was born in Glasgow. The family moved in 1915 to Greenock on the Clyde when James Bell was appointed editor of a local edition of the *Glasgow Herald*.

Three years later, when Sam was nine, everything changed with the sudden death of his father. The family returned home to Raffrey where the young Sam Hanna Bell discovered rural life and loved his excursions to Strangford Lough, the landscape which would shape *December Bride*. Within three years further upheaval would be caused by a move to Belfast. His mother supported the family with sewing jobs and taking in lodgers.

The only university for Bell was to read everything within reach – and he appears to have done that. The Linen Hall Library became his second home. His first collection of short stories, *Summer Loanen* (1943), most of which had originally been published in *The Bell*, was dominated by the changing settings of his childhood. His mentor Sean O'Faolain encouraged Bell to draw on the real life events that had taken place in a County Down community. The outcome was *December Bride*.

"I had heard my father speak about how he first heard that story of a *ménage a trois*", recalled Hanna Bell's only child, Fergus, in a conversation with me about his father: "And that although most of the company in which he had been were amused, he was horrified at the human tragedy of it."

Just as Bell so lovingly and meticulously conveyed the essence of the Presbyterian culture determining the world of the Echlins and Gomartins in *December Bride*, he would also immortalise Belfast in *The Hollow Ball* (1961), a novel about a footballer who leaves Belfast and attempts to make a playing career in England. Belfast featured in Bell's other fiction and non-fiction writings. He was to trace the Ulster heritage of US writer John Steinbeck in the 1980 documentary, 'West of Derry, East of Eden'.

When film director Thaddeus O'Sullivan came to make the screen version of *December Bride*, Bell, then approaching eighty, looked ideal for the part of Andrew Echlin, whose death sets the story in motion. Bell was invited to play the part in the movie but felt he was too old, pointing out that he certainly did not want to die by drowning as Andrew Echlin had in the novel. Sam Hanna Bell never saw the movie because he died in hospital, following a heart attack, a week before the premiere.

36

Mary
(1926)
by Vladimir Nabokov

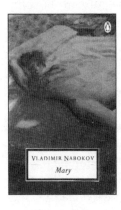

It is the stuff of a minor nightmare – realising you are trapped in a lift with the wrong person. Elevators, faulty or otherwise, were not all that common in 1925 when Vladimir Nabokov, a newly married young Russian émigré living in Berlin, began writing his first novel. *Mashenka*, which became *Mary* when he was working on its English translation, is as delicate as it is robust. It is a young man's study of bittersweet romance with an edge, in which Nabokov reveals his debt to Turgenev. This beautiful novella effectively straddles the magnificent nineteenth century Russian literary tradition and the modernist movement in which Nabokov would prove a significant player.

Mashenka was written many years before his second career began; in 1941, a year after moving to the US, he published *The Real Life of Sebastian Knight*, his first work written in English. Invariably placed shoulder to shoulder with Proust and Joyce, Nabokov remains an inspirational enigma; the sophisticated literary master who was also a major authority on butterflies. Images of these winged beauties flutter throughout the narrative which centres on handsome, exasperated Lev Glebovich Ganin.

As the story opens Ganin is standing in sudden darkness in a stalled elevator. With him is the annoyingly cheerful Alfyorov, another Russian. The two men are fellow boarders at a dilapidated boarding house in Berlin which is run by a tiny Russian-born widow of a German businessman. Nabokov leaves no doubts as to the pervasive gloom. "The pension was both Russian and nasty. It was chiefly nasty because all day long and much of the night the trains of the *Stadtbahn* could be heard, creating the impression that the whole building was slowly on the move. The hall, where there hung a bleary mirror with a ledge for gloves, and where stood an oak chest so placed that people naturally barked their shins on it, narrowed into a bare and very cramped passage."

Ganin has been threatening to leave for a while. Alfyorov has only just moved in and is awaiting the arrival of his wife, who is travelling from Russia. Podtyagin, an elderly Russian poet, is also desperate to leave. He has been attempting to secure permission to move to Paris where his daughter has settled. Another lodger, Klara, a young typist, has no dreams of escape. Her life is dominated by typing and long, empty evenings preoccupied with her hopeless love for Ganin, who has his own problems, including a tiresome girlfriend. "He no more knew what kind of external stimulus would give him the strength to break off his three-month liaison with Lyudmila than he knew what was needed to get him up from his chair." A pair of male dancers, "both as giggly as women, thin, with powdered noses and muscular thighs", share another room.

At meal times these displaced Russians engage in vague conversations and generally live within the confined worlds of their own situations, all of which is effortlessly sketched by Nabokov, displaying, even at this early stage his genius for subtle nuance and characterisation.

By chance Ganin discovers that the wife on her way to join Alfyorov is Mary, his lost love, whom Ganin had met some nine years earlier. Reliving memories of his youthful romance enables Ganin to finally break free of his stagnant relationship with the cloying Lyudmila.

The flashback to that distant summer of first love is atmospheric and vividly described, almost dream-like. There are echoes of Alain-Fournier's *Le Grand Meaulnes* (1913) in its evocation of lost youth, missed opportunities and a sense of longing.

Ganin, who has a shadowy political past, has no doubts; he believes his love has endured and that Mary will flee with him. Meanwhile Alfyorov is intent on securing Ganin's soon-to-be-vacated room for Mary of whose past he appears to know little.

Nabokov, an elegant maverick whose artistic manifesto championed the visual possibilities of prose, cleverly succeeds in making Ganin highly attractive and sympathetic through his efforts to help Podtyagin the old poet with his visa problems.

All the while in the background is Klara, who although she has mistakenly interpreted Ganin's reasons for being in Alfyorov's room, continues to love him. Klara and Ganin have an interesting rapport. It is to her that he confesses: "I must leave. This room, these trains, Erika's cooking – I'm fed up with it all." Memory continues to sustain him; he plots and prepares for a fantasy reunion with his beloved before Nabokov wields his realist's wand. The first signs of Nabokov's subsequent artistry announce themselves in this emotionally fraught, yet poised debut.

Vladimir Nabokov *(1899-1977)*

Vladimir Nabokov elegantly bridged several worlds; that of the aristocratic old Russia into which he was born in 1899, the European émigré cultural exodus he joined, and the new America whose innocence and naivety he noted and was able to channel.

As the child of privileged parents Nabokov was taught English and French. He did not write in English until he was forty. By then, he was already well established as a leading Russian émigré author of poetry, plays and novels, including *Laughter in the Dark* (1933) and had translated *Alice's Adventures in Wonderland* into Russian, and *Eugene Onegin* into English. On moving to the US in 1940 he began an academic career which would culminate in eleven years as professor of Russian literature at Cornell. He would also emerge as an international literary critic.

When he was forty-two he had a poem published in *The New Yorker*. That same year, 1941, his first novel written in English, *The Real Life of Sebastian Knight*, appeared and confirmed that Nabokov would be a dominant international literary force in his second language. His fiction is daring, stylistically adroit and linguistically rich; his criticism is astute and insightful. It was Nabokov who insisted writers and readers attend to both the complexities and resources of language.

Often criticised for being overly intellectual, too clever and addicted to trickery, it is wrong to suggest he fails to explore emotion; Nabokov does, and frequently at its most chaotically ambiguous. *Mary* (1926), is a rare work, a beautiful, traditional account of lost love recalled with equal measures of nostalgia and regret by an exasperated central character.

Nabokov's legacy is dominated by his most famous and most mis-read novel, *Lolita* (1955). Although considered by some to be a crazed sexual odyssey, it is in fact a celebration of art, style and cold wisdom. Admittedly, any discussion of love in relation to Humbert Humbert's obsession with Dolores Haze is heavy with issues of morality, yet art does transcend moral judgment. It could be argued that Nabokov, in common with his most obvious literary heir, John Updike, has always suffered censure because of the explicit content of his work.

It is too easy to dismiss *Lolita* as an erotic, comic romp. Far from being a conventional love story – despite Humbert's declaring "I loved you. I was a pentapod monster, but I loved you" – it is an ambiguous, multi-layered, repulsively beautiful and beautifully repulsive lament for innocence lost. As Humbert recalls of their journeys: "We had been everywhere. We had really seen nothing." Near the novel's close Humbert realises that were tough-talking little Lolita – whom he has reduced to a performing animal – capable of lucid thought she would probably be able to figure out, as he does, that whereas the playwright Clare Quilty broke her heart, he, Humbert, merely broke her life.

Lolita belongs to Nabokov's American trio, which includes the comic masterpiece *Pnin* (1957), dominated by its likeable title character. Humbert, for all his preoccupation with beauty, is really only concerned with surfaces, while Pnin is far more sympathetic. There had been a time when he had fretted over the exhausted students slumped over their books "fast asleep among the ruins of knowledge." He loses his college job, yet retains his dignity.

The third of that group is *Pale Fire* (1962). Half-poem, half-prose narrative, *Pale Fire* consolidates the resilience of the novel form, locating it in the realm of intellectual game crossed with detective story. The splendour of its language releases a series of fabulous images admittedly directed at the intellect, not the emotions. That conceded, it is a wonderful performance. Between these three novels, the entire bewitching Nabokovian repertoire is on display.

After fifteen years in the US and having played a significant role in the re-invention of the American novel, Nabokov returned to Europe and settled in Switzerland. There he wrote *Despair* (1965), a marvellous work and one with a powerful sense of the Russian masters, particularly Bulgakov, who had inspired him. Few writers have offered a better explanation of the world and sensibility which shaped them than Nabokov does in his memoir, *Speak, Memory*, which was published in 1967.

Playboy, tennis player, chess master, international authority on butterflies and artist, Vladimir Nabokov, with his fascination with perversion and perfection, theory and story, brings humour and humanity as well as cerebral game-play to inventive, daring fiction that both seduces and lingers in the imagination.

37 | The Tin Drum
(1959)
by Günter Grass

Sanctuary, at least for some people, may best be found in an insane asylum. From his white-enamelled metal hospital bed, under the watchful, if bewildered eye of his nurse Bruno, Oskar Matzerath sets out with the help of a family photograph album to tell his story and that of his country. Oskar, very much his own man despite his chosen lack of growth, elects to move between the first-person and third-person voice. Drumming is his way of detaching from his family and the events unfolding around him. He pulverises each new drum, replacements lasting mere days; such is the frenzy of the story unfolding; such is the reality he is intent on escaping.

So when he says in the opening pages of this angry, swaggering and earthy tour de force: "I'd like to have the bed rails raised even higher to keep anyone from coming too close," it is not that unexpected. Here is a postwar novel born of that war's legacy. *The Tin Drum* broke all the rules and invented a few more. The polemic is there but considering the boisterousness of the narrative, you often have to look for it. But not always; Oskar and his father stand outside the burning synagogue: ". . . civilians and men in uniforms were piling up books, sacral objects, and strange pieces of cloth."

When the young Grass began writing his flamboyant picaresque in Paris in the late 1950s he was a mason turned sculptor, visual artist and poet, intent on confronting the various versions of German history he had been taught, and had, by then, lived. *The Tin Drum* -combines history, horror story, burlesque cartoon and satiric fable with vibrant, subversive imagery. Stylistically it is light years removed from the stately narratives of the mandarin Thomas Mann.

Throughout the novel Grass appears to be looking more towards the freewheeling, organic word pictures shaping Cuban Alejo Carpentier's magic realism.

Oskar's odyssey began when he "falls" down the cellar stairs on his third birthday, determined not to grow and instead commence his career as a relentless drummer who "sangshattered" glass. This much is true. But his story began some years earlier, before he was born. In fact its roots are in the attempted conception of his mother. Cue to a Monday afternoon and his grandmother Anna, busy gathering potatoes in a Kashubian field. She stops to bake a few to eat and builds a small fire. After a while she decides to taste one: "and inhaling smoke and October air, stared with rounded eyes over her flaring nostrils across the field to the nearby horizon with its grid of telegraph poles and the top third of the bricks work factory."

Anna watches as a chase unfolds. She hides the quarry beneath her many skirts, four to be precise, and sets the police in the wrong direction. Though not exactly a love story, the fugitive, Joseph Koljaiczek, hiding under the skirts, in time becomes the father of Oskar's mother, Agnes. But Oskar with his storyteller's flair, makes the facts dance: "Anna Bronski, my grandmother, changed her name under cover of that very night's darkness, transformed herself, with the help of a priest who was generous with the sacraments, into Anna Koljaiczek, and followed Joseph, if not into Egypt, at least to the provincial capital on the Mottlau, where Joseph found work as a craftsman and temporary respite from the rural police." The city at the mouth of the Mottlau is of course, none other than Danzig. Oskar and Grass play games throughout; neither can ever resist a digression most of which are significant. Stories are told. Characters wander in and out. Sometimes they die, sometimes they don't.

Koljaiczek as a known arsonist is forced to assume the identity of a dead man. Even so, it is not enough and facing exposure he flees, most probably to his death by drowning, or possibly, and very unlikely, to a new life in America. "Called himself Joe Colchic, they say. In the timber trade with Canada."

The narrative races along, it is exuberant and confident, and in

2009, at the time of writing, the fiftieth anniversary of the publication of *The Tin Drum* has been celebrated with a new translation, one that conveys the sheer physicality of Grass's German with its rolling phrases, asides, an inventively rhythmic use of repetition, fairytale motifs and a wealth of linguistic jokes. Admirers of the novel will love Breon Mitchell's lively and faithful new translation, which has been supervised by Grass and is true to the whacky and the practical, which are hallmarks of Grass's comic vision.

Although generous with the details of all that went before him Oskar makes no apology about his particular interest in his story: "Since I'm burning to announce the beginning of my own existence . . ." He drums on. His story quickly becomes complicated as his mother marries the grocer Alfred Matzerath, but resumes her romance with her cousin Jan, leaving Oskar with two fathers. Jan is the romantic, but Alfred can cook. Oskar is a laconic narrator, with an eye for detail: "I first saw the light of this world in the form of two sixty-watt light blubs."

Returning to *The Tin Drum* confirms its influence over Salman Rushdie's 1981 Booker Prize-winning *Midnight's Children*. In Oskar, Grass has a witness whose story begins in childhood. As a baby he was already advanced. "I was one of those clairaudient infants whose mental development is complete at birth and there after simply confirmed." He could hear his mother softening her disappointment in his not being "a little lass" with a remark which would prove ironic: "When little Oskar is three years old, we'll give him a tin drum."

Come the birthday Oskar is taken with his image. "There, I have it now, my drum. There it hangs, brand-new, zigzagged white and red, on my tummy. There I am, self-assured, my face solemn and resolute, my drumsticks crossed upon the tin. There I am in my striped sweater . . . There my hair stands, like a brush ready for action atop my head, there, mirrored in each blue eye, a will to power that needs no followers. There I am back then, in a stance I found no reason to abandon . . . There and then I decided, there I declared, there I decreed, that I would never be a politician and most certainly not a grocer, that I would make a point instead of remaining as I was – and so I did, remained that size, kept that attire, for years to come."

Young Oskar is a defiant individual open to adventure, particularly sexual escapades. The comic often turns to horror as when an outing to buy fish includes the revolting spectacle of a submerged horse's head alive with eels being hauled up from the Baltic. Soon after this Oskar's comely mother dies, and becomes "poor mama" thereafter. Her death is the first of many. In a novel that never becomes sentimental Grass achieves moments of unexpected beauty. "Mama could be very cheerful. Mama could be very timid. Mama forgot things quickly. Mama nonetheless had a good memory. Mama threw me out with the bathwater yet sat in the tub with me. When I sangshattered glass, Mama sold lots of putty . . . When Mama died, the red flames on my drum turned pale . . ."

Throughout the novel Oskar engages in fairly graphic sex with a number of women. He sets off on a tour with Bebra's circus troupe and watches as Roswitha, his beloved, dies, killed by a stray shell in crossfire – and all because he declined to fetch her morning coffee. He also sees off of his fathers. Scores must be settled; Matzerath marries Oskar's Maria and the narrator sits in fury as his father assumes that baby son Kurt is his own. Oskar is soon being bullied by that boy. Hit by a stone at the grocer's funeral, Oskar has a growth spurt. More twists and turns. He sits for artists, becomes a jazz musician, finds fame. But always he is seeking something; love? security? answers?

Danzig caught between Germany and Poland is Oskar's tragic playground. The story is dense, a rollercoaster; Oskar is both monster and tragic hero. Above all he is a witness, angry and despairing. Near the close of the novel Oskar says: "I've run out of words now, but still have to think over what Oskar's going to do after his inevitable discharge from the mental institution. Marry? Stay single? Emigrate? Model? Buy a stone quarry? Gather disciples? Found a sect?" If there has to be the single greatest novel of the twentieth century, perhaps this raucously mercurial debut is it.

Günter Grass (1927-)

How to define Gunter Grass? All things to all men; novelist, visual artist, witness, 1999 Nobel Literature Laureate, commentator, polemicist, world traveller, poet, a tireless chronicler of Germany's clouded past and custodian of an uneasy present. At least, of the last mentioned role, he was until 2007 when he belatedly detailed his wartime membership of the Waffen SS, prior to the publication of his autobiography, *Peeling the Onion*.

Even if his wartime experience has tarnished his credibility as a moral conscience, there is no disputing Grass's contribution to our understanding of an impossible episode in human history. His war has always informed his darkly exuberant, experimental fiction. As a boy he had read Remarque's *All Quiet on the Western Front* (1929) and admits that as a fifteen-year-old bored teenager, he had seen war as exciting. In *Peeling the Onion* he writes, "I kept silent." He presents himself as neither a hero nor a victim. "As a member of the Hitler Youth I was, in fact, a Young Nazi. A believer till the end. Not what one would call fanatical, not leading the pack, but with my eye, as if by reflex, fixed on the flag that was to mean 'more than death' to us. I kept pace in the rank and file . . . I saw my fatherland threatened, surrounded by enemies."

In common with Oskar in *The Tin Drum*, Grass was a grocer's son. His sense of culture was complicated from birth. Born in Danzig, now Gdansk, he has always claimed that he lost his homeland at seventeen. His daring, colourful fiction is a search for it. His mother came from Kashuban stock; a member of a minority who at any particular time could be judged insufficiently German, insufficiently Polish. Her father and two of her brothers had died in the Great War; a third brother had perished during the global influenza epidemic of 1918. She ran the family shop and Grass at the age of eleven displayed a flair for collecting debts.

School did not excite him, but books did. His mother noticed this interest and encouraged it. He went to train as a stone mason and it led him to sculpture. His painting tended towards bold images in the style of Picasso and Max Ernst. Similar imagery would emerge in his writing, as did a consistent use of animals as powerful motifs: dogs, cats, snails and rats; to symbolise death and decay he summoned the toad. He is a fabulist who draws on the European fairytale at its blackest and often most comic, but for all the imaginative panache, the whimsy and the gags, he is remorselessly practical and political.

The Tin Drum made him internationally famous. The reaction in Germany to a burlesque exposé of the years spanning 1925-1955 was less enthusiastic. Oskar with the body of a child, the desires of a man and a nasty streak, shocked and repelled. Yet he was the equal to the society that had produced him. Grass followed his great big book, with a great small one, *Cat and Mouse* (1961), the second instalment of what would become the 'Danzig' trilogy, while the third volume, *Dog Years*, went further back in history to the Germany of 1917. Three narrators take up the story of a country racing towards disaster.

For his fiftieth birthday present to himself, Grass wrote *The Flounder* (1978). Taking as its theme mankind's communal stupidity, it is a study of feminism filtered through a 4,000-year survey of cooks. *The Rat* (1986) is an environmentalist polemic, while *The Call of the Toad* (1992) is the closest in style of all Grass's work to fellow German Nobel Literature Laureate, Henrich Böll (1917-1985). For once, Grass's characteristic comic flourishes are absent; *The Call of the Toad* takes an evocative and convincing look at post-1989 Europe in the form of a love story. Then there was his majestic post-unification Berlin picaresque, *Too Far Afield* (1995), in which two old men wander the streets of Berlin watching and remembering.

In 1999, the year in which he was finally, and so deservedly, honoured with the Nobel Prize, Grass published *My Century*, a sequence of one hundred stories, one for every year of the battered twentieth century, in which he told the story of his country and his relation to it. In ways, it is a salute to Germany.

His love of his country would also shape *Crabwalk* (2002). No doubt taking his cue from the great W. G. Sebald, Grass acknowledges the long-denied German war grief in what is a remarkable performance. Adopting a deceptively conversational

219

tone, *Crabwalk* is a dignified memorial which tells the true story of the Wilhelm Gustloff, a peacetime cruiser called into service to transport more than nine thousand civilian refugees and a thousand recruits. It was torpedoed on the night of 30 January 1945, losing all but a few hundred survivors. Grass maintained that the forgotten episode had had to wait more than sixty years to be recognised as a human tragedy because the victims were German.

A storyteller possessed of imagination and comic panache, Günter Grass is an original, as much a man of the Baltic as he is of Germany. For all his innovative fiction, his autobiography, *Peeling the Onion*, is as bluntly practical as Arthur Miller's *Timebends* (1987). Direct, gruff, ironic and matter of fact, it is a bit like the man himself, a realist with a long memory and his own ghosts to battle.

Nausea

(1938)

by Jean-Paul Sartre

A man sits in a café, watching a fly as it warms itself in the sunlight. The man, Antoine Roquentin, the narrator, who is preoccupied by writing a history book he has lost interest in, announces, of the fly: "I am going to do it the favour of squashing it." His companion, the Autodidact, a tormented older man, objects. But the matter has been decided: "I have relieved it of its existence." The fly's problems may be over; but Roquentin's are far from securing resolution. "Why am I here? – And why shouldn't I be here?" he ponders. "It is midday, I am waiting for it to be time to sleep . . . In four days I shall see Anny again: for the moment, that is my only reason for living."

This laconic, fluidly written debut is a study in alienation; it is also a statement of intent, and quite a comedy. Here Sartre offers an engaging introduction to his defining theory of existentialism. Roquentin is self-absorbed, depressed yet sympathetic; his relentless questioning of existence is above all supremely logical, even familiar.

Returning to *Nausea* – one of those seminal works first encountered as a school-going reader attempting to experience "serious" literature – is a revelation; it is even better on a second or third reading. Sartre's reputation has become so bound up with his philosophical theories and political causes, his famous ego, rampaging sexuality and the saga of his highly public private life, that it is unfortunately all too easy to forget the grace, playfulness and punchy wit which sustain *Nausea*.

Having travelled widely, the narrator, now a reluctant historian, has made a base in Bouville, a French provincial town. He spends his days drifting between the reading room in the library and the local café, all the while forcing himself to read Eugénie Grandet. He has begun to feel aware of a disturbing sensation, an unease he dubs La Nausée – the Nausea. He believes he should write it all down: "The odd thing is that I am not at all prepared to consider myself insane, and indeed I can see quite clearly that I am not: all these changes concern objects."

Within minutes this confidence has been undermined. In his first formal diary entry he concedes that being a historian is no preparation for psychological analysis. His elevated consciousness begins to respond to everything; he subjects the notion of being to relentless scrutiny. "Just now, when I was on the point of coming into my room, I stopped short because I felt in my hand a cold object which attracted my attention by means of a sort of personality. I opened my hand and looked: I was simply holding the doorknob."

Sartre conveys a suggestion of mild exasperation threatening Roquentin's efforts to maintain a balance between his thoughts and his fears. A measure of comfort may be gleaned from watching others. "I am alone in the midst of these happy, reasonable voices," he notes while sitting in the café. "All these characters spend their time explaining themselves, and happily recognising that they hold the same opinions." The dozy small town and its cast of colourful characters provide a vivid backdrop as the narrator observes, deliberates upon minutiae, remembers, experiences and attempts to define his freewheeling sensations.

Listening in the café to a recording of a jazz tune sung by a black girl has become a personal ritual for him. Late in the narrative, after meeting his former girlfriend, the somewhat altered Anny, in Paris, Roquentin returns briefly to Bouville and visits the café. The waitress offers to play the record. As he listens, Roquentin thinks of the American who wrote it, and imagines the man suffocating in the New York heat: "He is sitting in shirt-sleeves at his piano: he has a taste of smoke in his mouth and, vaguely, a ghost of a tune in his head."

In *Nausea*, Sartre the philosopher as novelist considers and explores the essence of existence and is doing so makes the reader think that bit more clearly, more deeply.

Jean-Paul Sartre *(1905-1980)*

More than fifty thousand people followed his coffin through the streets of Paris. Even more watched his funeral on television. His name and face were known to people who had never read his work. Jean-Paul Sartre was a great champion of causes and a believer in freedom. He was an intellectual, a career philosopher. If his story has become dominated in the public perception by his unorthodox "essential" love-without-commitment soap opera with fellow French thinker and writer Simone de Beauvoir, there is far more to him and to them than the casual sexual freedom which caused her untold grief. She was his devoted carer and they maintained a friendship that involved travelling together and working in different rooms, like schoolchildren doing their homework.

Most of his writing consisted of political journalism, opinion pieces and his philosophy, dominated by his opus, *Being and Nothingness* (1943). Yet he was never regarded as a journalist. He was a Marxist who had been in the Resistance. A complex mythology surrounds this unworldly, ugly, little man forever dressed in black polo necks who is acknowledged as the founding father of French existentialism. It is easy to forget that he was an ordinary schoolteacher until he was almost forty. He had his views on the Spanish Civil War and also on Algeria, Korea and Vietnam. Whereas Albert Camus died young and glamorous in a car accident, Sartre lived on, becoming a grumpy old man in slippers, more often than not accompanied by an equally depressed-looking de Beauvoir.

Sartre was always working; writing, editing, protesting, talking – yet he left a vast amount of unfinished projects behind him. His plays, even his finest, *Huis-Clos* (1945), never achieved the impact of Beckett's. Somehow in the midst of all the debating, all the philosophy and the messy affairs, Sartre the philosopher wrote one of the great novels of the twentieth century, *La Nausée* (*Nausea*, 1938). Narrated by the disgruntled anti-hero Roquentin it remains one of the set texts of youth, a novel so enjoyed that many readers are reluctant to re-read it. Rest assured, take the risk; all the humour, grace, intelligence and lightness of touch are there to be enjoyed again and again. Not only does it testify to Sartre's gifts it also celebrates his wit.

His autobiography, *Words* (1964), in which he recalls his adventures as the adored child of a young widow living with her parents, is delightful and often funny. It was published in the same year Sartre refused the Nobel Prize. This most conversational of autobiographies leaves one feeling Sartre is speaking directly to the reader.

As a child he had had long blonde curls. He suspected that his mother "would, I think, have liked me to be a real girl." Anyhow, his pragmatic grandfather left no doubts about his dislike of the curls. When Sartre was seven years old, the old man announced he was taking the boy out for a walk. "But no sooner had we turned the corner of the road than he thrust me into the hairdresser's saying: 'we'll give your mother a surprise.' I adored surprises. They were always happening at home . . . In short, melodrama was my staple diet and I watched with equanimity as my curls slid down the white towel round my neck and dropped to the floor, inexplicably dull: I went home proud and shorn."

Sartre's grandfather who was enamoured of the bookish child marched home in triumph; Sartre describes the homecoming: "There were exclamations but no hugs and kisses, and my mother shut herself up in her bedroom to weep; her little girl had been changed into a little boy. There was worse to come; while my pretty curls waved around my ears, she had been able to deny the existence of my ugliness . . . Even my grandfather seemed quite taken aback: he had gone out with his wonder child and had brought home a toad."

Considering his war experiences it is worth looking at Sartre's unfinished war cycle, *The Road to Freedom*; *L'age de raison* (*The Age of Reason*) (1945), *Le Sursis* (*The Reprieve*) (also 1945) and *La Mort dans l'ame* (1949) (translated as "Iron" not "Death" in the Soul, much to Sartre's irritation), in which a plausible hero, Mathieu, based on Sartre, confronts various moral dilemmas during wartime. The documentary style has echoes of Zola and of the American writer, John Dos Passos (1896-1970). Vital to an understanding of the narrative is Sartre's response to the compromises and betrayals of Vichy, as well as the wider developments on the international political stage.

A storyteller yes, a commentator and philosopher, yes; but ultimately Sartre was a witness.

39 | Wide Sargasso Sea
(1966)
by Jean Rhys

A fatalistic young woman spends her life hovering on the fringes of madness; initially as prime witness to her mother's and then when experiencing her own. Bred for tragedy in the oppressively lush setting of the West Indies, Antoinette, one of two narrators, recalls watching her restless young mother, Annette, rebel against a married life that is cruel and unforgiving. It began badly. Her father had married a second wife, her mother, a Martinique Creole beauty who, as a white West Indian, was considered an outsider. The narrator recalls her mother going riding each morning, indifferent to the resentful glances of the local blacks. But one morning her mother's horse was discovered dead, poisoned. Mother and daughter inhabit a slowly decaying house, once part of a fine estate but neglected now the slaves are gone.

Set in 1830, this daring, and daringly incomplete novel of thematic echoes takes as its central character one of literature's enduring enigmas; the mad wife kept locked in an attic by Mr Rochester in Charlotte Brontë's classic: *Jane Eyre* (1847). Rhys pushes the facts of Brontë's competent narrative to a higher art. Who was the woman in the attic? What really happened? She explores the mystery without attempting easy answers. It is a remarkable feat of imagination; the prose is lyric, hypnotic and intense. The dream-like nightmare mood sustains the prevailing contradictions, while the dialogue despatches truths, possibly half-truths, like so many darts.

The narrative festers with deep hatreds created by race, desire, sexual need and the dark messes often part of family histories. Destruction of self, of family, of community is its theme.

Antoinette, initially as a rejected child, establishes herself as the narrator we want to believe. She feels for Annette, her doomed mother, tracing her decline from the illness of her little brother, Pierre: "I don't know what the doctor told her or what she said to him but he never came again and after that she changed." Her mother disengages: "A frown came between her black eyebrows, deep – it might have been cut with a knife. I hated this frown and once I touched her forehead trying to smooth it. But she pushed me away, not roughly but calmly, coldly, without a word, as if she had decided once and for all that I was useless to her . . . and after I knew that she talked aloud to herself I was a little afraid of her."

The watchful family servant Christophine who knows everything, including black magic, remains influential even after she moves away. Annette, Antoinette's mother, marries Mr Mason. Evil prevails, the locals hate the family. Pierre's crib is set on fire. Annette turns on Mason and blames him for ignoring the dangers surrounding them. Antoinette describes watching the family parrot burst into flames. ". . . I heard someone say something about bad luck and remembered that it was very unlucky to kill a parrot, or even to see a parrot die." Ill fortune seeps through the narrative like blood. Her mother drifts further into madness while Antoinette enjoys temporary sanctuary in a convent school.

Time passes. Mr Rochester, another damaged child, takes up the story and marries Antoinette, only to allow gossip turn him against her. Rhys constantly shifts the focus. The hardened Rochester is far from idealised; he hates his lunatic wife but intends to keep her – her money has freed him of his unloving father. Antoinette emerges as the most appealing variation of the familiar Rhys woman, half-dead, desperate for love, passive, despairing, exploited, rejected and destroyed. In the closing section the action moves from Jamaica to England, to Thornfield Hall, where Grace Poole proves a tormented gaoler – and is obviously more insane than her prisoner. Antoinette, now Bertha Rochester, acknowledges her fate and seeks her destiny in the flames.

Wide Sargasso Sea ended a lengthy creative silence for Jean Rhys, who as a writer marginalised by being years ahead of her time, had been virtually forgotten. She resurfaced, approaching seventy-six, with this her fifth and final novel, an unforgettable, terrifyingly assured work, the one that finally balanced her personal and artistic obsessions.

Jean Rhys (1890-1979)

Personal and sexual humiliations drive the fiction of Jean Rhys, one of international literature's enduring prose stylists. Her subject was women who exist instead of living; her anti-heroines are victims dragging themselves from one miserable affair to the next. They drink heavily, weep and inhabit squalid hotel rooms. Their defiance is always short-lived, yet they survive. Rhys was an outsider and misfit; writing for her was both an agony and a lifeline. She created her own hell, imposing her horrors on all who associated with her, particularly anyone who tried to help.

Three failed marriages, a dead infant son, chronic drinking, a daughter who was passed from person to person, a history of violent behaviour and an inability to deal with people fuelled her paranoia. In spite of everything, she reached the age of eighty-eight, dying only three months short of her eighty-ninth birthday. Her five controlled and elegantly crafted novels record the bleakness of her life. True to the malicious irony which she was convinced pursued her, she only became famous in old age, long after her beauty, the one sustaining fact of her life – aside from her literary gift – had deserted her.

Ella Gwendoline Rees Williams was born on the island colony of Dominica in 1890 to a Welsh-Irish-Scottish colonial family headed by her doctor father, a moody rebel at war with himself. Her childhood memories of Dominica would later feature in *Voyage in the Dark* (1934) and her masterpiece, *Wide Sargasso Sea* (1966), which astonished critics, who also expressed surprise that she was still alive.

Rhys spent her first seventeen years on the island before travelling to England, which her extensive reading of English fiction had transformed into a romanticised dream country. She was quickly disappointed. Her shyness was interpreted as rudeness and her singsong accent was often mocked as an affectation. Although her father had at one time thought she was destined for a career in music, the nearest she came to that ambition was joining a chorus line at nineteen.

Lancelot Grey Hugh Smith – her first great love – was twice her age when she met him in 1911. As her biographer Carol Angier writes in a meticulously researched 1991 study: "He loved her. Briefly, reluctantly, confusedly, but he did." Passionate, intense, transitory love was the story of her life. Her first marriage took her to Vienna, and on to Paris, where she lived for many years.

There she wrote *The Left Bank* (1927), *Postures* (1928) – which became better known as *Quartet – After Leaving Mr Mackenzie* (1930), *Voyage in the Dark* and *Good Morning, Midnight* (1939). When she left Paris, she lived in obscurity in England; no wonder the critics had assumed she was dead.

It is difficult to understand her excesses; her anger, her tendency to physically attack people and invariably blame everyone else for her problems. However appalling the humiliation, she remorselessly turned it all into fiction. But if she seems a woman destined for unhappiness, it is fair to presume that her destructive relationship in Paris with the British writer Ford Madox Ford (1873-1939), who, in turn, involved her in his own cynical marriage, had marked her for life.

Her story is one of rage and bitterness. Rhys, the artist as monster, was narcissistic and paranoid, seductive, unforgiving, suspicious and profoundly unhappy. She was also possessed of, and apparently *by*, her dark, terrifying genius.

40 | Ethan Frome
(1911)
by Edith Wharton

Did fate ever treat an individual more cruelly than it battered Ethan Frome? Tormented by obligation and duty which combine to trap him in one hell, passion eventually places him in a second, even more unforgiving one. This is a tale guaranteed to unsettle; it is also Edith Wharton's finest achievement. All too often regarded, not entirely unfairly, as an acolyte of Henry James, Wharton, a satirical observer of the upper-class New York society into which she was born, set her heartbreaking novella in the bleak farming landscape of rural Massachusetts.

The grim fatalistic tone of the narrative surpasses the irony of another of Wharton's major works, *The Age of Innocence* (1920), in which love is destroyed by the kind of people "who dreaded scandal more than disease, who placed decency above courage."

The hard-working Frome is not without courage. When the narrator first arrived as an outsider in the small town of Starkfield, he noticed Ethan Frome. ". . . the sight pulled me up sharp. Even then he was the most striking figure in Starkfield, though he was but the ruin of a man." It was not merely his great height, "it was the careless powerful look he had, in spite of a lameness checking each step like the jerk of a chain." Bit by bit the narrator pieces together Frome's story, with information supplied by chatty townsfolk, outlining the appalling legacy of an accident which happened some twenty-four years earlier.

The narrative device of a visitor becoming privy to events occurring years earlier and which have since become part of local history has echoes of Brontë's *Wuthering Heights* (1847). Wharton weighs every word and draws her characters with precision. The narrator's curiosity sets the scene and establishes some sense of the small rural community in which an inhumanly harsh drama has been played out.

When the town's horses fall prey to an epidemic, the only unaffected animal is Frome's old bay. The narrator's urgent need of transport brings him to Frome. Foul weather causes him to invite the narrator to stay the night. Then Wharton allows the drama to unfold through a vivid flashback to Frome's youth as imagined by the narrator.

Wharton the city writer reveals the eye of a poet when she describes the winter landscape the eager young Ethan Frome strides across: "The night was perfectly still, and the air so dry and pure that it gave little sensation of cold. The effect produced on Frome was rather of a complete absence of atmosphere, as though nothing less tenuous than ether intervened between the white earth under his feet and the metallic dome overhead."

Within sentences Frome emerges as having something in common with the eponymous hero of Hardy's *Jude the Obscure* (1895); Frome had been at college but his father's death had put an end to his studies. His mother's illness had brought his cousin Zeena into the household to care for her. Ethan Frome thanked his cousin, some years his senior, for her devotion by marrying her. The young Ethan Frome walking through the snow has a lightness of heart; he is on his way to collect his wife's cousin, a charming girl, Mattie Silver, from a dance. Their mutual fondness is obvious.

Wharton incisively balances the contrast between this tenderness and the misery of Frome's marriage. Zeena has decided she is ailing from a number of illnesses. Obsessed with her health and various imagined threats to it, she rules the household with a snide viciousness. Her overnight absence caused by a visit to yet another doctor alerts Frome, now alone with Mattie, to the possibility of a very different life.

Anticipation underlies each casual exchange, each gesture. The sexual tension is palpable, as is Frome's romantic sense of decency.

All expectations falter with the sudden return of Zeena. The characterisation of the vindictive wife is a triumph for Wharton. Zeena's new plans make Frome, caught between passion and honour, determined to act. When he responds to Mattie's despairing plea for a final and dangerous moment of happiness, the outcome is catastrophic, laced with a chilling irony only too true to life.

Although invariably overshadowed by *The House of Mirth* (1905) and her Pulitzer Prize-winner, *The Age of Innocence*, *Ethan Frome*, sentence by sentence, image by image, is Wharton's most moving story.

Edith Wharton *(1862-1937)*

Born into a wealthy New York family, Edith Wharton was the daughter of a man who had never needed to work. Her literary ambitions surfaced while she was still a child and although her mother openly disapproved, she kept Edith's adolescent poems and had them published privately. Wharton always loved storytelling and grew into a sociable girl who adored dancing.

At twenty-three she married Edward 'Teddy' Robbins Wharton, a Boston socialite and friend of one of her brothers. The couple moved to Rhode Island and appeared set to continue a life similar to that she had always known. They often travelled to Europe, already familiar to Wharton having visited many times as a child. She first met Henry James (1843-1916) while in London. Her marriage to a spendthrift who proved inept at handing her money quickly became strained. Wharton suffered a nervous breakdown and then sought comfort in writing. Her first novel, *The Valley of Decisions*, was a lengthy historical romance set in eighteenth century Italy. It was published in 1902 when she was forty. She had by then written many short stories. James read *The Valley of Decision* but suggested she write about New York.

It was good advice; Wharton the writer came of age with *The House of Mirth* (1905). In it, she follows the career of Lily Bart, beautiful, witty and at twenty-nine unmarried. Although accepted by old money society, she has none of her own. Her parents are dead.

Suddenly, after years of rejecting suitors, she becomes aware of being in need of a rich husband. Although Wharton was married and middle-aged at the time she wrote it, *The House of Mirth* partly reflects her own life as well as the contempt she had for the society which had produced and sustained her. There was also the irony that it confirmed the adage: write about what you know. Wharton certainly knew Lily's world.

The influence of Henry James is clear; if one novel presides over *The House of Mirth*, it is *The Portrait of a Lady* (1881). By acting against convention on accepting an invitation in a single man's apartment, Lily risks exposure. She has many minor failings yet she also has commendable moral doubts. She wants to live nobly and makes the mistake of seeing goodness in the self-satisfied Lawrence Selden. The novel's power rests in the doomed Lily. *The House of Mirth* shocked New York society it also became a bestseller.

Wharton and her husband acquired a base in Paris. In 1908 she began a passionate affair with an American journalist living there. She separated from Teddy in 1911, the year *Ethan Frome* was published. Her least characteristic if most striking work with its rural setting and characters who are working people, it is a remarkable book of which she was justifiably proud. It is strange to think of her researching the landscape which she would evoke so well from the backseat of her chauffer-driven car.

Divorcing in 1913, Wharton spent the war years helping refuges and orphans. Her writing was supplanted by fundraising. She was becoming increasingly settled in France. *The Age of Innocence*, in which New York lawyer Newland Archer, destined for a conventional marriage, falls in love with Ellen Olenska, the estranged wife of a Polish count, but chillingly bows to society, was published in 1920 and won the Pulitzer Prize. The first woman to receive an honorary doctorate of letters from Yale, she died in France, aged seventy-five and is buried at Versailles.

An American scholar, Marion Mainwaring, using an eighty-nine-thousand-word manuscript and a detailed outline of the plot left by Wharton, edited, and completed a final novel, *The Buccaneers*, a social

41

Eugene Onegin
(1833)
by Alexander Pushkin

Consider the bored dandy, wayward, idle with little to do but strut his indolence:

"He dined, he danced, he fenced, he rode. / In French he could converse politely /

As well as write; and how he bowed! In the mazurka, 'twas allowed, / No partner ever was so sprightly." Wealth comes his way in the form of his uncle's country estate. So Eugene Onegin abandons St Petersburg society and heads for the provinces to sample the life of a country squire. Once settled there, a chance meeting brought about through his friendship with an idealistic romantic leads him to an offer of love, the declining of which will teach him a painful lesson.

There is nothing in literature to equal Pushkin's daringly sophisticated verse novel. Crafted with a technical brilliance and pace surpassing even that of Augustan satirist Alexander Pope, *Eugene Onegin* is as intense a study of a young woman's passion as it is a portrait of nineteenth century Russian life.

Composed and circulated in sections between 1823 and 1831 before being published in a complete edition in 1833, it is the major achievement of Pushkin's brief yet monumentally influential career during which he wrote many poems including 'The Bronze Horseman' (1833) and several perfect short stories. Often referred to as the "Russian Byron", Pushkin is the superior artist. It was he who gave his country its unique literary voice, one that balanced an evolving society heavily influenced by Western culture, particularly French and German, with Russia's rich folkloric tradition.

If the Russian novel has a specific birth, it is with the defining publication of *Eugene Onegin*. For all its clever observations, Pushkin's masterpiece is not a social satire; it is a subtle romantic tragedy with a bitter sting.

Onegin the socialite discovers the countryside to be eerily quiet. Soon in need of companionship, he finds it on meeting another newly established landowner; Vladimir Lensky, who, having been educated in Germany, is an avowed Kantian and an aspiring poet. He and Onegin strike up a friendship. Young Lensky is in love with Olga, a lively gentlewoman and, as he confides to Onegin, he has worshiped her since she was a child. Olga, who lives with her widowed mother, has an elder sister Tatyana, who "dearly loved romancing / Upon her balcony alone." Although it is obvious that Lensky and Olga are intended for each other, little notice is taken of the quiet, bookish, dreamy sister. Shaped by reading Richardson and Rousseau, Olga is ready for love. Unfortunately for her, she decides Onegin is her destiny.

In one of the most famous sequences in the novel Tatyana asks her old nurse about love and Nanny, speaking as a member of a social class far removed from the girl's, recalls: "But in my youth no one engaged / In talk of love. It was thought shameless" and describes the marriage-broker's insistence that the matter be settled as a business deal. "And I was just thirteen years old", adds the nurse. The older woman fears Tatyana is ill. But the poor girl merely splutters: "I . . . I'm in love." Her declaration of eternal passion is stated in an artless letter of heartbreaking eloquence sent to the unsuspecting Onegin.

He takes his time responding, each day that passes adds to her longing. Onegin's rejection is sensitive though emphatic, even ponderous; he has no desire to marry a naïve country lass. In order to leave no doubts as to his lack of interest, he flirts with Olga. The outraged Lensky challenges Onegin to a duel. Lensky falls dead, causing a remorseful Onegin to set off on a lengthy journey. Pushkin's graceful intensity of tone conveys the sense of an epic odyssey of self-discovery.

Throughout the story an opinionated, omniscient narrator oversees the characters, suggesting a better course of action for the protagonists. But fate has its own plans. Pushkin involves the reader; to read Eugene Onegin is to imagine being told the sequence of events in a number of breathlessly vivid instalments.

Tatyana sets off for Moscow where she acquires sombre maturity. Destiny eventually brings Onegin to a grand salon gathering. Ironically he falls desperately in love with the gracious hostess – an older, more refined Tatyana. Although still conscious of her old love for Onegin and willing to exchange her new grandeur for her former country life, she vows to remain faithful to her husband. "There Eugene, forsaken / Stood thunderstruck. He could not stir. / By what a storm his heart was shaken / What pride, what grief, what thoughts of her! . . ."

If ever there was a chillingly cautionary account of the destructive power of love, this is it.

Alexander Pushkin *(1799-1837)*

When Alexander Sergeyevich Pushkin died on 29 January 1837 from wounds sustained in a duel of honour two days earlier, Russia mourned the loss of its great poet, dead at thirty-seven. The wayward, impoverished noble, erstwhile expelled minor government employee and political exile remained dangerously touched by the taint of the Decembrists he had supported almost twenty years earlier. The authorities would not dare execute him, he was tolerated. Those same authorities were alarmed by the nation's grief when Pushkin died, as a result of his intemperate handling of a personal situation.

In life he irritated many who knew him, including Tsar Nicholas I and his successor, Alexander II. Pushkin, who had been ignored by his parents, in turn betrayed his friends, distressed women, embarrassed his family, outraged his in-laws and was generally unpopular. Not all of this was directly related to his rakish behaviour and pathological womanising; there were other resentments such as his African heritage which he never disputed. Pushkin's mother was the daughter of a black slave adopted by Peter the Great. Pushkin's short story, *The Moor of Peter the Great*, is based on this exotic ancestor.

Society delighted in the scandal involving Pushkin's beautiful wife, twelve years his junior, and her alleged lover, a French nobleman who was a professional soldier and man-about-town. The baron's blatant pursuit of the poet's wife was barely criticised as everyone was too busy jeering the cocky poet who was also rather ugly. It was all very eerie and appeared to have been foreseen with the death of Lensky the idealistic poet in *Eugene Onegin*.

But if Pushkin the man was disliked Pushkin the poet was loved – and still is. It could only happen in Russia. His is the presiding presence of Andrei Bely's wonderful novel, *Petersburg* (1916). Poet Anna Akhmatova revered him and through translation bought him to a wider audience, while Mikhail Bulgakov craved the master's lightness of touch and consummate knowledge of Russian literature.

At the beginning of the nineteenth century Russian intellectuals became intent on developing a national literary language. This language found its voice in the lyric genius of Pushkin, who had linguistic sophistication – and a close affinity with Russia's rich folkloric tradition. He also read the work of his peers. Pushkin wrote many poems, 'The Bronze Horseman' (1833) the greatest of these – probably the finest in Russian – remains iconic.

Dominating his splendid poetry and stories is *Eugene Onegin*. Whether seen as a long poem or a verse novel, it is a compelling study of a young woman's passion, and is also a vivid portrait of Russia. As compassionate as it is elegant, it is highly moral, preoccupying Russian readers as well as Pushkin during the eight years it appeared in instalments. *Eugene Onegin* proves the redundancy of comparing Pushkin to Byron – there is no contest; the Russian overpowers his English counterpart.

Consternation was expressed some fifty years after Pushkin's death when Tchaikovsky announced plans to base an opera on *Eugene Onegin*. It was felt that a musical version might lessen the profundity of the original. The libretto, based on the second half of Pushkin's narrative, does honour to both composer and poet in

Tchaikovsky's dramatic opera, first staged in 1879.

His own life may have been the stuff of farce, his death unnecessary, yet Pushkin's legacy endures; he gave Russia its literary voice, and in *Eugene Onegin*, a narrative which is exhilarating, wry and tender.

42 | More Die of Heartbreak
(1987)
by Saul Bellow

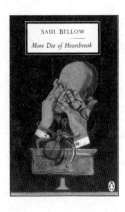

Kenneth, the straight-talking narrator, is worried about his absent-minded, increasingly restless uncle, even more worried than usual. Benn Crader, a botanist of world repute, has since the death of his beloved wife Lena some fifteen years earlier developed a messy addiction to women. Our narrator loves his uncle so intensely that he abandoned his native Paris to live in the drab Midwest, and has settled in Chicago.

Kenneth's father, an aging dandy who adores Paris almost as much as it apparently idolises him, can't understand any of this. But he is not overly bothered; in fact, he couldn't care less. Kenneth, by his own description, tall, goofy and none too handsome, was never the son his father had expected.

Bellow, the 1976 Nobel Literature Laureate, is one of the undisputed masters of twentieth century fiction and he invariably brought the soul of a philosopher, the mind of a street hustler and the timing of a stand-up comic to his punchy, vivid narratives. *More Die of Heartbreak* is a surprisingly little known classic, sustained by some of the sharpest, most exasperated and profound dialogue even Bellow ever concocted: "I haven't got second sight, Ken: all I've got is savvy."

Dominated by talk much of which is conspiratorial and soul-searching, this novel is fast and funny and physical – laugh out loud, and then, sigh some. The narrative revolves on a single theme, a perennial Bellow thesis suggesting that the cleverest people do the dumbest things in relationships. As Benn recalls telling a "newspaperman" who quizzed him about the increasing levels of radiation: "I think more people die of heartbreak." Kenneth has his own problems in the form of a sexually alluring former girlfriend who has his child but openly prefers men who tend towards physical abuse. The cause of Kenneth's desperate concern is Benn's latest romantic escapade, a sudden secret marriage to Matilda, the beautiful, if repellent, thirty-something, only child of the malevolently avaricious Dr Layamon.

Benn has not yet fully recovered from the experience of one lonely woman whose insistence on having sex with him caused her to expire of a heart attack in the middle of it. And then there was his last-minute escape from Caroline Bunge, a flamboyantly crazed millionaire who had had their wedding planned. Loyal, faithful and impressively patient, Kenneth listens and tries to help.

After all, who else but a devoted soul mate could possibly make sense of Benn? Kenneth is a fellow academic, though not a scientist. His field is Russian literature. He left Paris to be closer to his uncle and also to pursue his scholarly interest – Petersburg, 1913.

The conversations are miracles of humour and pathos; Bellow allows his feisty intellect to weave and parry literary references, art, history, politics, science, metaphysics, guilt and the ongoing chaos of sexual relations. The pages crackle with ideas and sensations as the bewildered central characters, Kenneth and Benn, attempt to make sense of life in general and their lives in particular.

Considering their intense closeness, Kenneth is hurt to be informed of Benn's marriage to Matilda only after the wedding. Bellow has created many convincing narrators but Kenneth is special – we share his panic. Benn in fairness is not thoughtless; he is merely terrified of his new wife and her scary parents. His father-in-law is pushing him into reopening a court case against an ancient enemy, a Crader relative, and Benn is nervous to begin excavating family history.

Benn's fears become ever more detailed. During a late-night phone call to Kenneth from the laundry room of his bride's fancy new apartment, the full truth emerges; Benn having reluctantly seen *Psycho* at Matilda's request, now realises she reminds him of the deranged killer in Hitchcock's movie. "I actually removed the phone from me," reflects Kenneth, "and wondered how such a thing could come out of the earpiece."

Written when Bellow was approaching seventy-two, *More Die of Heartbreak* graphically exposes what he refers to as "the post human era." All the linguistic fluency, wit, energy and shrewd understanding of exactly how many banana skins each of us is capable of skidding on lives and breathes in this timeless manic extravaganza of breathtaking range.

Saul Bellow *(1915-2005)*

His father couldn't read but he was proud of his clever son's books, while his mother died young, at fifty, leaving him hurt and angry. Saul Bellow's story is part of North American immigrant history. His parents had arrived in Canada, from Latvia, then part of the old Russian empire, and Bellow was born in Montreal in 1915. His family moved to Chicago when he was nine years old. It was that city, ultimately his personal theatre, which shaped his personality. Sorrow and hurt define his fiction, yet there is also life and humour, Bellow's Jewish humour with all its rich exasperation – and, as the years turned into decades, an increasingly sardonic tone of knowing regret.

His art has energy and a great deal of talking; earthy, metaphysical intelligence and profound simplicity. Early in his long career Bellow the streetwise philosopher identified, as had William Gaddis (1922-1998), the abiding source of US fiction: a dynamic, free-flowing language and diverse national vernacular and with it, believable dialogue. Life's chaos was his theme and to this he added an inherited measure of European angst to narratives which are snappy, conversational and invariably eloquent.

Dangling Man, his debut published in 1944, is a statement of artistic intent; sharp, cryptic, assured and engaged. Joseph awaits his call-up papers; he is in limbo, his life is suspended and no one need look too far for echoes of Dostoyevsky and Kafka. For Bellow, it was the beginning of his lifelong study of alienation as experienced by the eternal outsider – the Jew adrift in an urban landscape, be it New York or Chicago – struggling to become American despite the family ghosts of Eastern Europe. In addition to this search for identity, Bellow's convincingly flawed and human characters, sinners and schemers all – often emerging fully formed through one choice observation – battle the messy business of life.

At the close of one of Bellow's finest achievements, *Seize the Day* (1956), Tommy Wilhelm stands in a chapel at the funeral service of a stranger. He starts to cry. "It must be somebody real close to carry on so", a voice is overheard saying. But Tommy is weeping for himself, as the most human of Bellow's creations invariably do. Asa Leventhal in *The Victim* (1947), Bellow's second novel, is deeply troubled and wholly convincing. Ironically, Augie March, the all-American, all mouth central character of Bellow's baggy picaresque, *The Adventures of Augie March* (1953), is the least typical of his protagonists. While this third novel won the US National Book Award and made him famous, it was the book he shook off as his career and art evolved. For all its energy it now appears rather crude, far less nuanced than everything else Bellow wrote. *The Adventures of Augie March* is dated, whereas *Herzog* (1961), only eight years later, offers a profoundly felt portrait of a middle-aged intellectual in crisis.

Bellow, an artistic mentor to Martin Amis, whose interviews with him are masterclasses in literary journalism, won the Nobel Prize for Literature in 1976 when he was sixty-one. The honour came the year after *Humboldt's Gift*, his most Nabokovian novel and within months of *To Jerusalem and Back*, his non-fiction report of a journey to Israel.

Flash forward thirteen years to the May afternoon when I met him in his office at the University of Chicago, within weeks of his completing two superb novellas, *A Theft* and *The Bellarosa Connection*. The 'B' of Bellow had become unstuck from the door. I would like to say he seemed pleased to see me, but he wasn't. Weary and wary, he held his face in his hands as if to support his neck in the task. He had hooded brown eyes and a loud, hollow laugh, but his mood certainly lifted once he established he preferred having a conversation to being interviewed. His office was spartan; no pictures, no postcards – only books, books on every surface, and a sharp, black fedora hat. Although he never wanted his fiction to appear intellectualised, Bellow could not help being clever – here was an American intellectual capable of despatching the brightest of the Europeans in televised debate, and he did.

Death dominates his short stories, including superb works such as 'What Kind of a Day Did You Have?' and 'Leaving the Yellow House'. Throughout his career he drew on his own life and that of his friends. In *Ravelstein* (2000), the eponymous larger-than-life anti-hero, a once-poor academic made rich on publishing a bestseller, was based on Bellow's friend, critic Allan Bloom. Some critics objected to Bellow's apparent highjacking of a friend's life, but more recognised it as a fine novel.

Dominating his middle period is *The Dean's December* (1982), set in Bucharest, where a Chicago college dean has arrived at the bedside of his dying mother-in-law. It pits many of Bellow's big themes against his prevailing thesis, failed relationships. This question of love is again explored in *More Die of Heartbreak* (1987). Late in his career Bellow subjected the notion of truth to a forensic examination in *The Actual* (1997). It is yet another mercurial performance. He considered himself a romantic, and he was that and more. As shrewd as a professional card player, as subtle as a poet, Saul Bellow pursued greatness with open hunger and achieved it.

43 | The Charwoman's Daughter
(1912)
by James Stephens

Mary Makebelieve and her mother live in poverty in a room on the top floor of a Dublin slum. Mrs Makebelieve, a tall, fierce, black-haired woman with a large blade of a nose, is sustained by the powerful, desperate love for the child she continues to protect from the world. Full of chatter in the early mornings before she goes out to work, she returns exhausted, too tired to talk but always ready to listen to her daughter. Meanwhile Mary, her chores done, spends long hours wandering freely, window-shopping. Together, mother and child create fantasies for a future fit for a princess. But it is not easy living in a place where even the simple business of washing yourself means carrying buckets of water up so many flights of stairs.

James Stephens knew all about hardship, having been born into Dublin slum life. Possessing the grace of a poem and the force of a hard punch, *The Charwoman's Daughter* is assured, sophisticated social realism masquerading as a simple story, thanks to its author's inspired echoing of the traditional European fairytale. Stephens juxtaposes a powerful sexual theme against the realities of class conflict, yet the narrative never loses its lilting rhythms, nor does it slide into shrill polemic.

Small daily debates over which of her few dresses and hair ribbons to wear occupy Mary, as do her long, aimless walks about the city. Her hard-working mother is intent on extending her daughter's childhood into late adolescence. Mrs Makebelieve's simmering fury at their plight is hinted at in the reference made to the fine dresses and waistcoats she once made for wealthy young girls and fine young men, only to let her resentment goad her into tearing the garments asunder.

The charwoman scrubs and cleans for a constantly changing succession of employers, obviously moving from job to job because of her anger. Still, she is confident that her brother who went off to America in search of riches has not forgotten them. Mary, keeping a sharp eye on the ever-changing shop windows, drifts through her days and the city streets in an insulated dream-state which is finally perforated by her emerging sexual curiosity and the interested glances she notices from passing strangers. There is also the policeman's careful advance.

Mary's new awareness of him as a physically large male presence and not merely a symbol of authority capable of quelling the traffic, alerts her to an almost pleasurable fear: "she fancied she would not mind being hit by such a man . . . there was a terrible attraction about the idea of being hit by a man." Later, she considers "what an immense, shattering blow that mighty fist could give." The imagery is threatening and violent, suggesting size and control, the hunter and the prey. After Mary rejects the policeman, he is motivated by "a virus" which "was one half a passion for her body and one half a frenzy for vengeance."

The descriptions of the girl convey a remarkably controlled eroticism: Mary, now sixteen, emerges as an innocent object of desire with long fair hair flowing down to her waist "and when she walked about her room with her hair unloosened it curved beautifully about her head, snuggled into the hollow of her neck, ruffled out broadly again upon her shoulders, and into and out of her figure . . ."

Her fascination with the policeman's "tremendous body" and "calm, proud eye" overpowers her mother's need to keep her as an eternal child. Mrs Makebelieve has her own methods of sustaining her illusions. While at home she "would often desire her daughter to leave off her outer skirt and walk only in her petticoats to heighten the illusion of girlishness." Mrs Makebelieve has treasured motherhood and is struggling to preserve it; Mary is preparing to break free.

In this mix of fantasy and difficult reality, Stephens is also emphasising the hardship of Dublin slum life. Mrs Makebelieve falls ill but Mary is initially too preoccupied with her secret life to help. When she had to deputise for her mother and do the client's housework, the policeman, who turns out to be the nephew of the woman who owns the house, discovers Mary is poor and drops all pretence at gentlemanly seduction.

Writing in language which is winsome though formal and undercut by kindly irony, Stephens handles it all so subtly that he can allude to, rather than directly report, the policeman's probable role in the attack perpetrated upon Mary's other suitor, the thin, young lodger from next door with whom the girl chats freely.

James Stephens neither finished nor continued Mary's adventures, announcing, correctly, that "her chronicler may not be her guide . . . I, for one, having urgent calls elsewhere." And so he wrote his fantasy *The Crock of Gold* (1912), a far more famous work. Yet with *The Charwoman's Daughter*, he had crafted highly original social realism, beguiling in its optimism, if always unsettling in its psychological and quasi-erotic candour.

James Stephens (1880-1950)

James Stephens was an original, a storyteller who believed in equal measures of magic and realism. His early life in Dublin's northside slums had been harsh. Stephens's father had died when he was two and his mother's subsequent marriage did not improve the boy's situation; he was despatched to an orphanage from which he escaped.

He was resourceful and learned a useful skill, typing. A number of clerical jobs eventually led to a clerkship in a Dublin solicitor's office. In 1909 Stephens published his first book of poems, *Insurrections*. By then he had sufficiently impressed A. E., George Russell, to be invited by him to meet members of Dublin's literary inner circle, figures such as Yeats and George Moore. Stephens, who was born on 9 February 1880, liked to claim he shared a birthday with James Joyce, 2 February 1882. Whatever about the shared birthday, Joyce, in the event of his own death, nominated Stephens to complete *Finnegans Wake*.

Stephens's first novel, *The Charwoman's Daughter*, which had been serialised in the *Irish Review* between April 1911 and February 1912, was published in book form later that year, as was, in late November, *The Crock of Gold*, a daring fantasy, and a very different novel. Suddenly, or so it seemed, he was famous. He had also managed to publish his second collection of verse, *The Hill of Vision*. Further poetry would follow, but not the expected sequel to *The Charwoman's Daughter*. Instead he wrote his glorious hymn to nonsense, *The Crock of Gold*, with its shades of Lewis Carroll meets Edward Lear; to read it is to see the influence which would shape Flann O'Brien's subversive classic, *At-Swim-Two-Birds* (1939).

About this time Stephens set off to Paris, where he stayed until 1915 when he took up the post of registrar of the National Gallery in Dublin. All the while he was becoming a literary man, concentrating on short stories. He had also become friendly with Maude Gonne and is mentioned in her correspondence with Yeats. It was Gonne who would inform Yeats in 1917 that Stephens was "seriously ill with pneumonia."

He was an important witness to an event which changed Irish history, the Easter Rebellion in 1916. His first-hand account, *The Insurrection in Dublin*, became a classic. *Irish Fairy Tales* (1920) and *Deirdre* (1923) prove he never lost his interest in the imagination.

All the idealism that had inspired the Irish Revival and later the Easter Rebellion, the ultimate romantic gesture, began to be lost in the harsh realities of political compromise. Disillusioned literary figures, including Stephens, left Ireland. In 1924, the year of the publication of *In the Land of Youth*, he resigned from the National Gallery and moved to London. He then became a founder member of the Irish Academy of Letters.

There was a subtle flamboyance about him; he continued to write poetry, while the stories in *Etched in Moonlight* (1928) are strongly realist. Stephens had many talents including broadcasting and worked for the BBC between 1928 and 1931. The verse collection, *Strict Joy*, was published in the year he left the BBC, with a final collection, *Kings and the Moon*, in 1938. Despite his graceful simplicity

Stephens could also strike a Blakean tone. He would remain suspended between the worlds of Gaelic myth and Irish reality. Stephens was wise; more than that, he knew the value of fun: "It's easy to have brains, as they call it, but it is not so easy to have a little gaiety or carelessness or childishness." He died in London on 26 December 1950. One of the most intellectually alive of Irish writers, he is also one of the most consistently overlooked.

44 | Empire of the Sun
(1984)
J. G. Ballard

Shanghai 1941, on the eve of the bombing at Pearl Harbour and for an eleven-year-old boy his closed world of church services, choir practice, secret cycle rides and making model aircraft has acquired a subplot: war. Jim dreams about it, the images of events at Dunkirk are locked in his imagination through the newsreels he watches. Even the Dean of Shanghai Cathedral duly hauls out an antique projector to show his choirboys more footage. Everyone is obsessed with watching a war that appears to be taking place elsewhere. Young Jim is interested in all of it and has a particular fascination with burning aircraft falling from the skies.

Jim is living as an English boy, the son of English parents moving within an England located in the international settlement. Waited on by passive Chinese servants, the English in Shanghai go about their lives under the expressionless gaze of Japanese soldiers. Daily life has its own brutality, most of it endured by the Chinese; they are executed in public, their dead bodies litter the streets, their funeral parties place the newly dead adrift in the water only for the tide to return the corpses. Jim sees everything and is always asking questions.

Matter of fact, direct and ironic, told from the point of view of a growing boy, not a soldier, *Empire of the Sun* is a narrative of dramatic images, evoking all the chaos, contradictions and the horror with laconic detachment. Most of all it examines how a child's mind works. It is unlike any of Ballard's other books. Although based on his experiences, it is not autobiographical. Instead, Ballard unleashes his surrealist flair on the destruction he witnessed, all the while sustaining a neutral, remote tone.

The youngster watches as the insulated routine he knows falls asunder. From the outset, Ballard makes it clear that this resourceful, very English boy is an innocent alien in the city in which he was born and raised. He doesn't speak the language, and doesn't like the food, while England remains the home he has never visited.

A propaganda battle is going on; the German and Italian war films screened in the public theatres are very different from the Pathé newsreels arriving from England, which give the impression that "despite their unbroken series of defeats, the British people were thoroughly enjoying the war."

The situation in Europe is going badly for the English, yet Jim's parents and their friends continue with their social engagements. Sitting in their big Packard car en route to Dr Lockwood's fancy dress party, their chauffer, Yang, drives over an old beggar's foot. Every journey is now overseen by Japanese soldiers. One of them runs his bayonet across the windshield "as if cutting an invisible thread." The family sit still "as the slightest move would produce a short pause followed by violent retribution." The tension of the parents is juxtaposed with the eager curiosity of the boy alert to all the changes.

At the party Jim meets Mr Maxted, an architect-turned-entrepreneur and father of his best friend Patrick, who has already left for Singapore with his mother. He is a brilliant study of an Englishman abroad, "who faced reality across the buffer of a large whisky and soda." Maxted, a likeable, raffish character with a habit of falling into swimming pools, though only, as Jim reflects, when they are safely full of water, mentions that he has heard Jim has resigned from the cubs. "Jim doubted if there was any point in explaining to Mr Maxted why he had left the wolf-cubs, an act of rebellion he had decided upon simply to test its result. To his disappointment, Jim's parents had been surprisingly unmoved. He thought of telling Mr Maxted that not only had he left the cubs and become an atheist, but he might become a communist as well. The communists had an intriguing ability to unsettle everyone, a talent Jim greatly respected."

Jim soon becomes bored with the party and sets off to what is for him a magical place, the abandoned Hungjao Aerodrome. As he runs across the field he notices yellowing skeletons and is struck "by the contrasts between the impersonal bodies of the newly dead, whom he saw every day in Shanghai, and these sun-warmed skeletons, everyone an individual . . . Jim felt his cheeks and jaw, trying to imagine his own skeleton in the sun, lying here in this peaceful field within sight of the deserted aerodrome." The boy has become immune to death, it is unsettling as is the entire narrative. Ballard brings his deadpan humour and exact imagery to a chapter of history without losing the sense of story. His sinuous prose embraces the oddness of it all, including the grotesque brutality. *Empire of the Sun* also contains Ballard's most convincing dialogue, much of its making effective use of the specific nuances of British social class.

Throughout the novel there are many instances in which the questing boy remains oblivious to danger. He is intrigued by everything, including the enemy. Following the attack on a British ship, he is separated from his parents and eventually wakes in a children's ward in a hospital run by the French. A ward sister intent on his bed sends him home. This is when his adventure really begins.

Ballard's Jim and Twain's Huck are light years removed from each other, yet Jim shares Huck's individuality. When Jim returns to his ransacked home and rests in his mother's bedroom where the spilt talcum on the floor suggests the steps of a crazy dance made by various footprints, he almost seems vulnerable. Chinese servants no longer defer to him and consider him the enemy. But the boy survives, quickly learning how to win favour and food.

Eventually he loses his bike and his freedom. His three-year-stay at the Lunghua Internment Camp dominates the middle section of the narrative. For Jim it is a playground. While the adult British internees such as Mrs Vincent regard the contented boy with suppressed horror, he revels in his situation and sees the Japanese as heroes. Inmates die, are barely buried in the dusty earth, the living are clothed in rags and they are all starving, yet Dr Ransome expects Jim to do his Latin homework.

Even in the camp, a sense of England emerges. The adult

characters are foils to Jim. Power-shifts dictate the action. In one of many stark set pieces the internees are marched to a stadium which had been built for an Olympic Games that was never held. Here Ballard the novelist makes symbolic use of the massive explosion overpowering Hiroshima. Slowly the reality penetrates Jim's thoughts. He experiences guilt and wonder. Ultimately, through the slow death of a young Japanese pilot, he confronts life and death.

Its profundity lies in its detachment. There is no pathos, no sentimentality. This is an astonishing novel of vicious happenings; most of the characters are reduced to onlookers. Ballard's familiar imagery of decay and abandonment are here harnessed to acts of outright brutality. In the character of Jim he has a survivor, but more importantly, he has created an objective consciousness who responds with the clinical inquisitiveness of a scientist let loose in a very weird lab.

J. G. Ballard (1930-2009)

Seldom has any writer created a world so mesmerisingly his own as that of the master of the obsessional psychological novel, J. G. Ballard, whose chosen territory is extreme states of mind. His characters are stuck in elevators, marooned under deceptively ordinary motorway by-passes, are afflicted by strange viruses, experience the zero zone of modern hospitals and deserted shopping malls, or are bombarded by an unending succession of odd things falling from the sky. Drained swimming pools become sinister spaces, as do ordinary houses.

In *Cocaine Nights* (1996), a vicious tennis machine fires balls across empty tennis courts. Whatever the situation, however surreal the landscape, there is always the familiar Ballard character, alienated, at the mercy of private obsessions, and more often than not, potentially insane.

Ballard, British literature's singular maverick visionary, was a subversive original in possession of an imagination that had, admittedly, been given a shocking head start – incarceration in a wartime Japanese detention camp. It left him the memories which would eventually inspire *Empire of the Sun* (1984). Yet, for years he had looked elsewhere, less to the past and more to an imagined future which has eerily become increasingly real. His weird, inventive, futuristic work bypassed conventional science fiction. *The Drowned World* (1961), *The Drought* (1965), *The Crystal World* (1966), *The Disaster Area* (1967) and *The Concrete Island* (1974) shared a cult following long before Ballard was shortlisted for the 1984 Booker Prize with *Empire of the Sun*, which became his first international bestseller.

Before that came *Crash* (1973), a pornographic morality play exploring the sexual fulfilment of the car crash for characters who, weary of ordinary dangers, are seeking new thrills. This offbeat narrative marked the beginning of what would become a major preoccupation for Ballard, the dangers of increased leisure time, a theme which would in turn be replaced by another – random violence.

In person Ballard was unusual; an edgy combination of loquacious, urbane, very English affability, jolly and civil, though given to sudden leaps from his chair, almost barking with defensive sharpness should he decide to dispute something, or perhaps, stress a point. Not all that unexpected perhaps, of a man who had witnessed so many nightmares, and invented many more. His wartime boyhood was full of rotting corpses, bobbing about the waterfront in Shanghai while he watched occupying soldiers who were capable of murder as easily as they would yawn.

Day of Creation (1987) set in Central Africa is a fine example of his lucid madness at work. The narrator Mallory, one of Ballard's habitually crazy doctors, accidentally creates a river. Mallory is a drifter and a dreamer intent on irrigating the Sahara. It is an erotic, dream-quest populated by a cast of crazies and sustained by Ballard's deadpan humour and characteristic visual imagery.

Born in 1930, into a cosmopolitan, sinister Shanghai of extremes, to British parents, Ballard grew up within the protected insularity of the international settlement, watching poverty, disease, death as though they were routine aspects of an ongoing television drama. He never learned Chinese as the native servants all spoke English.

He remained untouched by the culture of the country in which he had spent his first sixteen years.

He was seven years old when the Japanese invaded China. Prior to the bombing of Pearl Harbour, life continued as before. Ballard's parents and their friends still drove about in their big Packard and Buick cars. Then, everything changed. He and his parents were evacuated and moved to Lunghua camp. *Empire of the Sun* tells some of the story but it also tells it as a novel; *Miracles of Life* (2008), his beautiful, moving and candid memoir, fills in the gaps of a life that ran parallel to his literary career.

Arrival in grey, wet England introduced Ballard to a homeland he had never seen. He discovered class, and most specifically a working-class culture of which he had been unaware. He studied medicine and not surprisingly given his wartime experiences, was drawn to psychiatry. But his wife's shocking sudden death in 1964 while on a family holiday in Spain caused him to stay at home with their three children, becoming a full-time parent and writer.

Ballard's laconic, visionary, apocalyptic fiction combines the fantastic and the logical; he is an heir of sorts to Lewis Carroll and Conrad, and also to Orwell and Greene. His experiences left him marginalised and different, an outsider. He chose suburbia and would remain in his modest semi-detached house in Shepperton, near Heathrow airport, until his death in 2009. Through his sittingroom window he often glanced towards at the sky, as if waiting for something to fall from it.

For all his understanding of popular culture, he was a dreamer and a romantic. When I met him in that by-now-famous house he spoke about the loss of his beloved dog. For months, Ballard had dreamed of his dead pet and woken, calling "Polly, Polly" to the dog, who in the dream had simply walked away – causing Ballard to wake, screaming his name. "Then one night, in my dream, he stopped and looked around at me. That's when he finally said goodbye and the dreams ended."

45 | Hunger
(1890)
by Knut Hamsun

Feeling hungry is a commonplace human experience; food is a basic need. But extreme hunger, starvation, results in being no longer capable of digesting food. The narrator of Hamsun's groundbreaking, urban novel is neither a beggar nor a typical unemployed drifter; he is an aspiring writer – arrogant, intense, frenetic, educated, desperate – and starving.

The streets of Christiania, now Oslo, have become his private battleground. His thoughts are chaotic, torn between his wild plans for literary success and his outraged awareness of his body weakening, failing. At first he believes his problems will be solved by his next article. He offers stories to editors and waits for what he thinks will be certain triumph. Waiting, the endless waiting, is dominated by his craving for food.

Even now, more than a century since its first publication, *Hunger* remains devastatingly fresh and relevant. It is one of those timeless rites-of-passage or outspoken outsider as anti-hero novels. It is also a lucidly nightmarish narrative introducing the self-conscious into fiction, for the narrator the story is about him. It is *his* story; the characters he meets exist only in relation to him and his problems – he has no intention of saving mankind, only himself.

There are no heroics, no social polemic. Hamsun, born Knut Petersen into a Norwegian peasant family, had worked at a range of labouring jobs before eventually, through *Hunger*, establishing a literary career which continued long after he won the 1920 Nobel Prize for Literature. His reputation suffered because of his support of Nazism. Yet the younger, decidedly apolitical Hamsun who wrote

Hunger was an introspective authority on physical hardship and humiliation having experienced both as a young man.

Hamsun had graphically lived the life he gave to the narrator of *Hunger*. Those long months wandering about the city, pestering editors and fleeing unpaid landladies as recalled by the narrator, a peevish, egotistical individual who is not interested in our sympathy, reflect Hamsun's aimless decade of wandering through Norway and the US. The narrator begins his account with a tone that suggests a sense of detached wonder: "All of this happened while I was walking around starving in Christiania – that strange city no one escapes from until it has left its mark on him . . ."

Starvation has forced him to pawn everything he owns, stopping short of his spectacles. "I was becoming more and more nervous and irritable, and several mornings lately I had been so dizzy I had had to stay in bed all day. Occasionally when my luck was good I took in five kroner or so from one of the newspapers for an article."

It all begins rather conversationally; the narrator appears to be sharing his memories. Hamsun then introduces an inspired element of mounting frenzy: "How steadily my predicament had got worse . . . I didn't even have a comb left, or a book to read when I felt hopeless." The more exasperated he becomes the more he echoes Dostoyevsky's Underground Man in *Notes from Underground* (1864) and to some extent Raskolnikov in *Crime and Punishment* (1865-1866). But Hamsun's narrator, although he does think, looks no further than his personal embarrassment and the slights to which he feels he has been subjected.

There are several lively comic set pieces, such as when he attempts in vain to pawn his green blanket. "For God's sake, be careful . . . Two delicate vases are inside. That package has got to get to Smyrna!" Abandoning journalism, the narrator begins to write a play and realises that his mind is overwhelmed by lines of dialogue to be uttered by medieval monks. Yet all the while hunger, gnawing like rats, intervenes. A candle briefly becomes more important than food; he needs light to write by. There is also the practical difficulty of attempting to sit down to write when you are homeless, without lodgings. He considers eating his finger so he bites it but quickly decides to abandon that particular enterprise.

The narrative voice is direct; the exasperation compelling. Although the central character is concerned only with his story, his survival, his candour proves unexpectedly engaging. It is as if he feels his suffering is a necessary test. He explains what happened and how he felt as if he were compiling a report.

Having failed locally, he decides on flight, and approaches a ship's captain, asking for work. He explains that he has no experience "But as I said, give me a job, and I'll do it." The skipper agrees to give him a chance. Our hero bids farewell "for now" to Christiania, noticing that "the windows of the homes all shone with such brightness."

Hamsun's finest novel, *Mysteries*, was published in 1892. He would continue writing until his death in 1952 aged ninety-three, yet *Hunger*, with its tormented, angry narrator at war with himself and an indifferent city, remains his most famous work.

Knut Hamsun (1859-1952)

He made no apology; he courted no favours. Norwegian Knut Hamsun did not set out to save the world, or even change it through his autobiographical fiction. Instead, he concentrated on how people act; he was a realist who drew on personal experience and sensation. Instinct, not intellect, drove him. He rejected the work of his countryman, playwright Henrik Ibsen (1828-1906), which he considered polemical and overly concerned with social issues. Ibsen had a reforming zeal; Hamsun believed in the subjective, after all, as he saw it, it as a more honest representation of the way we conduct ourselves. Few novels reflect this subjectivity as relentlessly as does Hamsun's forceful debut, *Hunger* (1890), in which the egocentric narrator rails against the heavens and everything else in his quest towards recognition.

Hunger, with its urgency and energy, is an individual work despite its echoes of Dostoyevsky's Underground Man. One of the earliest and most influential urban novels, it features what would become a familiar Hamsun character, a driven, anti-heroic obsessive, in this case an aspiring writer, reduced to pawning his vest, and ultimately, the buttons from his coat. *Hunger* established Hamsun as a pioneering modernist.

In 1886, about two years before he began work on it, he wrote and published *A Lecture Tour*. A short story with an interesting variation on the subsequent novel, which also reflects Hamsun's flair for exasperated asides.

"I was going to give a lecture on modern literature in Drammen," begins the narrator. "I was short of money, and this seemed to me good way to get hold of a little. I didn't think it would be all that difficult either. So one fine day in the late summer of 1886 I boarded a train bound for that splendid town." The sting comes as early as the next paragraph: "I didn't know a soul in Drammen, nor did anyone there know me. Nor had I advertised my lecture in the papers, although earlier that summer, in an expansive moment, I had 500 cards printed, and I intended to distribute these in hotels and bars and large shops, to let people know what was in store for them. These cards were not wholly to my liking in that they contained a misprint in the spelling of my name; yet I was so comprehensively unknown in Drammen that a misprint was neither here nor there."

On arrival in the town he decides to call upon the local newspaper editor. "Arensten the editor was naturally not in his office, so I visited him at home. I told him my business, that I had come in the service of literature." In the exchange that follows, it is possible to hear the effects of the time Hamsun spent in the US Midwest: "Not much interest in such things here," says the editor. "We had a Swedish student come last year with a talk about everlasting peace. He lost money on it."

The narrator remains on the attack: "I'm going to talk about literature," he repeats.

"Yes," says the editor. "I realise that, I'm just warning you, you'll probably lose money on it." The narrator shrieks silently to himself: "*Lose* money on it? Priceless! Perhaps he thought I was a salesman travelling for a firm."

Among the obstacles hindering the narrator is the presence in the town of a rival lecturer, a dandy who is an anti-spiritualist and though hampered by speaking "a horrible mixture of Swedish and Norwegian" he wins the audiences because, as the narrator reports, "he pulled a string of handkerchiefs out of his nose, produced the Jack of Clubs from the pocket of an old woman sitting near the back . . . and made a table walk across the floor without touching it."

Hamsun published three volumes of short stories but abandoned the form about 1906 leaving him to concentrate on novels. Many of them feature small town life, a world he was to discover.

He was born Knut Petersen in the Gudbransdal Valley of central Norway but the family moved to the Arctic north, to a farm called Hamsund. He would later adopt it as his name. The young Petersen herded cattle and hated school. By the time he was twenty he had written a novella and brought it to Oslo, then Christiania, to a publisher who rejected it. He would spend the next decade travelling and taking up labouring jobs, initially in Norway and then, when he was twenty-three, in the US.

His experiences there helped him write *The Cultural Life of Modern America*, a scalding, often funny book. *Hunger* was published the following year. It established Hamsun the novelist. His next novel, *Mysteries* (1902), a vivid account of one young man's destructive pursuit of the impossible, is even better. The central character, Nagel, arrives at a coastal town and begins to impose his personality on the citizens. The "mysteries" of the title refers to his quest but also to his contact with others. His search destroys him and leaves those with whom he had associated, bewildered.

Hamsun's other work includes *Pan* (1894), *Victoria* (1898) and *Growth of the Soil* (1917). He won the Nobel Prize in 1920. He continued to write during what proved to be a long life – he lived to be ninety-three – but his later fiction failed to retain the energy and subversive voice. More importantly, his support in old age of Nazism discredited him. Years have passed and critics have returned to his finest work, much of it written in the earlier part of his life. *Hunger* is his most famous book; *Mysteries* is his finest.

Petersburg
(1916)
by Andrei Bely

An extremely nervous son is expected to assassinate his father. It has been carefully planned – well, about as carefully as a group of somewhat haphazard radicals can manage to organise anything.

Meanwhile, the targeted father, Apollon Apollonovich Ableukhov, an elderly, high-ranking government official, has his own problems; his health is not good and his wife who "now and then used to play Chopin (never Schumann)" has run off to Spain – all very embarrassing. Yet the old man, although discreetly concerned about his son's increasing distraction, continues to attend to his duties, sharing his puns and bad jokes. In the streets outside, a great city shaped by history and the ubiquitous presence of its creator, Peter the Great, emerges from the fog and the darkness to shimmer and seduce with its wealth of stories.

Petersburg is a daring, flamboyant performance. Set over several days in 1905, the fast-moving, witty narrative reflects the atmosphere of revolution which the poet Andrei Bely, one of the central figures of Russian symbolism, appeared to place in a religious rather than political context. Pushkin's spirit presides over the action, with Bely paying homage to the pioneering father of modern Russian literature throughout.

Pushkin's long poem, 'The Bronze Horseman' (1833), provides the subtext, while Bely bows to Dostoyevsky, albeit humorously, particularly in the quasi-philosophical exchanges between the aspiring, slightly crazy revolutionaries.

Bely also nods to Tolstoy; old Apollon – in common with Karenin, the dull husband of his doomed heroine Anna in *Anna Karenina*

(1873-1877) – is a bureaucrat; he too has large ears and he also has an unfaithful wife named Anna. Bely celebrates the Russian literary tradition with a wealth of references and allusions. Published four years after his debut, *The Silver Dove* (1909), the earliest twentieth century Russian novel, *Petersburg* proves an imaginative, sophisticated, original and innovative second novel. Most importantly, it also bids a stylish farewell to tsarist Russia.

Central to the narrative is the prevailing issue of Russian identity and the mood of change then affecting Russia: Petersburg the city provides the stage, yet this novel is also about a country. "Those were foggy days, strange days. Noxious October marched on with frozen gait. It hung out dank mists in the south. October blew off the golden woodland whisper, and that whisper fell to earth . . . Now the ploughmen had ceased to scratch at their lands, and abandoning their harrows and wooden ploughs, they assembled in small clusters in their huts. They talked and argued . . . thus it was in the villages . . . Thus it was in the towns as well . . . Everyone feared something, hoped for something, poured into the streets, gathered in crowds." Not surprisingly, Apollon Apollonovich, representing the old order, "had a fear of space."

Petersburg soon becomes more than a backdrop; it is a major character. "Petersburg streets possess one indubitable quality: they transform passers-by into shadows. This we have seen in the case of the mysterious stranger." Bely ingeniously exploits the near hallucinatory quality of the light illuminating this eastern city built on a vast marsh. The myth of the city adds an additional life force to the story.

While Nikolai Apollonovich, the terrified would-be assassin, paces his bedroom and agonises about his gruesome task, a homemade bomb is passed around in a sardine can; fancy dress costumes and reported sightings of a large domino in the city add to the confusion.

Bely's extravaganza took everyone by surprise, including the censors who were waiting, red pens poised. He was forced to make cuts. Although initially written between 1913 and 1914, and then reworked for publication in 1916, the definitive version of *Petersburg* was not published until 1922. The first of the big city novels, this virtuoso performance, which so influenced Mikhail Bulgakov's Faustian romp, *The Master and Margarita* (1928-1940), remains playful, exciting, mercurial and very funny, standing as it does between the extraordinary nineteenth century Russian literary achievement and the dawning of literary modernism.

Andrei Bely *(1880-1934)*

Andrei Bely's influence on modern Russian literature is two-fold. As a Symbolist poet, a friend, rival and, in time, critic of Aleksandr Blok, he dominated Moscow's literary and intellectual circles; and as the author of *Petersburg*, the novel that led Nabokov to rank him alongside Joyce, Proust and Kafka, he was assured literary immortality. Published in sections between 1913 and 1914, and as a complete work in 1916, *Petersburg* is an urban epic. Though not on the scale of *Ulysses*, and taking place over several days, not one, it is nevertheless the first great city novel, expanding as it does the urban setting of Hamsun's *Hunger* (1890). *Petersburg* is as committed to the search for the essence of that hallucinatory city as *Ulysses* was to finding Dublin's soul. The revised *Petersburg* was finally published in 1922, the same year as Joyce's earthy anti-epic.

Just as the statue of the Bronze Horseman, depicting Peter the Great, founder of modern Russia, appears to oversee Bely's novel, eventually to emerge as its most perceptive character, *Petersburg* overshadows his other work, including his first novel, *The Silver Dove* (1909).

Born Boris Nikolayevich Bugayev in Moscow in 1880, Bely changed his name to spare his father, an internationally respected mathematician, any embarrassment because of his Symbolist associations. He first became a published writer in 1902 while still at university and followed four short prose pieces, his 'Symphonies', with a novel, *The Silver Dove*. It had been intended as the first part of a trilogy to be called 'East or West'. When he first began work on *Petersburg*, he saw it as the second part of the trilogy.

There would be no trilogy. Instead Bely set off on lengthy travels, including a long stay in Berlin, returning home to launch what he hoped would be a Symbolist revival. His efforts came to nothing. But he settled in Moscow and remained influential, although his work appeared in only minor journals. He wrote five subsequent novels, including *Masks*, published in 1932, two years before his death at fifty-four. Along with his fiction, he left extensive memoirs and critical writings, all hoping to make sense of the Russian reality.

The Silver Dove and *Petersburg* redefine Russian fiction. One is a rural work, the other an urban tale. Together they address the fundamental questions that dominate Russian literature – national identity and the dilemma of a country torn between its traditional rural self and the cosmopolitan attractions of Western culture. There is also the tension of the religious versus the secular. Bely's two major narratives link the nineteenth-century novels of Gogol and Dostoyevsky with the increasingly surreal twentieth-century vision of Zamyatin, Bulgakov, Platonov and Venedikt Yerofeev.

Admirers of *Petersburg* should read *The Silver Dove*. Set in a landscape of small villages and modest homesteads, it is a whimsical, if oddly prophetic novel driven by Bely's awareness that Russia was facing a future built on fear and change. It follows the misadventures of Daryalsky, a decadent poet and something of a stock romantic hero who may have slipped from the pages of Turgenev. Wearied of life as a city intellectual, he joins a mystic sect, the Silver Doves, led by a carpenter named Kudeyarov. Think of Christ; no, think more intently of Rasputin. Bely was to later make this bizarre connection himself as information surfaced about the evil priest's dangerous hold over the Tsarina and its subsequent impact on Russia's last imperial family.

Bely's prose style and tone in *The Silver Dove* is far more traditional than it is in *Petersburg*. The narrative voice is gossipy, ironic, knowing. "Daryalsky – surely you notice something about my hero's name? Look here, it's Daryalsky – you know the same Daryalsky who two summers running rented Fyodorov's cottage with his friend. Wounded by a maiden's heart, two summers running he sought the surest means of meeting the young lady he loved here . . ."

But it is not a comedy. Beyond the offbeat dialogue, the parody, the injections of melodrama and earthy humour, there is the sinister activities of the sect's leader. *The Silver Dove* is a portrait of a country facing upheaval and transformation. From 1905 until the revolution in 1917, Russian intellectuals such as Bely experienced crippling disillusionment. For all the sophistication of *Petersburg*, certainly a modernist masterpiece, the Bely who wrote *The Silver Dove* had already realised that idealism would have no hope in the society Russia was about to become.

47 | Death in Rome
(1954)
by Wolfgang Koeppen

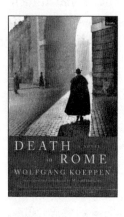

An unplanned family reunion with a difference takes place in this daringly well-choreographed exploration of the twentieth-century German dilemma. Here are all the defining elements of the nation of Goethe and Beethoven; music, war, guilt, racism, God, romance, mythology and history, always history. Koeppen tells his story with an unnervingly candid mixture of irony and regret. If it is polemic, it is polemic as high art. The strange, dreamlike narrative structure, spanning two hectic days, ebbs and flows between snappy observation, symbolism and long, flowing phrases, interspersed with the contrasting preoccupations of an uneasy family unit, each member of which has their own ghosts and memories.

Young Siegfried Pfaffrath has come to Rome for the performance of his new symphony. Personal doubt stalks his every waking moment. "Wrong, the music sounded wrong, it no longer moved him, it was almost unpleasant to him, like hearing your own voice for the first time, a recording coming out of a loudspeaker, and you think, well, so that's me, that braying twit, that phoney . . . in particular it was the violins that were wrong, their sound was too lush; it wasn't the unearthly wind in the trees . . . it should be more tormented, more passionate . . ." Siegfried feels like crying, yet the conductor Kürenberg reassures him. The nervy composer, though troubled, manages to respond to the richness of Rome. Koeppen not only describes Siegfried's sensations, Siegfried also articulates his thoughts and fears.

The conductor's wife looks on. She knows that Siegfried "has come from my home town and he writes symphonies and his grandfather may have played the harpsichord or the flute, but his father killed my father, who collected books and loved listening to the Brandenburg Concertos." Siegfried's estranged father is also in Rome. Formerly a holder of high office under the Nazis, the grandly named Friedrich Wilhelm Pfaffrath has managed to reinvent himself sufficiently to have resurfaced as a respectable bürgermeister. He and his wife are accompanied by their other son, Dietrich, already a civil servant in the making.

Pfaffrath's brother-in-law, Gottlieb Judejahn, a former SS general, personifies the unredeemable face of Nazism, (and do note the ironic use of "Jude" meaning Jew in the name). Symbolic intent is evident in the names Koeppen gives the central characters. Drawn rather like a caricature by George Grosz, Judejahn is repulsive; convinced he sees in every Italian woman's face a Jewess deserving to be killed. Holed up in a hotel with a mangy cat named Benito for company, Judejahn, refuses to accept he was on the losing side. He swaggers incessantly; fantasising about murder, victory and sex. Meanwhile his son, Adolf, has given up being a soldier and is preparing to become a Catholic priest.

Wolfgang Koeppen lived a life that spanned the German century. In the 1930s he published two novels, including the beautiful *A Sad Affair*, an autobiographical love story. He went abroad and was never drawn to Nazism. Nor did he idealise his detachment and returned to Germany before the war. During the 1950s he published three openly political, courageous and stylistically ambitious novels; *Pigeons on the Grass* (1951), *The Hothouse* (1953), which is a superb study of post second World War apathy, and *Death in Rome*. While his countrymen preferred to forget what had happened, Koeppen confronted a past that was all too recent. His candid engagement with that history informs his fiction. "Do you believe in war?" asks Pfaffrath of Judejahn. Koeppen pursues this question incisively, aware that it is the key to so many questions: "Judejahn said he always believed in war, what else was there to believe in? Pfaffrath too believed in a new war, it had to come, justice demanded it."

Long ashamed of his family, Siegfried continues to fret. Having agreed to meet his cousin Adolf he realises he has forgotten the arrangements: "Was it noon or was it later?" he wonders. For the composer, his cousin has been reduced to an unhappy reminder of their shared history.

"He took me back to the oppressiveness of youth, the past, family, morning exercises and lessons in patriotism in the Nazi academy", reflects Siegfried, "and even though Adolf had, like me, immediately dissociated himself from those days . . . the whiff of family still clung to him . . ."

Published in 1954, five years before Günter Grass was to unleash *The Tin Drum*, a bravura debut which continues to resonate across international literary boundaries, Koeppen's symphonic, remorseless tale brilliantly filtered through his carefully orchestrated prose explains a nation to the world and to itself.

Wolfgang Koeppen (1906-1996)

He had two literary careers, possibly three, should his belated rediscovery during the 1990s count as one. He found writing an effort and was fortunate in securing publishers who believed in him. Wolfgang Koeppen is a vital element, the bridge which sees twentieth-century German fiction moving on from Alfred Döblin's writer as witness, to the towering presence of Thomas Mann, on to the fabulist, burlesque polemic of Günter Grass and the novels of ideas so beautifully and profoundly shaped in the elegies of W. G. Sebald.

Timing was never Koeppen's strong point. After all, writing a gorgeous romance in 1930s Germany and having it published by a Jewish publisher was not such a great idea. Hardly surprising that *A Sad Affair* (1934), an openly autobiographical account of his obsession with a young cabaret performer, was banned.

An element of at best distraction, at worst chaos, always hovered over his life. He was born in Greifswald, a Baltic coastal town. His father was a married doctor who had no further interest in the boy's mother and less in the child. Young Koeppen's education petered out and he drifted between odd jobs and bouts of unemployment. He became involved in freelance journalism, writing for left-wing publications and in 1931, he moved to Berlin. *A Sad Affair* irritated critics as well as the authorities. Koeppen drifted off to the Netherlands. Before war broke out he returned to Berlin and spent the war years writing film scripts that earned him enough to live on, yet were never made. He moved to Munich and settled there.

Central to the man and the writer is that he was never involved in the war; if ever there was an uncompromised witness, Koeppen is it. "It is perhaps my only boast," he once said, "not to have served in Hitler's armies for a single hour."

Whatever about his haphazard approach to life, he is a literary stylist who read Proust, Kafka, Woolf and Faulkner as they became available and had read *Ulysses* in the first German translation in 1926. In a remarkable postwar trio of novels written in the 1950s, he openly tore away the protective layer insulating a nation which was not only defeated but disgraced. *Pigeons on the Grass* (1951) takes place in Munich on a single day and consists of fragmented episodes. *The Hothouse* (1953) followed and then *Death in Rome* (1954). Koeppen the outsider exposes his society in deliberate, precise narratives. Resisting any tricks or fanciful devices, his candour is direct.

The publication of *The Hothouse*, with its brooding honesty, sent the critics scurrying for cover. No one was prepared for its fearless exposure of postwar German hypocrisy. A tauter version of Ivan Klima's wonderful *Judge on Trial* (1978), *The Hothouse* is a portrait of a society suspended in a mindless apathy of acceptance. Set in Bonn, which is referred to throughout as "the city on the Rhine," it follows a grim journey towards realisation as experienced by an idealistic politician named Keetenheuve. He is an intellectual and as he attempts to deal with the corruption surrounding him, his humanity proves his downfall. Within that failure, however, resides a muted grandeur.

Koeppen depicts Bonn as a seedy hell, inhabited by liars and fools. The cunning are blatant hypocrites and conceal their Nazi past, while the ordinary merely decide to believe that nothing in fact happened, it is all rumour. His writing is sharp; the observations are despairingly idiosyncratic and the characterisation as exact as could be expected of a writer who knew what had gone on and was unafraid of writing about it.

The sympathetic Keetenheuve is a quiet hero, no saint perhaps, but without stain, a saviour; he returns to Bonn with no war crime to either hide or defend. He has memories but no secrets, just a social conscience and his personal grief in the death of his troubled young wife. This is his only guilt, that and thinking. He also dreams a dreamer's dreams: "He would have liked to visit America. He would have liked to see the new Rome for himself. What was it like, America? Big? Free?" Even a man as good as Keetenheuve is compromised by having witnessed so much and is too aware of the corruption.

Koeppen's rage is controlled; the interior monologue-like narrative pulsates with a regret that is both public and private. There is also a convincing sense of moral and physical exhaustion. In one of the most intense and dramatic scenes in a novel of such moments Keetenheuve shares a taxi with Korodin, a former colleague, now a political opponent. "They sat together in silence. It splattered and flashed, and sheets of rain swathed the tops of trees like fog, but the thunder boomed feebly, as though the storm were already tired or still far off." It is an outstanding, allusive novel, and as utterly individual as is its successor, *Death in Rome*.

Koeppen, who once described *The Hothouse* "as a German fairytale" – a fairly loaded description considering the menace of many of the stories collected by the Brothers Grimm – is a truth-teller who never abandoned his artistic sensibility. He never ran for cover, nor did he fight obscurity. His rediscovery is due to astute publishing decisions to commission translations of his work from as gifted an interpreter as poet Michael Hofmann. It is sad, though, to think of this original writer sitting in Munich writing travel books and random pieces of journeyman journalism, almost forgotten. It was not until the final years of his long life that Wolfgang Koeppen's achievement would finally be acknowledged.

48 | The Go-Between
(1953)
by L. P. Hartley

During the hot, hot summer of 1900 young Leo Colston, a recent victim of school bullying, is invited by a classmate's mother to the family's country estate in Norfolk. Part idyll, part excursion into the English class system, the visit becomes a harrowing rite of passage into adult duplicity. Half a century later, the man who was once that boy happens upon a long-forgotten diary and remembers the period recorded within its pages. L. P. Hartley's beautifully brutal Jamesian tale begins with one of the most famous sentences in literature: "The past is a foreign country: they do things differently there."

Hartley evokes an Edwardian England pivoted between major conflicts, the still resonant Boer War and the first tremors of future global upheavals. For Leo, the new century brings a determination to improve on the previous year during which his father had died suddenly and he, Leo, had been so ill that his caring mother decided his health to be permanently at risk. Looking back at his young self, he recognises a clever, romantic boy who tended to live in his imagination. His belief in his mastery of the dark arts had caused him some bother at school. When his tormentors quite coincidentally appear to pay for their wrong doings, Leo begins to fear his powers yet enjoys the new-found respect of his peers. The invitation offered by the wealthy mother of Marcus Maudsley, one year younger and not a close friend, introduces Leo who is genteel if poor to a world of servants, social ritual, languor and secrets.

The imposing Mrs Maudsley is watchful and formidable; her husband is a shadowy, detached, though equally impressive presence. Leo quickly falls under the spell of their daughter, Marian, edgy, beautiful and remote, who takes an unexpected sudden interest in her little brother's house guest. Slowly and carefully the astute Hartley, as if opening a door into a gallery of wonders, conveys the sense of a mind almost reluctantly beginning to engage with memory.

Having long suppressed this episode, the older Leo, once he begins to remember, recalls everything; the heat, the domestic tensions, the glances, the minor embarrassments – it all returns with chilling clarity. The result is an astonishingly graceful performance and a seminal example of an English writer engaging with memory, regret and that all-prevailing theme, the loss of innocence.

Hartley assembles a well-drawn ensemble cast and although the narrator's memories focus on the family members and the rival suitors, a significant background hum is created by the other house guests. Most inspired of all is the ingeniously vicious banter which passes between Leo and Marcus, a precocious satirist with a superior command of French. He notes each of Leo's social gaffs: "Only cads wear their school clothes in the holidays. It isn't done . . . And, Leo, you mustn't come down to breakfast in your slippers. It's the sort of thing that bank clerks do."

The temperature continues its relentless ascent. Leo's sturdy Norfolk jacket and winter garments are too heavy for comfort. Marian decides to improve his wardrobe. Her unlikely concern thrills Leo. She, however, has urgent messages to pass on to the local farmer, Ted Burgess. The house guests are finally joined by Trimingham of whom there had been much talk. Although he is badly disfigured by war injuries, Marian's mother regards him as her future son-in-law. He is also a viscount and by nature as well as birth a gentleman. Leo takes a liking to him but has mixed feelings about Burgess, handsome, physical and volatile, who also has messages in need of delivery.

Marcus takes to his bed, allowing Leo to concentrate on performing his postal errands. His idealised notion of his importance to Marian is destroyed on realising the nature of her association with Burgess. Hartley confers high symbolism on a cricket match and the impromptu concert which follows. Leo's dreams collapse: "I feared for Lord Trimingham, I wept with Marian, but for Ted I grieved."

The boy's ordeal shapes his life. Retaining all its original charm and menace, this outstanding study of paradise lost and innocence betrayed and betraying, triumphs through Hartley's elegant irony and may well have influenced Ian McEwan's impressive novel, *Atonement* (2001), which also explores similar themes. Both novels are about children being introduced to adult duplicity. *The Go-Between*, however, is a special book. Whereas McEwan concentrated on a life-long burden of guilt, Hartley's novel is more subtle in that it explores complex feelings of regret haunting a convincingly damaged narrator who has never recovered from that initial betrayal of trust.

L. P. Hartley *(1895-1972)*

Although it was claimed that he had been named Leslie in honour of Virginia Woolf's father, Sir Leslie Stephen, L. P. Hartley was never to become part of the Bloomsbury set – possibly because he was simply too normal. There was also, of course, the fact he was friendly with the Asquiths, a connection not likely to garner him much favour with Woolf and her associates. His father was a solicitor who then became the director of a brick works. The family was comfortably middle class, yet Hartley learned early in life about the layers and realities of British social class. It was a theme he would make perceptive use of in his fiction, culminating in *The Go-Between* (1953), his finest novel.

He attended Harrow and then went on to Balliol College, Oxford, where he read modern history. At Oxford he became friendly with Aldous Huxley. In 1916, Hartley joined the British Army and was commissioned as a junior officer. Owing to poor health, he was never to see active service and was invalided out. On his return to Oxford in 1919 he settled into a literary life, writing short stories and poetry while establishing what was to be a long, distinguished career as a fiction reviewer. His first book, *Night Fears*, a collection of short stories, was published in 1924.

By then he had already suffered a nervous breakdown. Yet Hartley enjoyed his position within the literary world. He was also given to writing ghost stories. In 1944, he published his first novel, *The Shrimp and the Anemone*, about a childhood summer spent by the sea in Norfolk. It was to be the first part of a trilogy chronicling the early life through to adulthood of Eustace, who must contend with an unexpected inheritance and a demanding relationship with his sister Hilda. *The Sixth Heaven* (1946) followed, and then, within a year, *Eustace and Hilda*, which won the James Tait Black prize. The trilogy, particularly the concluding volume, was considered a major breakthrough for Hartley, as well as being a significant contribution to British postwar fiction.

Hartley's growing status was consolidated on the publication of *The Go-Between* in 1953, in which an elderly man unexpectedly, and somewhat reluctantly, revisits a childhood experience. It is an extraordinary book and one interesting to consider alongside William Maxwell's *So Long, See You Tomorrow* (1980), in which another aged narrator recalls a damaging childhood episode.

The Hireling (1957) sees the widowed Lady Franklin re-emerge after two years of reclusive guilt to share her secrets with the driver of the title. The hired man feels compelled to invent his own history, causing the two central characters to become involved in strange fictions.

A quiet man of British literature, Hartley divided his time between the West Country and Venice. Yet this very English writer's most obvious literary kindred spirit is Henry James. In common with James, Hartley explored how an individual's behaviour can change when confronted by an unfamiliar social context. Young Leo Colston's arrival at Brandham Hall in *The Go-Between* may not, on the surface, appear as dramatic an experience as that inflicted upon American Isabel Archer when she is introduced to British class rituals at Gardencourt in *The Portrait of a Lady* (1881). But Hartley was as aware as James of the subtle pressures of contrasting, and conflicting, social contexts. Both writers shared a fascination with innocence corrupted and corrupting.

Hartley was to make a life-long study of the often duplicitous contradictions which underline – and undermine – human behaviour.

49 | Oblomov
(1859)
by Ivan Goncharov

It is easy to dream of a glorious and romantic future, if far more difficult to achieve anything like one. Ilya Ilyich Oblomov spends a great deal of his time daydreaming when not actually engaged in his preferred occupation, sleeping. Yes he is idle – lazy beyond belief and he finds the mere business of existence too taxing to contemplate, yet Oblomov is undeniably human. As he lays on his sofa, issuing half-hearted orders to Zakhar, his slovenly servant, this lazy, apathetic likeable central character attempts to keep his mind clear, mainly because thinking, for him, is exhausting.

The son of a long-dead landowner, Oblomov, gentleman and failed civil servant, suspects that the estate is being badly managed yet he can do nothing about it, as taking action on anything has never been his strength. He must also vacate his apartment. Small wonder he would rather go back to bed.

Even by the dauntingly high standards of the nineteenth-century Russian novel, *Oblomov* is unforgettable, as funny as it is heartbreaking. It is also an intriguingly philosophical book, taking as its central theme apathy and the collapse of one man's life. Goncharov, stylistically poles apart from his elegant rival Turgenev, sidestepped the violence and the radical politics of Dostoyevsky. Nor was he drawn to Tolstoy's panoramic vision – although the narrative does evoke a colourful sense of Russian life. After all, miles away from Oblomov's flat in Petersburg, are the serfs working on what remains of the family estate.

Goncharov, a career civil servant who was familiar with the

workings of censorship, concentrated on the ordinary, making effective use of domestic ritual and daily life as lived by a small group of characters, including two very different women in love. The vivid comic exchanges between Oblomov, an engaging, if detached anti-hero with no ambition beyond his next nap, and the feisty, old family retainer Zakhar are brilliant, as are the descriptions of the visits made to Oblomov's messy apartment by his various friends. But it soon becomes clear that his lifestyle is not only chaotic, it is dangerous. Although little past thirty, he is slowly killing himself as he slides deeper into a deadly inertia.

He may be too lazy to fulfil social engagements yet Oblomov is possessed of "an honest and faithful heart" and friends call, attempting to lure him out. He is also prey to a cynical scrounger named Tarantyev who becomes increasingly sinister.

Acting as a foil to all of the crumpled paper, dust and crumbs in the flat, is Stolz, a brisk man of action and Oblomov's boyhood friend. They love each other with an intensity of which only exact opposites are capable. Through Stolz, Oblomov meets Olga, an idealistic romantic who is as impressive as she is terrifying in her passion. Their relationship pivots on confused emotions as well as possibly the most interesting dialogue exchanged between aspiring, ill-suited lovers. As Oblomov forcefully encounters his feelings for her, he also becomes aware of social pressures. Further complications develop when he is tricked into agreeing to take new lodgings.

In 1849, a decade before the novel appeared, Goncharov published a long section, 'Oblomov's Dream', from it. The self-contained segment presents an idealised celebration of the protected childhood world our Everyman anti-hero knew growing up on the family estate. The ease of a country life where clothes and food were supplied by willing hands dominates his memories of that time, years when he had no responsibility.

It becomes possible to understand Oblomov's dilemma and the sense of honour which prevents him from accepting the romantic happiness which is his for the taking. Through chance and his inherent laziness, he drifts towards another form of comfort which reminds him of his past. Meanwhile, his friend, the organised, directed, super hero Stolz, discovers affection can become love.

Goncharov succeeds in steering the narrative through a number of lengthy philosophical dissections of love and metaphysics which could have been written by Goethe. Oblomov remains sympathetic and his final meeting with the bewildered Stolz is subtly underplayed by Goncharov who conveys many emotions. This poignant, richly layered tragic-comic study of one man's acknowledged inability to battle his personality, also explores love in its many guises against the colourful background provided by a Russia caught between tradition and imminent upheaval.

Ivan Aleksandrovich Goncharov (1812-1891)

James Joyce would have approved; in *Oblomov*, Goncharov wrote a novel that transfigured the commonplace and is not concerned with war, or madness, or bursts of violence. It is instead a masterful study of the ordinary. Can a lazy man of no ambition become a hero? Yes, or at least, he does in this singular tragic-comedy. Oblomov is Everyman at his most unexpectedly heroic and, as his creator would confess, composed of parts of himself and parts of human nature as he observed it.

Goncharov was born in 1812 in Simbirsk, a small town on the Volga. His father, a wealthy grain merchant, died when the future writer was seven years old leaving Goncharov's brisk-mannered mother to take over the business. The young Goncharov's education was organised by a family friend who ensured he was sent to a local boarding school attended by the sons of the gentry. It was there that Goncharov first studied English and French. When he was ten he was despatched to Moscow to study business at a commercial school. But he was not a business tycoon in the making and was more interested in languages. Having passed the university entrance exam, he began studying languages and remained indifferent to the revolutionary feeling gathering momentum all around him. But then, many of the student intellectuals made a point of excluding members of the hated merchant classes, such as Goncharov, from their political circles.

On graduating Goncharov returned to Simbirsk and became private secretary to the provincial governor. A few months later he set off for St Petersburg and joined the Ministry of Finance, initially as a translator. Goncharov was on the way to what would prove a long, undistinguished career in the civil service. He became friendly with an arty family, led by artist Nicholas Maykov, father of the future poet Apollon and Valerian, who was to become a leading critic. The family circle published a magazine. One of the two stories Goncharov published in it contained the sketch of a man of "unexampled and methodical laziness and heroic indifference to the bustle and turmoil of life" – this character would become his most famous creation – Oblomov.

Goncharov's first novel, *An Ordinary Story*, was published in 1847 when he was thirty-five. Its theme is the tension between the landed classes and the newly emerging bourgeoisie. Within two years, the long, romantic, reflective section of *Oblomov* known as 'Oblomov's Dream' was published in the *Contemporary Russian Review*. Work appeared to have stopped on *Oblomov* for a few years, probably because of its implied condemnation of serfdom. Goncharov was a civil servant alert to, and respectful of, government attitudes. He also knew how censorship worked and had no wish to appear on a list of banned writers.

In 1852 he joined a round-the-world expedition as secretary to the vice-admiral; it would take him to Japan and London. Goncharov's account of the trip ran to two volumes. The more liberal regime of Alexander II which began in 1855 may have encouraged Goncharov to return to writing *Oblomov*. When it was finally published two years later, its simplicity, cohesion and attention to realistic detail made him famous throughout Russia.

The early signs of paranoia which would dominate the final twenty years of his life had begun to manifest themselves. In 1860 he accused Turgenev of stealing his plots and conspiring against him. On resigning from the civil service in 1867, Goncharov turned to his most ambitious novel, *The Precipice*, which was published two years later and proved a failure. His final years were spent brooding in his

Petersburg apartment. Although so utterly unlike the other major nineteenth century Russian writers, Goncharov, born in the same year as Dickens, stands alongside them because of an irresistible, somewhat Dickensian novel which is profound, sympathetic and beguilingly human.

50 | Adventures of Huckleberry Finn (1885)
by Mark Twain

Mark Twain
Adventures of Huckleberry Finn

OXFORD WORLD'S CLASSICS

Racism and slavery are major themes in this timeless comic picaresque, the tale of a lively young boy none too keen on the efforts made by the Widow Douglas to "sivilize" him. Huck Finn is one of literature's immortals, half-anarchic innocent, half wised-up abused son of a vicious drunkard. Equally remarkable is the boy's companion for much of his odyssey, Jim, Miss Watson's runaway black slave. Jim has his superstitions and why not? In common with Huck, he is also a dreamer and one possessed of true compassion who promises himself that as soon as he gets to a Free State and earns some money, he will buy his wife out of slavery and then together they will work to buy their children's freedom.

For all the polemic, it is a tremendously funny book, as truthful and as deliberate as anything Dickens wrote. In fact there are many echoes of Dickens in the pace, the vivid characterisation and the feel for dialogue, not forgetting that neither Dickens nor Twain entertained any delusions about the goodness of humankind.

Mark Twain, born Samuel Langhorne Clemens, came from Southern stock that had moved from Virginia to the slave-holding lands of the Louisiana Purchase and on to Hannibal, Missouri, where he grew up. His father died when he was twelve and he was the apprenticed to a printer. Twain was an open-eyed realist immune to all the romanticised cant about Southern chivalry. Having served briefly in the Southern army, he knew what living in the South meant for anyone born black. That charged word "nigger" is used freely throughout the narrative by both black and white characters precisely because the word was common usage at the time and no amount of politically correct hindsight can, or should alter that. Books should be read in the context of the period and culture in which they were written.

Twain was sharp and shrewd, having a strong moral sense, comic flair and timing in abundance – not forgetting a well-developed commercial instinct. *Adventures of Huckleberry Finn* was the sequel to *The Adventures of Tom Sawyer* (1876), which had been promptly banned from the children's section of the Brooklyn Public Library because of the "questionable character" of Tom Sawyer, a boy with a creative attitude towards the concept of truth.

Adventures of Huckleberry Finn shares Walt Whitman's celebration of the American vernacular, admittedly in a most specific way. Twain prefaced the story with a detailed explanatory note outlining the number of dialects he had used as he did not wish readers supposing "that all these characters were trying to talk alike and not succeeding."

Huck's comic language and unique world view are spectacularly well served by a dialect which injects the narrative with an energy and pace sustained throughout a sequence of burlesque encounters and happenings. When caught out by Aunt Sally, Twain's inimitable boy narrator memorably reports: "My heart fell down amongst my lungs and livers and things, and a hard piece of corn-crust started down my throat after it . . ."

And yes, like many a hero, Huck is an inventive liar who has been influenced by Tom Sawyer, himself shaped by the romantic adventure yarns he has feasted upon. Huck is acutely aware of not being as "well brung up" as Tom. Twain allows Huck moments of insight, such as when he debates with himself the matter of helping Jim escape; the boy knows that he is stealing a commodity – Jim is Miss Watson's property. Huck is equally conscious that Jim is a human being. When faced with either informing Miss Watson – spinster sister of the Widow Douglas – of Jim's intended flight or of assisting him, Huck decides to help, declaring to himself: "All right, then, I'll go to hell."

Elsewhere, when watching thieves preparing to rob the Wilks

family, a disgusted Huck recalls, "It was enough to make a body ashamed of the human race." He thwarts the criminals. Twain, however, ensures our hero is no goody goody, and defiantly creates an overwhelmingly human boy; independent, careless and daring.

Set in the Mississippi Valley some years before the Civil War, Twain's classic tale juxtaposes the pastoral innocence of the riverbank with the growing corruption threatening the nation's mighty north-south turnpike, the Mississippi. Drifting down that mythic river on their raft enables Huck and Jim to form a convincing, unsentimental bond.

Despite the claims of Melville's magnificent, though strongly European saga, *Moby Dick* (1851), here is the first great American novel. "If I'd knowed," declares Huck, "what a trouble it was to make a book, I wouldn't a tackled it." Thankfully he or at least Mark Twain did, securing immortality for them both.

Mark Twain (1835-1910)
He entered the world as Halley's Comet raced across the night sky, and took his leave of it seventy-five years later when the comet returned as if to guide him on his way. Samuel Langhorne Clemens was fifteen when Nathaniel Hawthorne published *The Scarlet Letter* (1850). Herman Melville's epic masterpiece *Moby Dick* appeared the following year. Both Hawthorne and Melville crafted major pioneering works of American literature, but it was Twain, the American Cervantes, who would write the first great American novel, *Adventures of Huckleberry Finn* (1885).

Twain the man, sharp, funny, opinionated, with a preference for cigars and white suits, who made a fortune only to lose it, remains one of the most immediately recognisable American writers, thanks to his keen gaze, wayward mop of white hair and assertive moustache. The British have Dickens, and America has Twain, America's definitive American whose life spanned the Pony Express and the arrival of the motor car.

No one ever loses faith in Huck Finn, a true subversive realist; no one outgrows his story, and it is, most emphatically, Huck's story;

Twain allows him to tell it his way, in his voice, and in his words. You may lose empathy with Holden Caulfield, but not with Huck, he's with you for life. "I had first read Huckleberry Finn when I was seven," writes the gifted British writer Jonathan Raban in *Old Glory* (1981). "The picture on its cover, crudely drawn and coloured, supplied me with the raw material for an exquisite and recurrent daydream. It showed a boy alone, his face prematurely wizened with experience. (The artist hadn't risked his hand with the difficulties of bringing off a lifelike Nigger Jim.) The sheet of water on which he drifted was an immense enamelled pool of lapis lazuli. Smoke from a half-hidden steamboat hung over an island of gothic conifers. Cut lose from the world, chewing on his corncob pipe, the boy was blissfully lost in this stillwater paradise."

Such memories of the book inspired Raban to journey down the Mississippi, and America, on an aluminium raft to write *Old Glory*, an extraordinary travel book born of a dream that remains a dream as much as Kenneth Grahame's *The Wind in the Willows* (1908), although while Grahame drew on the English class system, Twain paraded his feel for vernacular speech and specific American dialects.

Twain had grown up in a slave-owning town, in a slave-owning household. His father, a justice of the peace, sent "slave-stealers" to jail. Twain the writer could see the evil of slavery and made this clear in his work. He was fearless at exposing people who considered themselves Christian and law-abiding yet acted otherwise. In common with Dickens, the young Clemens had experienced the raw side of life. His father's land speculations went wrong and his death forced the future writer to leave school at twelve. By seventeen, he had begun a varied career which included a range of occupations from typesetting, to piloting a river boat, two weeks of action on the Confederate side in the Civil War, gold mining, and journalism. His debut story, 'The Notorious Jumping Frog of Calaveras County', was published in 1865. For his pen name he took "Mark Twain", river-speak meaning a twelve-foot depth of navigable water.

His first major commercial success was a satirical travel book based on a trip to Europe and the Middle East. It sold an estimated 100,000 copies. His collected works would eventually span twenty-nine volumes. Twain married the daughter of an upstate New York coal baron. They moved to Hartford, Connecticut, establishing a large family hone which remains a place of literary pilgrimage. Hannibal, Missouri, his boyhood stomping ground, has also kept its magic.

The blind Argentine writer Jorge Luis Borges (1899-1986), agreed in 1982 to lecture at Washington University in St Louis. There was a condition; his hosts had to take him the two-hour drive to Hannibal. Once there, Borges was determined to thrust his hand into the waters of the Mississippi. He had to touch the river, for him it was the essence of Twain's writing.

Having once humorously refuted as "greatly exaggerated" news reports of his death, Twain and Huck Finn, are destined to live forever.

51 | Crime and Punishment
(1865-1866)
by Fyodor Dostoyevsky

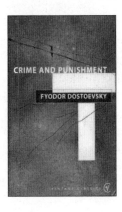

A disgruntled one-time Petersburg university student is starving and too embarrassed to risk an encounter with his long-suffering landlady. But no, he has now gone beyond caring. He decides to kill an old pawnbroker, a nasty operator who has contempt for her customers and subjects her poor sister Lisaveta to appalling treatment. The pawnbroker's death will liberate the long-suffering sister, and this will be a good deed.

Raskolnikov, displaced and alienated – *raskolnik* is Russian for schismatic or dissenter – is indeed divided. His waking hours are passed in furious internal debate, as he searches for his vision of a higher good. Or so he thinks. The reality is less lofty; he not only despatches the old woman he also kills Lisaveta who unexpectedly arrives while he is still at the murder scene.

Metaphysical thriller, profound detective story and a psychological study of tragic pride and epic guilt, *Crime and Punishment* is the defining literary achievement of the nineteenth century. It cast its cohesive presence over all that would follow, from Kafka, an admiring successor, and the reluctant Conrad – who criticised Dostoyevsky for being "too Russian" although *The Secret Agent* (1907) and *Under Western Eyes* (1911) are clearly influenced by this great novel – to Thomas Mann and on until the present day.

It was Dostoyevsky who identified and constructed the troubled modern imagination, and who, most compellingly, continues to stalk that imagination. Tolstoy was the historical novelist with a panoramic overview of society as well as of the relevance of reason; Dostoyevsky's fantastic realism looked inwards. He was the psychological visionary who understood violent suffering, wrote with a hallucinatory energy and created unforgettable, troubled, at times, deranged characters who express themselves in frenetic philosophical exchanges. Then there are the passages of horrific, hysterical, exasperated, often unintentional, comedy. Only William Gaddis is quite as screamingly, darkly funny.

Dostoyevsky realised that Western Romanticism became more extreme when adopted by the hyper-emotive Russian spirit. His involvement in a secret intellectual circle, influenced by several European radical thinkers, led to his arrest. A last-minute reprieve spared his life but cost Dostoyevsky four years in a Siberian labour camp and a further five as a soldier on the Mongolian border. Drawn to Balzac and Dickens, he would surpass both through his unnerving intensity and flair for suspense. *Crime and Punishment*, framed by despair and hope, was conceived as "the psychological study of a crime." Dostoyevsky was painstaking in his exploration of Raskolnikov's chaotic reasoning.

St Petersburg is the setting, as ever that mythic, mystical city central to Russian writers, from Pushkin to Joseph Brodsky. For Raskolnikov, it is "the embodiment of some blank and dead spirit", while another major character, the depraved Svidrigaylov, newly returned after seven years in the country courtesy of the wealthy wife he killed, considers it home to invariably disturbed citizens. It is a chaotic place of nightmares, extremes, revolutionary ideas and feverish thinking.

Raskolnikov is arrogant, contradictory, relentlessly intellectual and interestingly, unsympathetic. He does not have to deny his crime because he is not a suspect. His conversation is often bewildering as he announces to his loyal friend Razumikhin: "But it's only illiterate peasants or inexperienced greenhorns who flatly deny everything when questioned by the police. A man who's had some education and experience of life will always do his best to admit all the external and incontrovertible facts. Except, of course, that he will try to find other reasons for them . . ." Elsewhere he tells himself: "The old woman was only an illness . . . I didn't kill a human being – I killed a principle!"

By the time his mother and sister Dunya arrive in St Petersburg, Raskolnikov has met Marmeladov, a disgraced alcoholic civil servant whose second wife has in desperation encouraged Sonia, his daughter by his first marriage, to become a prostitute. Sonia, gentle, kind and a devout Christian, is the moral centre of the novel. Dostoyevsky moves his characters through vividly described set pieces, filled with recriminations, tears, illness, family funerals and the inevitable, metaphysical debates.

Although Raskolnikov largely conducts his investigation as a quasi-philosophical personal exploration, he does have extensive assistance from one of Dostoyevsky's finest creations, the eccentric examining magistrate Porfiry Petrovich, given to sudden barks of laughter and a digressively conversational style of interrogation. He could as easily have strolled out from the pages of Dickens and his approach to his police work is reminiscent to that of Bucket, the personable detective in *Bleak House* (1852-1853). Meanwhile Svidrigaylov, bored, cynical, and secretly privy to Raskolnikov's confession to Sonia, stages a dramatic farewell.

Dostoyevsky became increasingly drawn to mysticism yet in *Crime and Punishment*, with its theme of redemption through truth, he determined modern literary consciousness.

Fyodor Dostoyevsky *(1821-1881)*

It was a life lived at breakneck speed. Even before he stared death in the face in the form of a firing squad, Fyodor Dostoyevsky knew too much about violence and terror. His father was a doctor and their home in Moscow was filled with his rages. When Dostoyevsky was sixteen, his mother died. His father became a heavy drinker and in an attempt to retrieve the family's lapsed nobility, acquired a modest country estate of five hundred acres, about one hundred and fifty kilometres from Moscow.

At the estate, in 1839, a year after Dostoyevsky had begun his studies at the Military Engineering Academy in St Petersburg, his father was beaten to death by his serfs. The murder no doubt had an effect on the then student. Long before he began to write about vicious deeds and frenzied behaviour, Dostoyevsky had lived through such episodes. His imagination was sustained by inner, as well as outer turmoil.

No writer, with the obvious exception of Shakespeare, has left a legacy to match that of Fyodor Dostoyevsky. His pioneering psychological influence and philosophical self-doubt influences writers everywhere, in all traditions. He introduced an almost crazed interior intensity to fiction. Born into an age of revolution, he grew up questioning everything, including himself. A product of the intelligentsia, he had been inspired by romantic, revolutionary ideas sweeping in from Western Europe. Tsarist Russia remained backward, a feudal, autocratic society, unfairly divided between nobles and landowners; far removed from those privileged classes were the poor, exploited on the land and starving in the cities.

In common with other young aspiring radicals in the 1840s, Dostoyevsky lived in squalor and talked ideas. He soon lost interest in his military career and in 1844, at the age of twenty-three, abandoned his studies, intent on literature. The first thing he discovered about being a writer was poverty. His debut, *Poor Folk* (1846), took a direct look at the experience of being poor. It was a resounding success. Dostoyevsky was immediately celebrated. His next novel, *The Double* (1846), was radically different and introduced the psychological dimension which would become central to his work. However, neither the critics nor the reading public were ready; it did badly. But Dostoyevsky's position was assured and instead of being disappointed he looked to the German and French romantic movements and joined in the discussion of Western liberalism.

Those ideas would draw him into the revolutionary fervour of 1848. Within a year his enthusiasm almost cost him his life. He had become involved with an intellectual circle led by Mikhail Petrashevsky, a foreign office official who was promoting the ideas of various European radicals, in particular, Charles Fourier. A tsarist spy informed on the group. Under Nicholas I, tolerance was at a low. Several members, including Dostoyevsky, were arrested and placed in the Peter-Paul Fortress in St Petersburg.

Under cross-examination he refused to answer any questions but in a written statement defended the ideas of liberalism. It was a dangerous gesture. A military court imposed the death sentence on him. There is some debate as to whether the tsar actually intended for the executions to be carried out, but either way, Dostoyevsky and his comrades were stood before a firing squad. At the last moment, a reprieve was read out.

It was almost irrelevant. Dostoyevsky had experienced a moment of extreme terror; extremes dominate his work, from remorse and guilt, to self-disgust and the feeling of being emotionally pulverised.

Instead of death, he suffered four years in a Siberian labour camp. He would write about it in *Notes from the House of the Dead* (1860-1861) and it influenced the description of Raskolnikov's imprisonment at the close of *Crime and Punishment* (1866), while the mock execution features in *The Idiot* (1868). Dostoyevsky spent much of his prison term alone, the vestiges of social rank and his own solitary temperament kept him apart from the prisoners, many of whom were serving criminal, rather than political, sentences. He became embittered, underwent a spiritual crisis and also developed the epilepsy that would trouble him for the rest of his life. His ordeal in Siberia was followed by five years serving as an ordinary soldier on the Mongolian frontier.

During this period he was denied freedom to travel or publish. When he finally returned to St Petersburg in 1859, great changes were evident. The new tsar, Alexander II, was far more liberal; for a while life seemed more open. But for Dostoyevsky there was further hardship. His wife, whom he had married while on military service, was ailing and the magazine he began with his beloved brother Mikhail quickly ran into debt. In the midst of all this chaos, he developed a destructive passion for gambling. His wife died, leaving him to care for her son by a previous marriage and Dostoyevsky also had to deal with Mikhail's death and assume responsibility for his widow and family. Writing offered his only practical solution, but to make it pay he accepted impossible deadlines.

The pressure that life and his personality placed on Dostoyevsky was beyond comprehension. The great South African novelist, J. M. Coetzee, imagines the Russian's hell on earth in *The Master of Petersburg* (1994), a superb study of personal turmoil. Dostoyevsky's writings also reflect this. *Notes from Underground* (1864) articulates the dilemma of the thinking man, trapped by circumstances, venting his spleen. It is funny, Dostoyevsky often is, such is the force of his exasperation. Underground Man entered fiction and would be heard through Hamsun and Kafka and beyond.

Notes from Underground also marked the beginning of an unsurpassed sequence of immortal novels; *Crime and Punishment* and *The Gambler* (1866), *The Idiot*, *The Possessed* (1872) and *The Brothers Karamazov* (1880). All were written in haste, at times in a frenzy. The pressure he worked under was similar to that experienced by Dickens, whose work he had discovered while a prisoner in Siberia. In common with Dickens, he died young, suffering two massive haemorrhages probably related to undiagnosed tuberculosis. He was sixty. On the morning of the day he died, he calmly announced to Anna, his second wife, with whom he had been happy: "Today I shall die." And he did.

Dostoyevsky is far more than an inspired storyteller; he is a thinker, a visionary, a moral conscience and yes, the giant at everyone's shoulder.

52 | The Recognitions
(1955)
by William Gaddis

For far too long this novel had to contend with two major obstacles: its length and its alleged "unreadability". While it may be close on one thousand pages, *The Recognitions* is a mercurial European novel of ideas, written by an American. It is a dialogue-driven work: the mixed-up characters talk and shout, parry and fret. They may confess but they don't exactly confide. Most of them are bewildered by truth; the need for it, as well as the pursuit of it. There has to be a battleground, and if life itself is not enough, take a world in which lies and contradictions abound: art.

Set in the art scenes of New York, Paris and Spain, it is a quest like no other. The narrative itself recognises the implausibility and impossibility of originality in art or even in thought. The idea of thinking about the purity of art preoccupies the characters. Is Gaddis being clever? No, the tone of the novel is more despairing. While the characters toss up more one-liners than the Simpsons, beyond the bravado, there is fear and unease.

At the broken heart of it all is the counterfeiting of art. Upon a grim thesis, "nothing is real," the plotless yarn races in circles, or so it seems. Characters wander in and out, snatches of conversations are overheard, interrupted and some are even continued. Ideas surface; only to disappear and re-emerge later, along with references to music, books, artists and history. It is an endless movie; the reader is a voyeur, privy to sufficient information to figure out what is going on. The characters continue speaking, arguing, lamenting. If Gaddis wrote plays they would go on for days.

Wyatt Gwyon, the troubled young painter of genius in *The*

Recognitions, has many problems, not least his wife, a relentless social climber. Her days are preoccupied with meeting the famous. Eventually he has enough: "What do people want from the artist that they don't get from his work. What's any artist, but the dregs of his work? The human shambles that follows it around?"

Gwyon is not alone in his exasperation. Elsewhere, Otto, a writer intent on the languid, indifferent Esme, walks with her around Washington Square and attempts to quiz her about her feelings. He compares speaking with her to tying a knot before a mirror: "I know just what to do and then do everything backwards." It is one of the best scenes in a novel of set pieces, as Gaddis's tales tend to be. Yet this is a stark moment of truth in a narrative concerned with its absence.

Gwyon has become a forger, it pays better. The fact is originality is impossible. Otto can't shake this from his thoughts either: "Like a story I heard once, a friend of mine told me, somebody I used to know, a story about a forged painting. It was a forged Titian that somebody had painted over another old painting, when they scraped the forged Titian away they found some worthless old painting underneath it, the forger had used it because it was an old canvas. But then there was something under that worthless painting, and they scraped it off and underneath that they found a Titian, a real Titian that had been there all the time. It was as though when the forger was working, and he didn't know the original was underneath, I mean he didn't know he knew it, but it knew, I mean something knew . . ."

Some of the characters scratch and stab at understanding, others glide on deceived or deceiving or both. You listen so intently to their garbled conversations, half finished comments, or the fragment of a sentence that may drift in over the noise, and it is a noisy book, that the knowing narrator seems a busy body, a guide you may need, but don't want. The centre holds, albeit, horribly, horribly well, as it does in his other novels. Gaddis disputes the notion of originality and yet is an original.

The Recognitions is an ambitious book, inflated by an outraged sensibility. But it is also a spiritual book engaged in a search for truths that may be disputed by every passing speaker with an opinion, but truths which still endure. It is a vast painting brought to life; a marathon movie with no intermission. Above all it is a questing, investigative novel that speaks loud and fearful, not always all that clearly, but with a voice that has lost neither its energy nor its urgency. This apocalyptic novel opens the door to the genius of William Gaddis.

William Gaddis *(1922-1998)*

Some writers take years to become an overnight success; others take a good deal longer. When William Gaddis's first novel, *The Recognitions* (1955), was singled out in 1986 as "one of the great under-recognised modern novels" by British academic and novelist Malcolm Bradbury, he unfortunately attributed it to another US writer, William Gass. The satirical moralist Gaddis would have been amused by the irony of a novel so intently concerned with the truth and counterfeiting in art being passed off as somebody else's work.

Before Thomas Pynchon, there was William Gaddis, a writer who had set out to change the world with his first novel. Instead, he alienated critics and returned to obscurity for a further twenty years. The approach was the same but this time the novel was slightly shorter, a mere seven hundred and twenty-five pages. The topic was a good one, money. *JR* won the 1976 National Book Award but not all the critics were happy; one of them likened reading it to being "trapped in a phone box for seven hundred pages with a maniac screaming down the line."

Money is the first word of the novel and the central character, the JR of the title, is an eleven-year-old financial wizard who builds an empire inspired by junk mail and sustained by frantic calls made from phone booths. He is Huck Finn catapulted into the age of greed while an unlocatable radio blares on in the background providing a perverted accompaniment to the proceedings. Of course it's funny and of course, it's horrible. It is a narrative of voices, all shouting the jargon of public relations, bond trading and high finance. Alive with irony and anger, it too slipped away, while more than ten years later, Tom Wolfe's inferior Wall Street yarn, *The Bonfire of the Vanities*, would enjoy international success. Gaddis's "soundtrack of the now" remains a major influence on Don DeLillo.

A third novel followed, *Carpenter's Gothic* (1986). At a mere two hundred and sixty-two pages, reviewers were relieved. It is a frenetic comedy featuring the scheming attempts of Paul, a traumatised Vietnam veteran turned PR guru, to launch a hick preacher as a media star. When two people drown during a staged river baptism Paul decides to repackage the tragedy as an event and begins negotiating the movie rights. His antics are watched from the sidelines by his timid, asthmatic wife Liz, who is desperate for love and friendship. She also happens to be an heiress. The couple are based in a rented mausoleum of a Carpenter's Gothic-style mansion on the Hudson. Paul plots his crazy projects, while Liz wanders about, answering the persistently ringing phone and engages in lengthy conversations with her wrong-number callers. Meanwhile Paul's hopes rest in the support of Teakell, "the best US senator money can buy."

In person William Gaddis seemed every inch the courtly Southern gentleman when I interviewed him in 1994. But he was a streetwise New Yorker with a ravaged face and a sense of humour, who as a student at Harvard, had once noted the arrival of a bright young fellow named John Updike. Gaddis, whose favourite novel was Goncharov's *Oblomov*, left without a degree. True to his individuality he did not go to Paris, he headed for Spain. Asked about the critical failure of *The Recognitions*, Gaddis, looking back over a gap of forty years, could at last laugh about it. But at the time he felt angry and frustrated. After all, as he recalled, he had been confident at publication that he would win the Nobel Prize. He didn't.

He was born in Manhattan and his parents divorced when he was three years old. Gaddis always attributed his ear for dialogue to this, convinced he had learned to listen at an early age. After the failure of *The Recognitions* he worked as a speechwriter for corporate executives, a fact-checker for *The New Yorker* and a cowpoke in Arizona and Wyoming. The most appropriate of those jobs is the fact-checker, as Gaddis's fiction is full of detail; every digression, every aside comes complete with a vast amount of information.His decision to take on the legal system in *A Frolic of His Own* (1994) won him his second National Book Award and happy readers. "Justice?" it begins, "You get justice in the next world, in this world you have the law." Oscar Crease, a lowly history professor, is convinced that a play he once wrote about his grandfather's Civil War experiences has been hijacked by a Hollywood film-maker. He is advised that there is no copyright on the Civil War. But Crease is determined. He becomes involved in another action. He has been run over. There is a catch; he was hit by his own car while he was hot-wiring it. Meanwhile Crease's father, a judge, almost a century old, has taken to handing down increasingly offbeat judgments. The latest concerns the rights of a small dog trapped within a modern sculpture. There are eighteen legal actions in progress, most of them ridiculous, yet Gaddis sustains them all.

His final work *Agapē Agape*, published posthumously in 2002, is a celebration of the player piano. In keeping with his life's thesis about art and the value of ideas, it is also a metaphysical discourse about many things, including Gaddis's regard for the Austrian writer Thomas Bernhard. Most importantly of all, it represents his artistic leave-taking. This is Gaddis's manifesto and the work most closely related to the ideas about art and truth explored in *The Recognitions*. Make no mistake about William Gaddis, his deliberate method is always contained within the apparently random chaos.

Gaddis encapsulated a dilemma; for many readers he arrived too soon, for others, he was too late. Joyce had got there first. But it was Gaddis, an admirer of Dostoyevsky, who perfected the technique of the exasperated one-sided telephone call, as well as the accurate depiction of vividly random inarticulate speech. He uses language as spoken to reveal the excesses, the corruption, and the sheer panic of society.

Brief Suggested and Selective Reading List

General Background to Nineteenth-Century Russia
Life on the Russian Country Estate by Priscilla Roosevelt (1995)
Anyone with an interest in nineteenth-century Russian fiction must read this book.

Natasha's Dance: A Cultural History of Russia by Orlando Figes (2001)
Exhilarating survey of a history, a culture, a people, a literature.

Background to Central Europe
Danube by Claudio Magris (1986)
A graceful, reflective and informative journey through the contrasting histories and cultures of central Europe.

The Snows of Yesteryear by Gregor von Rezzori (1989)
Although a memoir it is included here for its rich evocation of central Europe.

Biographies
Kafka by Pietro Citati (1987)
Biography is often a minefield, but at its best, as in this intelligent, playful work by Citati, a living sense of the subject emerges.

Jane Austen by David Nokes (1997)
There are many bland studies of Austen, but this one from Nokes has an edge and offers vivid social history.

Samuel Beckett: The Last Modernist by Anthony Cronin (1996)
Stylish and perceptive, one great Irish literary man considers another.

The Brontës by Juliet Barker (1994)
A passionate, though admittedly, exhaustive study of a remarkable clan.

Virginia Woolf by Hermonie Lee (1996)
The definitive biography; this is a polished, assured and intelligent exploration of a pioneering and troubled modernist – and has the advantage of being written by an astute textual critic.

Jean Rhys by Carole Angier (1990)
Rhys needed a sympathetic biographer and found her in the fair-minded Angier.

Thomas Mann by Ronald Hayman (1995)
This is the first biography to make use of the 5,000 pages of diaries Mann ordered to be kept secret until twenty years after his death.

Sartre: Writing Against by Ronald Hayman (1986)
Hayman's detailed, quietly sympathetic account of the life and work of the great French thinker also comments on twentieth–century French intellectual life.

Fyodor Dostoyevsky: A Writer's Life by Geir Kjetsaa (1985)
This is a great book, worthy of its subject's overwhelming humanity.

Dickens by Peter Ackroyd (1990)
The larger-than-life Dickens deserves a larger-than-life biography; this lively romp catches the sheer energy of the supreme storyteller.

Solzhenitsyn by Michael Scammell (1984)
Published while Solzhenitsyn was still alive, this is respectful and polite, yet highly informative.

Tolstoy by A. N. Wilson (1988)
Good on the writer as a man of contradictions and even better on the society.

Max Perkins: Editor of Genius by A. Scott Berg (1979)
The "genius" refers not only to Perkins but to the rich stable, Fitzgerald, Hemingway, Thomas Wolfe, Ring Lardner etc, he managed; vital background to the twentieth–century US literary world.

Henry James – A Life by Leon Edel (1985)
This single book is a distilled version of the classic five-volume study published between 1953 and 1972.

Journalism and Essays

What I Saw: Reports from Berlin 1920-1933 and *The White Cities: Reports From France 1925-1939,* both by Joseph Roth (Granta, 2003 and 2004)
Roth was a great observer and saw things others missed. His writing is wry, intelligent, always informed and often profound.

Orwell's Collected Journalism (Various editions available)
He was a committed witness and a fearless commentator.

Orwell's Essays
A new Penguin edition, *Shooting an Elephant,* includes 'Charles Dickens' and 'Decline of the English Murder' and is more than useful.

It All Adds Up by Saul Bellow (1994)
He was not as versatile as Updike; nor was he as interested in everything but Bellow had opinions and this book is a key to how his mind worked. It includes pieces ranging from 1948 to 1990.

Memoirs

Speak, Memory by Vladimir Nabokov (1967)
Elegance personified, this likeable memoir surprised many readers with its candour as Nabokov explained the society which shaped him.

Words by Jean-Paul Sartre (1966)
Childhood revisited with irony and sharp wit.

Peeling the Onion by Günter Grass (2007)
The lull before the storm: Grass published this memoir which takes his life from birth up until and during the writing of *The Tin Drum.* Revelations about his service with the Waffen-SS caused outrage, with many believing his wartime past should have been dealt with years before.

Miracles of Life by J. G. Ballard (2008)
Written in the knowledge that he was dying, Ballard retraces the journey that brought him from wartime Shanghai, to "home" in an England he had never lived in, and on to life as a single parent and a full-time writer.

Gathering Evidence by Thomas Bernhard (1985)
The life and times of a central European intellectual, Bernhard explains his world, and to some extent, his work.

Note: publishers not listed as available editions vary